T0374177

JESUS' MOUNTAIN

BETTY SWAN LUCKEY

WESTBOW
PRESS®
A DIVISION OF THOMAS NELSON
& ZONDERVAN

Copyright © 2022 Betty Swan Luckey.

All rights reserved. No part of this book may be used or reproduced by any means, graphic, electronic, or mechanical, including photocopying, recording, taping or by any information storage retrieval system without the written permission of the author except in the case of brief quotations embodied in critical articles and reviews.

This book is a work of non-fiction. Unless otherwise noted, the author and the publisher make no explicit guarantees as to the accuracy of the information contained in this book and in some cases, names of people and places have been altered to protect their privacy.

WestBow Press books may be ordered through booksellers or by contacting:

WestBow Press
A Division of Thomas Nelson & Zondervan
1663 Liberty Drive
Bloomington, IN 47403
www.westbowpress.com
844-714-3454

Because of the dynamic nature of the Internet, any web addresses or links contained in this book may have changed since publication and may no longer be valid. The views expressed in this work are solely those of the author and do not necessarily reflect the views of the publisher, and the publisher hereby disclaims any responsibility for them.

Any people depicted in stock imagery provided by Getty Images are models, and such images are being used for illustrative purposes only.
Certain stock imagery © Getty Images.

Scripture marked (KJV) taken from the King James Version of the Bible.

Scripture marked (NKJV) taken from the New King James Version®. Copyright © 1982 by Thomas Nelson. Used by permission. All rights reserved.

Scripture quotations marked (NIV) are taken from the Holy Bible, New International Version®, NIV®. Copyright © 1973, 1978, 1984, 2011 by Biblica, Inc.® Used by permission of Zondervan. All rights reserved worldwide. www.zondervan.com The "NIV" and "New International Version" are trademarks registered in the United States Patent and Trademark Office by Biblica, Inc.®

Scripture quotations marked (NLT) are taken from the Holy Bible, New Living Translation, copyright ©1996, 2004, 2015 by Tyndale House Foundation. Used by permission of Tyndale House Publishers, Carol Stream, Illinois 60188. All rights reserved.

Scripture marked (WEB) taken from the World English Bible.

Scripture quotations marked (FNV) are reproduced from First Nations Version, copyright ©2021 by Rain Ministries Inc. Used by permission of InterVarsity Press, Downers Grove, IL. All rights reserved.

ISBN: 978-1-6642-7271-2 (sc)
ISBN: 978-1-6642-7272-9 (hc)
ISBN: 978-1-6642-7270-5 (e)

Library of Congress Control Number: 2022913126

Print information available on the last page.

WestBow Press rev. date: 07/18/2022

CONTENTS

DEDICATION

"Is to My Children, My Grandchildren, and to my Great-Grandchildren, with our God's Blessings!"

As arrows are in the hand of a mighty man; so are children of the youth. Happy is the man whose quiver is full of them! they shall not be ashamed, but they shall speak with the enemies at the gate"
Psalm 127:4-5 KJV

How can a mother ever find words meaningful enough to express the honor God bestows us when He gifts us with a precious new life to hold in our arms, a part of ourselves, an extention of our own being, an expression of Himself and His mighty power. He is the Life-giver, and to borrow a few of my favorite words from my new favorite song, He *is* the "Waymaker, Miracle Worker, the Promise Keeper, the Light in the Darkness, my God, that is Who You are!" Hallelujah!

When each of our four children were born, three daughters and one son, my husband Gary and I took turns holding them for the first time and with each new baby, we both were unable to hold back the tears of gratitude to God, the Creator, and tears of awe. Such a moment, it was just like at our wedding ceremony, when we had looked into each other's eyes, and we were unable to hold back holy tears of joy which flowed down our cheeks as we repeated our wedding vows before the congregation. It was so sacred, too awesome for words, and most Holy.

There would never be a day in their lives when we could not have been more proud of our children. No one in this world escapes the common disappointment, discouragement, the ups and downs and life's challenges that we all experience, and that at any day you might encounter, but we were altogether oh, so blessed! Some people might call us 'lucky", but we called ourselves "Blessed" by God. We were a bonded family of intense unconditional love, forgiveness, acceptance, and daily open communication filled with hysterical humor on the part of everyone!

Our family unity was and is, a perfect template for the arrival of wonderful grandchildren and great grandchildren. As if life could get no better, another little one would come to make our lives even more complete and full. With each new one you experience your love expanding larger and so amazingly, like you never knew possible. The contentment it gave us to receive each one, to hold and hug, filled our hearts and put smiles on our faces, with memories that still do!

Photo left to right:
Elizabeth (Libby) Joy Luckey Fraund, Nikole (Niki) Lynette Luckey Brothen, James Tifton Luckey, Sheryl (Sheri) Kaye Luckey Bjorn

May the Lord use the contents of this book, my autobiography, some family history, and the powerful faith God has given me to help minister to others, be an anointed blessing to every reader. And I dedicate it to my family for always loving me and helping me try to be a good mom, grandma, and great grandmother.

To my late husband Gary Wayne Luckey, in Heaven,.... to our children, Libby Luckey Fraund, Sheri Luckey Bjorn, James Tifton Luckey, and Niki Luckey Brothen,......to our grandchildren, Justin Savacool (in Heaven), Sean Savacool, JT and Tiffani Luckey, Ernie and Daphne Brothen,......to our great grandsons, (JT's sons), Landon and Luke Mack Luckey, with love immeasurable, ... to God be the Glory!

"Sheri Luckey Bjorn"

FOREWORD

Truth is stranger than fiction. *That is how I begin to describe the life experiences* of Elizabeth (Betty) Swan Luckey, my Mother.

From my earliest memories, I witnessed the intermingling of the *unseen,* with the seen, the *supernatural,* with the natural, as this wife and mother of four, threw herself into the arms of Jesus and trusted Him with her life.

A woman, with a *real* life, with a *real* God, who spoke to her in such a *real* way, that she could not deny that **God is truly who He said He is,** and she *trusted* Him at His Word.

This "knowing" was evident in her life and is to this day. God's personal interaction with her are seen in these pages. Her heart is that you, too, will embark on an eternal journey with your Creator, *who loves you,* and is interested in every detail of your life.

"Greenlawn Memorial Gardens, Peachtree, North Carolina near Murphy"

THE DEVIL WANTED ME DEAD, Y'ALL!

"But you are a chosen generation, a royal priesthood, a holy nation,
*God's own special people, that you may **proclaim the praises** of*
Him who called you out of darkness into His marvelous Light!"
1Peter 2:9 (NKJV)

Sometimes I sit at my late husband's graveside up on the mountain in the Smokys, surrounded by even more awesome mountains. I enjoy the lovely park bench placed there by the Little Brasstown Baptist Church, which, conveniently for me, they located right between Gary's grave and his brother Glyn's. Thank You, Jesus. I use the private solitude to collect my thoughts, talk to the Lord, and enjoy the views, singing Cardinals, fragrant blossoms, and usually, release some of my emotions, all while taking in the awesome clean, fresh mountain air.

I remember hearing that when the great comedian, Bob Hope, was on his death bed, it was reported his grandson was sitting by his side and asked his grandfather a question something like this: "Dad, we have discussed some things pertaining to your final arrangements and funeral instructions, but you have never told us *where* you would like to be buried". To which it was said, Bob Hope replied, "I don't care, Son, *"Surprise me!"*

Well, I suppose it's no surprise where my final bones will rest if Jesus doesn't return first to take us all home, together, at once, in the "rapture". I would have a graveside service right here where the photo above was taken. Brother Jerry Morrow, my Notla Baptist Church pastor and friend, would offer words of comfort and inspiration and maybe a humerous story or two we'd shared through the years.

We actually had so many, like the day I left my wallet at home and put an "IOU" note in the collection plate, for some reason it really struck him funny. Oh, and the time I had arrived late for the church service and the back door was accidently locked. As I waited with my walker, I called Linda May, who was already singing up in the choir loft, and when she saw the text light up, left her seat up there in front of everyone, and let me in the door. I heard folks laugh as they had wondered at how she'd known to go do that, but was I glad she did.

That reminds me of the night I was in a police drug investigation class and one of the officers, a deputy, on the last row had his hand up, for *a very long time,* to ask a question, and the instructor, who was also employed by the same Sheriff's department as the deputy, kept calling on others with *their* questions, and unknowingly, *ignoring* the man in back. As he was answering one of the other student's questions, the classmate said quietly, to the rest of us, "I'll fix *him!*"

The officer called his dispatcher on his cell phone and told her to "contact" him (the instructor,) immediately! Right away the teacher checked an urgent message he'd just received on his *loudly* beeping pager and then looked toward the back of the room to see the very tired, up-lifted hand. Everyone had howled. That worked!

But the funniest thing yet, was one day in church with Gary. Well, it's funny to me now, but it sure wasn't then.

The Sunday morning service had come to a close following the benediction prayer, with the exciting announcement for everyone to meet, right then, downstairs in the fellowship hall, for a church luncheon and everybody, especially visitors and all, were welcomed to join us there for an over abundance of good country vittles. Gary had already left my Shepherd's pie down in the dining hall before the service had begun.

Since I was using a walker due to the knee replacements I'd been avoiding, I preferred to give the congregation a head start in that direction. At the top of the stairs we shoved the walker to the side. Gary and I followed behind all the folks, with two deacons right behind us, picking up the end of the line that was descending slowly down the staircase to the basement. All of a sudden I *heard* **and** *felt* the elastic around my waist in my panties snap in half!

Now, I'll have you know that on that particular day I was properly attired in a long mid-calf jean skirt, but immediately wished it was the jeans I'd worn. *My problem was that the underwear began to slowly descend down my legs faster than we were able to walk down those stairs!* That wasn't the worst of it...I could already see, from my high vantage point, since I was standing on an upper step, the people all seated below at tables, were *watching* *everyone* as they were coming down the stairs! They were about to see a sight they'd never forget, and that was, a bird's eye-view, of Betty Luckey's **oldest pair of underwear falling around her ankles to her feet**!

With no further word of explanation, I whispered to my husband, who was holding one of my hands to help steady me, "We have to turn around and get to the truck immediately!" We excused ourselves to the deacons behind us, as we passed them on the top stairs. I hurried out the back door, sorta' leaning on the walker, clutching my skirt, "as if" to not drop my purse and Bible, and scurrying away, "as if" to have forgotten our Shepherd's Pie at the house, or *something*.

Once outside in the parking lot, I had quickly scooped up the little bundle of old black satin, with the ravels, that had me shuffling along, looking like an ole grandmaw Penguin, stuffing the panties in my purse. I told Gary we were going home; that, there was no way I intended to eat at a conservative, country mountain church dinner, without my panties on!

I had said to Gary, "Please don't ever tell anybody what just happened!" to which he replied in his Southern drawl, shaking his head, "Oh, ya' shor' don't have to worry yo're purdy lil' ol' head about *that* 'un!"

Well, Pastor Jerry, on second thought, maybe you better leave that story out of the cemetery officiatin'. I guess you might say that's a bit personal; but, so is every page ahead of us in this whole book, and I shoot from the hip, folks, so hang on, here goes!

It's easy for me to relax there at Greenlawn Memorial Gardens, though, and to reminisce a lifetime "dedicated to God". Well, that's what the books say my name "Elizabeth" means, and sitting there I can see clearly the name already engraved in the marble with my birthday on it, along with Gary's name. People sometimes say, "Oh Betty, doesn't it make you *too sad* to go over there and to have to *see that?*" and I can say confidently, and *with joy*, "Nope!"

I will tell you why. It's a grave marker, a memorial declaring, not death, but LIFE *eternal!* Gary, Glyn, his dear wife Pam (a best friend of mine), are not there, either, but rejoicing in Heaven and one day I'll be there with them, too. Now, you see why this place is not so bad....it is a **living** memorial to our family about a *LIVING* God and **His** *"Resurrection"*, *LIVING* **Power**! Hallelujah! The tomb of Jesus in Israel is empty, too! I mean to tell you, His *is* **really** *empty, without a single bone!* I saw a living illustration of this one night in a cemetery near Nashville.

I was driving home from my security job at Trinity Broadcast Network (TBN) to Lulu Roman's home. She is the famous HeeHaw commedianne we watched every Saturday night for many years when we were younger, and it was where I was living at the time. As I passed a cemetery, I could see from the corner of my eye a huge hillside cemetery aglow with candle-lit paper bag lanterns on every grave, causing me to stop suddenly and then back up slowly and into the front entrance.

Each lantern cast a golden ray of flickering "sunshine" on the name of each person who had been buried there. Well, I should probably call it, "**Son**-shine"! The sight was incredibly awesome, and was something I had never seen before! How in the world had they been able to secure a lit candle on every single grave there, I did not know. The undertaking, (not meant as a play on words), would have appeared to be impossible, and yet there it was and I was feasting my eyes on an indescribably beautiful and inspiring sight to behold.

Just as I began to think it was one of the most remarkable things I'd ever seen, and could not get better, it did! It was just starting to snow and little snowflakes began to sprinkle, sparkle and dance all over my truck and in the air, and I knew the Lord had enabled me to see this wonderment just in time, "for such a time as this", (which is one of my favorite phrases ever). And I thanked Him for such an exciting, joyful, expression of everlasting Life!

I didn't have a camera, and so I immediately called (Nashville's famous heavy metal pastor, who feeds the homeless), "Pastor Bob", family members and others, who, at that late hour may well have been asleep already. I excitedly told them to get dressed and into their cars and get over there before day, or before the snow flakes put out the firelight and bring their cameras. I never knew if they ever did go, but I didn't need a camera to forever remind me of its incredible affect, to see an entire hillside become a living memorial of happy warmth and joyfulness.

Of course it made tears come to my eyes at what a happy representation it seemed of the Glory of resurrection into eternal life. I thought of how each grave over there stood for a family's loved one, and how the dark cemetery on a cold night would be a lonely and sad place to look at, especially as Christmas celebration time was drawing nearer; but instead, it had become transformed into a lighted happy landscape with lively flickering flames and dancing snowflakes which were now visible in the misty glow and the place looked very much *alive!*

I called the cemetery office the following day, (even though I'm not for sure which one it was), and they explained how their cemetery patron group had enlisted other groups as well, and a huge troop of volunteers had filled small paper sacks with a bit of sand and placed the candle upright in the sand and lit them all at about the same time. The candles were lit by even more volunteers who helped and a ceremony of dedication was provided by area pastors that same day. They said it was a December sixteenth tradition, a Christmas season celebration, of sorts, to bring joy to the families and others who would see it, that the Savior of the world was born who would then rise from the dead and offer everlasting life to all who would believe.

If it was Mount Juliet Memorial Gardens, and I'm pretty sure it was, that's where Charlie Daniels was laid to rest just a couple of years ago, close to when my husband Gary passed away. We had been to at least two of his live concerts before, in Florida, and he was one of Gary's favorite singers. Among his hit songs Charlie did were "Country Boy Will Survive" and "Devil Went Down to Georgia", but my favorite was one live performance, when he sang "How Great Thou Art". He didn't have the special backup music like in his recorded songs, but I think he gave his rendition of that hymn more energy and put so much more of himself into it, and the Holy Spirit, than I had ever heard him sing and play before.

Charlie made several statements before he passed away from a massive heart attack in July of 2020. One was that, **"I stand with Jesus!"** Another was that, it is not the government or the media we follow, but the "God of *the Bible, our parents, and our pastors followed.* On another occasion he expressed how in his life he had mistakenly failed to follow God like he should, but that he had returned to his faith, and now was proclaiming that, it is *faith* we need to live by! His devotion and appreciation of our country, military and patriotism, was unmatched, and that had made him one of Gary's heros, and mine.

Charlie had known what it was to be a man with doubts in his past, as many do, so how do we know for sure Jesus arose again after having been crucified? We can accept it by faith for lots of reasons, from how it was prophesied by men of God centuries before, written in the scrolls in which God gave His Word, and it became God's Word, and how it makes sense that Jesus was and *is* God's Word come in the flesh. How those ancient prophecies then became true and did so exactly as they were predicted, and because there were ample first hand witness accounts of this, and I could go on.

And here is another major issue: when we believe it by faith, the Holy Spirit has a way of confirming it in our Spirit. He verifies it in multiple ways that never stop. In my lifetime, they get stronger and more frequent, and by now, I don't wish or hope it's all true, or just think it probably is, no, *I know in my knower.... it's true!*

I know this, and I can be assured of it, because from up on mountain tops, *Jesus lets you see forever,* about what you can see, and especially what you *can't see.* Now, and in these pages I will show you what He showed me, they'll include wonderful things I learned from lessons with eagles, Indian chiefs, high places (and some low ones), proving true, the validity of the *living* Word of God.

That reminds me of something funny He said to me once: I had prayed, "Well, Lord, I don't think anybody's actually reading my book, (the first one). He replied, "Yeah, Betty, I know what you mean, they're **not reading *mine,* either!**" We both had laughed. That's a pretty good example of the relationship I have always shared with Him, and still do, Hallelujah!

I'm not sure at how early an age you begin to discover your identity, who you are and what you're about, but I can pretty well recollect some images and visions, experiences and impressions, that all first got started in my "wrapped in a blanket" baby stage. I can actually remember being held warmly snuggled in a blanket and passed around between family members. I also vividly recall riding in a stroller along western New York State walkways in parks and city sidewalks, looking up at the trees.

I had always loved it outdoors, being out in the fresh air and sunshine. I would rather be out, rather than inside, when I was a little girl, right up until this day in my senior years. Mother said I loved trees, watching them move in the breezes, smelling the leaves and pine needles, and I still do. In fact, I delighted my entire life seeing trees and *mountains,* and in this book I'll be telling you about a few of them that impacted my life and that up until now, I have told only a few folks about.

The Lord first spared my life when my mother was in a long and difficult labor with me in Jamestown, NY, because my doctor was not there to deliver me when needed. He was way too inebriated and could not be sobered up enough to perform the delivery and with not another physician available. Phone calls went out to everyone to pray.

Our family Weakland Chapel radio broadcast shared the urgent prayer request. They kept my mother stablized as long as they possibly could, when the tipsy elderly man arrived in just the nick of time and delivered me healthy and strong, Praise the Lord! The name of our radio program was, "The Hour of Power" and they said God showed forth a powerful answer to prayer when I was born, when we allowed me to live that night.

I would hear this story repeated throughout my lifetime concerning my intoxicated doctor who delivered me and I don't doubt it probably helped to create in me an early anti-alcohol attitude that would stay with me. If it was the initial attempt for an enemy, such as Satan, to attempt to prevent my birth, he was using booze to do it and I resisted drinking it my whole life. I will be telling you in this book what crisis happened when I didn't resist it. Well the Bible says we have to be sober and vigilant because the devil stalks about trying to destroy us.

I was named after my Aunt Betty, the Rev. Betty Weakland (Bixby), the childhood evangelist who preached from the time she was eight years old, nightly, across the whole nation. They also had that daily radio program, she and my Grandfather, Rev. Dr. Joseph Roy Weakland, (who I called "Papa"), shared, on which they announced my birth on March 16, 1943, in Chautauqua County, NY.

I was born in a hospital that was built on the site of the first recorded Iroquois Indian encampment and there is a historical marker there to confirm it, located on the area's highest hill, a part of the Appalachian Mountain range. I suppose you could say that within these pages, I will be escorting you from the *first* Indian high place, where I arrived on earth, to God's *last* Indian mountain He is climbing hand in hand with me on, (and now *with* you), on "Jesus' Mountain"!

My mother wrote a poem the week I was born that has been tossed about in collections of important documents and papers for almost eighty years and I miraculously came across it today in an old file folder of my mother's:

Betty "Winsom" Swan
On an Indian hill, on a frosty morn,
Our baby girl was born;
Her Dad had prayed
The whole night through,
And when her cry was heard,
He named her Betty Winsom **Swan,**
For she would spread the Word!
by Dorothy Weakland Swan, (March 18, 1943)

The famous Seneca Indian Chief Cornplanter settled on the "mountain top" where I was born, and the official historical marker says his camp was there in the late 1700's. It was between 1797 and 1830 when they lived there before they retreated to the Alleghany Indian Reservation at Salamanca. That was where I would meet later in life and become befriended by, the Chief's direct descendant, the Rev. Ralph E. Bowen, and his wife, Dee, who would come visit me and stay in my home in Florida.

They said the announcement of my birth, caused a flurry of excitement in the family and in the church family. Local residents of the Jamestown community, who were members of Papa's Baptist church, the Betty Weakland Chapel, sponsored the popular radio broadcast. You must remember there was no television in those days. The Weakland Tabernacle was built to seat approximately 2,000 people, due to the influx of parishoners who were longing to be in church during the war years.

The country was reeling with bad news brought about by the Depression, and World War II, with local soldier boys returning home in boxes to their grieving families. News about the new baby girl to my parents, Dorothy Weakland Swan and Sherman Winsom Swan, was a welcome escape from all the sad reporting of the day, and baby gifts began to flow in to the Weakland family.

My Grandma Weakland, the grandest Gospel pianist I ever knew, said every day when the postal deliveries arrived it was like a baby shower in our living room, so many wonderfully handmade baby blankets and clothes, they were happily able to share them with other new mothers in the community, who also were in need of them. Little dresses would continue to be sent to us throughout years to come, by generous seamstresses in the audience who were blessed by the family ministries and wanted to show their appreciation. God's Blessings in my life began from its start and I began to know Him, not just for **presents,** but for the mighty and powerful gift of faith and His very own ***Presence!***

From as early as a two year old, they would have me stand on a chair in front of the microphones at church services and at the radio studio and have me sing songs like "Praise Him, Praise Him, All Ye Little Children, God is Love!" and "Jesus Loves Me This I Know". My favorite was "A Sunbeam, a Sunbeam, Jesus wants me for a Sunbeam!", but the audiences only laughed at me because when I sang that one, I thought the word was *Zombie,* "Jesus wants me for a Zombie!" Of course I had no idea what a zombie was, but a sunbeam shined for Jesus and I knew from the beginning that I always wanted to do that!

I will always remember singing "I'm in the Lord's Army" (written about 1936, Public Domain, according to Google), as I would march and act out all the lyrics:

"I may never march in the Infantry, Ride with the Calvary, Shoot the artillery, I may never fly over the enemy, but I'm in the Lord's Army! I'm in the Lord's Army, I'm in the Lord's Army, I may never..." and so on. After singing those words through 2-3 times, then my best part was to end it and to snap to attention, salute, and shout loudly, **"Yes,** *Sir!"*

Sometimes I'd sang it with all the other little children and march, and they say it was quite a sight. I remember the people crying though, because it was war time and all the funerals left everyone with a very tender, hurting, heart and mind. Watching the people in Ukraine in the news reports lately, brings it all back to me and I keep on praying for miracles for their aid.

My mother frequently sang duets with Aunt Betty and my dad, who had become well known in his own right, playing his trumpet. They ministered in music at church services and radio broadcasts when he wasn't away serving the country at an Army Air Force Base. I recognized their notoriety at an early age as complete strangers would rush to greet us in public, calling us by our first names, and referring to me as "Oh, there's little baby Betty!", even long after my babyhood. I can remember frowning and whispering indignantly, to my mother when I was four, "I'm not a *baby*! How come all the people keep calling me *a baby*!?" lol

My Dad was a full blooded Swede whose parents' families had immigrated from Sweden. The Jamestown, New York community included a large population of Swedish settlers, many who attended the Zion Covenant Church there. That's where my daddy's father, Lawrence Warner Swan, served as a spokesman, similar to the role of a Deacon for the congregation. He was also a great Sunday school teacher of the Bible. He would officiate at the services, introducing the pastor, and also guests in the audience.

When we were in attendance we would stand and be welcomed with much applause by their church members who were already familiar with us on the radio. I was always so proud of my Grandfather Swan, who would speak in both Swedish and English from the podium. Grandma Swan would join him near the front door after services, greeting the people as they left. She had also served as hostess in the fellowship hall for dining events sponsored by the church.

Everyone was always so glad to see my dad, the young Swedish trumpet player who had grown up in their congregation, and who, together with his two best friends, formed the "Cathedral Trumpeteers" playing beautiful harmony on their three trumpets.

The Cathedral Trumpeteers won the biggest competition for talent on the Major Bowes radio broadcast, listened to by the country coast to coast. It was the "American Idol" of their day. The win spiriled them to fame and even an invite to perform in an exclusive New York night club, which caused reason for their families to pray about the matter before allowing them to consent. Three young Swedish boys raised strictly in their conservative homes were not accustomed to attending events with alcohol. After much discussion, they agreed it was an opportunity of a lifetime to get to play there and also a chance to give a Christian testimony they might not otherwise be privilaged to give.

My dad would share with me what it was like to be thrust into the limelight, to walk on stage at the club packed with standing room only. It was an audience wanting to see the fellas in person who had achieved such a great award, who they had only before, just heard on the radio.

Daddy said the three prayed together backstage, and then when facing the brightly lit, colored floodlights and enthusiastic crowd, they played their very best renditions of the hits of the day, the love songs, the patriotic war music, and then it was time to close with the last song. My dad thanked them for coming and the club for inviting them. Then he told the crowd they could only give God all the credit for the wonderful things He was doing in their lives and for their success. Then he said they would like to close the show by playing their favorite hymn, "The Old Rugged Cross".

In perfect harmony, with anointed chords that vibrated through their very beings, the boys played with eyes closed, belting out that beloved song of the ages, loved by so many. It told the story of God's love for us, so great He gave His only begotten Son, Jesus. Daddy said during the first verse it was so silent you could hear a pin drop, then quite a stir as the crowd began to stand up beside their chairs at their tables.

Opening his eyes, he saw it looked as if every soul there was standing with tears rolling down their cheeks, many wiping their eyes or their eye glasses with their linen napkins, for the remaining stanzas. Then breaking into wild, thunderous applause and shouting, even as the trio left the building, the standing ovation continued as they made their way across the parking lot to their car.

Daddy said that night he prayed, "Thank You, Lord, only to You is due all the glory. May I dedicate the rest of my life serving you and bringing Your good news to all who need to hear it!" He would say that what had started out being a concert, ended up being *"church"!*

He joined the Army Air Force where on guard duty one night he heard the voice of God call him to be a preacher and pastor. My parents would then attend in Louisville, Kentucky, the Southern Baptist Theological Seminary where he graduated, and mother completed all the Christian Education courses, before accepting the pastoral positions at several small, Kentucky churches.

While at the seminary, I was a student as a four and five year old in the kindergarten that trained young Christian women to become ministers and workers in children's education. I came down with Scarlet Fever while I was there and my doctors at the hospital feared they would lose me. The entire seminary body had special prayer for me at their weekly chapel church service that packed the auditorium that day. When they prayed, my fever miraculously broke, and I was well! God had used me to create a miracle for all the future preachers, pastors, missionaries and Gospel musicians to share in and to witness first hand.

"Thank you, Lord, for sparing my life. Thank You for giving me a true story to tell with this book, which I ask You to anoint, that readers may come to know You, Jesus, as our Healer, Savior, and wonderful Friend, our Life Giver."

I chuckle to myself as I type here today, 79 years of age, as I keep pausing to look out at the horizen completely surrounded by glorious mountains gleaming in the North Carolina sunshine, feeling like I'm still the "little baby Betty", wrapped in the blanket shawl, watching the trees, and thanking God for being so good to me.

I thanked God for not only sparing my life when I was born and then again in kindergarten, but later, as a young mother. I was almost electrocuted as I stood barefooted on a damp terrazo floor I had waxed that day, when I took hold of my refrigerator freezer door and was momentarily grounded. The following day the Palm Beach Post Times Newspaper had me pictured on the front page by my fridge and the headline read, *"She's as 'Lucky' as Her Name"*.

In that fearful panic I had promised my Creator that if He would spare me I would serve Him the rest of my life and tell the whole world about His Son Jesus. *It felt as if I had been thrust from my kitchen floor up into the gates of Heaven* where I asked to return to my family, and It was granted. My Dad had me checked out at the hospital and officials from Florida *Power* and *Light* verified to news reporters the voltage should have killed me. Thank God, He had *His* Power and *His* Light operating in my life!

In 2016 the doctor removed a small spot of malignant cancer from a breast and in 2020 God spared me again when He brought me through 10 days fighting for my life in the Blairsville, Georgia, hospital with Covid19, with pneumonia in both lungs. (The hospital is only fifteen minutes from my North Carolina house.) A month later the virus would then take my dear husband, Gary, and leave me widowed; but, the sadness, the tears of grief and mourning, He faithfully replaced with total peace, *and* a mission to get this book written.

When I took the specialized course on "patrol officer pursuit," offered to all law enforcement officers once, I think I was Florida Highway Patrol instructor, Max Shell's, star pupil, if I do say so myself, lol. Probably because I was the only female in the class, he would frequently encourage me when I was being tested for a grade on driving skill and the clock time in which we would have to accomplish the manuever. It paid off, and my scores exceeded those of my male classmates. I think the teacher's theory was to allow some healthy competition between the sexes and I would sometimes hear the fellas saying, "Ok, guys, don't let the lady show us up, now!" However, the instructor's support served to boost my confidence when I was driving at that time, not just in the class, but everywhere, and it still does.

Why am I telling you this? Because there are some close calls I have now when no one is with me and I try to avoid ever mentioning them. It will be an especially sad day for me, if I ever have to hear people tell me I'll have to quit driving "at my age". One of my favorite quotes was when my late grandson, Justin Savacool, told a room full of people, "If you ever have to get somewhere in record time, like an airport, ya gotta have my grandma drive you there! I guarentee you....she'll get you there in time!"

I would want Lt. Shell, (who had probably achieved an even higher rank, since that time), now to know, that he is responsible for saving my life all these years, many times over, in dangerous situations. I have had semi's headed right toward me in my lane, I have had wrecks occur immediately before my truck, I've had passing cars crowd me into the shoulder of the road, when there was no shoulder. I have had a car pull out into my lane at high speed and disappear and reappear in my rear view mirror!

I thank God He led me to make the moves it required to prevent what would have been the inevitable crash; but, I also have to thank Him for putting me under that master driving instructor. I think I put on some pretty hot, spit-firin,' breath-ketchin', trick-ridin', rodeo shoutin' routines in my truck, that woulda' made him down right proud! ("Jus' sayin'") lol.

Max was the noted media celebrity of the day, who gave daily televised driver information on public service announcements for many years. God used him to help me manage on the road, so many times, the unique skill it took to stay alive. Thank You, Jesus! That is precisely what the Bible teaches us, "how to manuever safely, as we travel in a very unsafe world".

I was very honored once to be invited by a dear friend, Seminole Indian, Wallace Tommie, nicknamed, "Waldo," to attend the annual Green Corn Dance, near Yeehaw Junction, Florida. Only tribal people were allowed to be there and even some of my close Christian Seminole friends were no longer attending like they had in former years, and who had grown up always looking forward to it.

My tribal pastor had explained to me that originally it was held with strict rules and restrictions, such as the prohibiting of alcohol on the grounds, but it was still a gathering utilizing all the oldest songs passed down through generations that would only be sung at the yearly event. Waldo told me he remembered all those old songs in the native Indian languages, because his father and grandfather had helped officiate using them long ago. He had been asked to come and help lead in those dances since he had been taught by his elders and could still recall all of the words. He had given me the directions of how to locate it and had instructed me to find the Deer Clan camp when I got there and they would be expecting me.

When Gary and I arrived in the heavily wooded and secluded ceremonial grounds there was a flurry of excitement going on. Late spring and early pre-summer storms had saturated the wet ground, so the first thing we noticed was how many trucks were already stuck in the mucky clearings. We were told if we hurried we could catch the next "ride" deeper into the woods, so I quickly parked under a couple of really tall old pine trees and prayed that the frequent lightning wouldn't strike one of them and hit my Ford F150 four wheel drive truck.

Did you ever wonder just how many people a big front-end loader can hold? No, I hadn't either, but I was about to find out. I *heard* our "ride" coming through the palmettos before I *saw* it, yep, a nice *huge*, John Deere dirt-hawlin' piece of heavy equiptment with a long haired Seminole driver holding a beer in one hand, grinning from ear to ear, announcing he'd be right back for the next load, to climb aboard wherever we could and to hang on tight!

We had so many folks on it I lost count. They were in and on the bucket, in and on the cab, the top, the front and the back! Some of the people were just hanging off the sides with only one foot on the thing holding on to a someone else so they wouldn't fall off. As I observed the huge ruts we were navigating through, I could see why no one's four wheel drive trucks were of any use. All the way through the woods to the camps the rain had let up just long enough for us to get to the thatched roofs made of cabbage fans (palm fronds), but what had not let up, was the outrageous lightning!

Every time a lightning bolt clicked around us from all four winds, that even lit up our faces, with each blinding flash, followed by the thunderous crashing of ear deafening thunder, not one soul ever expressed a single sign of fear, concern, terror, or alarm! It occurred to me that had I been the only, (well I'm sure I was not, but had I been), the only Christian on the front end loader, I didn't want to be seen as the *fearful* one of the bunch. I belonged to and represented Jesus Christ Who tells us to **never** fear! So I didn't. I would see Gary cringe or almost want to cover his cowboy hat with his arm as he flinched, and jump once or twice, but he, too, even got the spirit of the thing and acted really brave. Why, it was as if the Seminoles looked forward to this yearly event just to dance openly in the most severe and dangerous lightning God had ever created! One girl sitting in the bucket beside me said it would rain like this every year but would stop and start during certain songs.

The first thing we did was try to find Wallace, who was right where he was supposed to be, but was asleep on the wooden platform, so we went on back to the Deer Clan camp, keeping warmer by the fire there, in the now dark night with occasional light showers. Only the sound of the rumbling thunder was heard in the distance, and then sometimes, Waldo's familiar voice above some singers.

We were welcomed by the clan mother at the camp and as I sat alone by the fire two young Indian men, probably in their twenties, took chairs next to me asking me about my faith, because they'd heard I was a Christian. Gary had disappeared when a pickup truck filled in the back with men asked if he wanted to join them, and I saw him leap into the bed waving me goodbye. They had said people were stuck all over the place so they had a chain and planned to pull everyone back out. Well, they sure got the right fella, Gary was an expert at that, too.

Later he would say what fun, not work, it had been. Now me? I was *working* as I shared my testimony and tried my best to answer questions and Bible trivia. It was very enjoyable, but would have been more fun if I had Jack Van Impe, or Ken Copeland there beside us in the firelight, two of my favorite on-fire Bible teachers at the time.

The two inquisitive, polite, congeniel and hospitable men began to question me on every Biblical issue, theory, concept and teaching they had ever wondered about. They had just recently given their hearts to Jesus at a church at the Hollywood reservation, but had needed someone who could help with a few answers. Now I was certain I knew why the Lord had sent me there to the Green Corn Dance. I could only thank God and praise Him for this unique opportunity to be doing precisely, the ministry He had called me to do.

He had also taught me to never, ever again, be fearful of lightning, He is with me. And should He ever use it to bring me to Heaven, well then, that's ok, too. It just "don't" get better'n that, to be here and then all of a sudden, be there with Jesus in Heaven, how ever He chooses to bring us Home. This chapter I entitled, "The Devil Wanted Me Dead, Y'all".........but he "don't" get me, till God is ready for me, and God is the Life-Giver and the Life sustainer, and the provider for Life *eternal*! I like the bumper sticker I had once, *"DON'T LEAVE EARTH..... WITHOUT JESUS!"* and I always liked it that an inmate came up with a good acronym for the word, B.I.B.L.E., *"basic instruction before leaving earth!"*

On the way home from the Green Corn Dance, in the early morning hours, just before dawn, Gary and I pulled up to the house, sleepy, but happy. Gary said, "I really had a good time tonight with those ole Seminole boys, pulling everybody out of the muck...kinda like that song says, the "mirey clay". "Yes, that's what I was doing, too Gary, helping two young fellas all night, who want to go into ministry, learn how to help others do the same thing, spiritually". Then we sang together "He Ransomed Me", (written by Julia H. Johnson 1849), where the lyrics say..........

Hallelujah! What a Savior, Who can take a poor, lost sinner, lift him *from the miry clay, and* set ME free!

"I will ever tell the story, shouting, 'Glory, Glory, Glory! Hallelujah Jesus lifted me!"

He is still "lifting us" up where we belong. I used to like to listen to Buffy Sainte Marie, a great Cree Tribal member and songwriter, who made it famous, when she sang her song....."where the eagles cry, on a mountain high, *Love lift* us *up where we belong!"*....only I had thought the lyrics said, *Lord,* lift us up, so that's how I still sing it....well, *God is Love!* ("Up Where We Belong" was written by Buffy St. Marie, Jack Nitzsche, and Will Jennings in 1982).

God wasn't ready for me to come Home yet, and He has at least one last assignment for me to fulfill and it is to tell you many things in the pages that follow. Thanks for joining me on our journey.... *to Jesus' Mountain.*

MY HOLY MOUNTAIN

The Lord says "...But whoever takes refuge in Me, will
*inherit the land and possess **My holy mountain**"!*
Isaiah 57:13c NIV

Now you may find this hard to believe, but even as a very young girl I began to love my Bible and to enjoy reading it like the other kids devoured comic books and the like. I treasured it. As I learned to read and write in the first and second grades it was my Bible that I wanted to learn to read.

A funny side note about my first words I ever wrote, my first one was "BEER"! (lol) We were living in Louisville, Kentucky at the Southern Baptist Theological Seminary where I was enrolled in the beginning kindergarten class and my parents were studying to graduate. On every trip across the city, passed all the stores and bars, there were bright, colorful flashing lights that said, "BEER". I would sit in church beside my mother while my dad was preaching, drawing on her church bulletin, or program, and would write all over it, "beer". Probably because my name started out with "Be" and so did the word "beer", it had been easy for me to remember how to spell the word I had seen flashing everywhere, so I did.

As I was practicing my letters this one Sunday, Mother noticed it and whispered that it was not very appropriate for a little Baptist preacher's girl to be writing that in church and that if I ever spelled it on paper again, I should probably include the word "NO!" So I then wrote "BEER NO" everywhere. It was my first sentence and to this day I have not tasted it.

Well, once I started to have a sip at a pizza restaurant but wrinkled up my nose at it. I was ready to go into labor and we decided to feed the kids before taking me inside the hospital to have Niki. One sharp bearing down pain caused me to lift Gary's glass up to my lips but I immediately decided I'd rather feel the labor pains than taste a drink that smelled like my furniture cleaner!

I remember way back then I even removed old prior bulletins from the pages of mother's Bible and added "NO" to each word where I had written beer. This story would follow me throughout my lifetime as my teenagers sometimes teased me as they left the house on dates, "Bye, Mom, Love you! Don't worry,..."Beer, no!"

I had a small New Testament I loved to carry around when I was little, and I recall even having 'BEER NO' written on the inside covers but I could hardly wait to be able to copy down whole Bible verses. I would use Scripture to practice on paper, finally being able to write: "For God so loved the world". What I'm trying to explain is that, I had such a strong desire to read the Bible, that it had even motivated me to learn to read and write.

Much later in life I once surprised a little boy in an Everglades migrant camp, by giving him a new Bible, and he hugged it, kissed it, and then danced around the farm field with it, prompting me to pray, "Oh Lord, forgive me if ever I fail to cherish your Holy Word like that little kid." I think maybe it may have been the best present he had ever been given and he expressed true delight with it as he jumped around, running in circles, and happily singing. Well, that probably best describes how I have *always* felt about my own Bible.

This may be the finest way to start an introduction to you of who I am, and how probably **I started out, early on, a little *differently* than most of the other kids around me.**

I would end up actually carrying my black Bible to school with me from grades one to twelve, right on top of my school books. I had even carried my little white bridal Bible with me underneath my white roses bouquet down the aisle at my wedding when I married. Did I understand everything in it? No, of course not, but, I understood the happiness and peace it gave me to even just have it with me and to read it. Now I make sure I am no where without it. Like Prophet Robin D. Bullock always reminds us, "No soldiers or warriors go into battle without their 'Swords'!", and in case you haven't noticed yet, *every day's* a battle.

My Bible was to be, and is, my sword, guidebook, mapbook, rulebook and comforting inspiration and what I was to base my faith on. It contained the very words of Jesus, who was and is the Rock I would stand on trusting Him to show me the way, the truth and the life. This Bible was His Word and is *the* Word. I loved it that it said that only *Jesus*, the *only* begotten Son of the living God, *and that He is the Way, the Truth, and the Life.* I even have that verse on the back of my new Jeep pickup truck. On the back just above the state tag, I have John 14:6 KJV, where Jesus answered and said, *"I am the Way, the Truth, and the Life; no man cometh unto the Father but by Me".* The front tag simply reads: "John 3:16".

Carrying a Bible with you anywhere in public causes people to notice it and take note, (remember it), not that I wanted people looking at me. I wasn't trying to draw attention to myself at all, but I certainly wanted to know, both then and now, that I am always doing everything possible to point others to Jesus. I usually keep a Bible on my dashboard, until I turn a corner too fast, anyway.

I always had a bumper sticker or two proclaiming the name of Jesus. I had one once, that said, "I know the way if you are lost". My favorite for many years was when I was parked in the police station parking lot, between the patrol cars where all my officers would see it, I had my bumper sticker displayed prominently, *"REAL men, love Jesus!"*

Yesterday my daughter needed to drive my Jeep into town and referred to it as the Gospel "billboard". Come to think about it, none of our friends have asked to borrow our Uhaul-type cargo trailer since I plastered two huge Bible verses on it, one on each side, the kind and size designed for truck tail gates.

Let me share with you what happened when I had carried that Bible in high school along with my books, and every day when I passed one of my classmates. I would always say "Good Morning" or "Hi" and call him by name. For three years I did this *every day*, as I smiled and he never once responded except to just look at me. Every day, I repeated the same thing regardless.

Many, many, years later after we had graduated, I saw his name on the front page of the newspaper. He had tragically run over his little boy accidently as he was leaving for work, saying goodbye to his wife who was standing in the doorway. They had not seen their toddler run out the door and go behind his daddy's truck. I wept as I put the paper down and found his address in the phone book.

That very day I drove to his home, parked in front and as I walked up toward the open front door with only the screen door closed, I could hear him excitedly say to his wife......"It's Betty Swan!...*I told you she'd come!*"

I prayed, "Thank you God for sending me to his home and to the funeral, what if I had not gone!?" It proved that whenever we stand up for Jesus, or represent Him in any way, we never know how He will use it to minister to hurting people for Him. I learned to never be offended *ever,* when someone didn't respond to my friendliness and it was only one example of that, there would be many more.

From the time I learned to read, it was exciting to open the Bible up randomly and see just what I had turned to. It has always been the perfect Word for that moment in time. After all, I believed what it said and I had faith to believe I could trust its Author to know, as I opened up the pages spontaneously, exactly which verses were meant for that very moment. I wasn't very good at memorizing stuff but I disciplined myself to do it and the scripture I memorized early on, was probably the most valuable thing I ever did for myself (and others!).

Maybe only once it backfired on me when I was teaching in my adult Sunday school class at the Indian reservation, and someone challenged me to just open up the Word right then to see what it might say, so I did. Bad idea, it was Amos 4:1a, and in that New Living Translation (NLT edition). I think it said, "Listen to me, *you fat cows!*" It taught me to be more respectful of the Holy Scripture and not allow myself to 'tempt the Lord, my God'. From then on, I only did that after sincere prayer asking Him for a passage to read. Of course, God loves to also tease me, sometimes like that, though, so we all finally quit laughing, and it was ok....and that same week I also started a new diet, and I think maybe everyone in the class did!

For many years and right up until we left to move to the mountains, I was teaching for many years, the adults at First Indian Baptist Church and the class was pretty much evenly divided between men and women. It had begun in the first classroom at the beginning of a long hallway located behind where the piano is inside the sanctuary. So that had to be when I first started the class about 1990. That class eventually grew too large and by the time we had left Florida to move to the mountains, we had to meet inside the sanctuary to hold the group.

But soon after we first had started that class, one morning I had the husband of the minister's daughter in attendance, and just as I had closed with prayer, he asked me a question in front of everyone as we all stood to leave. I have to admit it threw me for a loop, lol. Our lesson had been about one of the prophets in the Bible. Now, I can teach a Sunday school class and follow the literature and share it, but I am not a Bible "scholar" who *studies* the Bible, and in fact, I have sometimes had problems retaining even who did what in God's Holy Word. I am ashamed to admit. But I will never forget when Juan Rodriquez, a very well educated man I have respect for, posed a question.

"Mrs. Luckey", he had said, "Do you believe that there are prophets like that today?" At once I had every eye looking at the teacher for an answer. I don't even remember what the bland sounding answer was exactly, that I came up with, but it was something about God being so great He can speak through anyone or at anytime He chooses. Well, I knew that wasn't particularly the answer he was looking for, and I knew I didn't have that answer, for one reason, I had never wondered about it myself. Not until *last week!* **Now this is maybe some 30 years later!** I texted Cyndi for his phone number and I called him up.

"Hello Juan! This is Betty," I said boldly, "The answer is YES!"

I could hear him laughing. I explained to him it was not until this year I had a most definite opinion on that subject and his name is Prophet Robin Dale Bullock from Warrior, Alabama. I proceeded to explain to Juan that I had begun to listen intently to him and had been even YouTube-ing his back videos and church services he shares with his wife of 42 years, also named Robin, who is the pastor. I added that the reason I had to call him was because *God told me to.*

Minutes before, Prophet Bullock had just preached and revealed another of the most amazing revelations, and I was so excited, I thought I heard the Lord **audibly** say, "Call Juan and tell him!" I resisted thinking he would think I was nuts, after thirty years, when at that moment, Robin stopped what he was saying, looked directly at the tv camera and said something to the effect, "Didn't God tell you to do something?" And as I sat there dumbfounded, the Prophet adds, "well you better do it, now!" I thought I'd fall off my rocker! That's when I did it. I called Juan.

I told Juan that I wasn't always so quick to ask everyone I knew to watch Bullock, or some of my other favorite prophets, as well, because the political message that is included is a strong one, and that I already knew a percentage of my friends and some family, were not going to appreciate it, in fact, would about disown me. But look what happens to our country when we sit back and don't speak out fast enough?! I knew this because when I had attempted it, some close to me had already said it would alter our closeness from then on, so now I had been trying to be more discreet. (Shame on me).

It's a hard and hurtful thing to be almost 80 years old and think your loving family might allow our differing political opinions to separate us and make us distant! Kinda like being stuck between a rock and a hard place, that's how divided our nation is and it makes me cry...and pray.

Well, half of me is being discreet not to offend and the other half is too motivated with joy, prophetic inspiration, and exuberance not to shout it from the rooftop! After I listen to Robin D. Bullock, and also, Rabbi Jonathan Cahn, Brother Perry Stone, and Pastor Jentezen Franklin, and Kat Kerr, I feel the same way. We actually have Prophets among us and God has sent them for us to listen to. No, I don't worship man, and at any time these awesome people can let us down, being human, because only Jesus has that authority in my life, and theirs, (to be worshipped), and they will be the first to agree.

Well enough of that everybody, I said what I needed to say about it and I can't afford to lose you before I get to all the good stuff, in the following pages, the reasons I wrote this book. We are in the middle of Spiritual warfare and I have some of the stories you may need to hear. Everything *you have read to this point was to help set the stage* so you'd watch this production my life has been, with a greater *understanding.*

Way back "in the day", the routine at the start of the school day was to stand with your whole class, saying the pledge to the flag and the Lord's Prayer together. Just prior to that, the teacher would call on a student to read a Bible verse from the Bible on the teacher's desk. This little daily ritual was probably dreaded by most students because of shyness, or fear they'd mispronounce unfamiliar words, or nervousness in general and rarely was there a volunteer.

I was usually the appointed reader, which I loved, and what the class did not know, was that I would silently pray for God to have me turn to the right verse He wanted read. I merely opened the Book and would glance down at the verse on the page that sort of jumped out at me and then read it. It was miraculously always so appropriate that every day I looked forward to the verse that the Lord was going to have us share. If I would see that the following verse or two were also especially meaningful, I would include them also at my own free will. I'll bet the teachers thought I had the verses planned, but I never did, and the Lord was so faithful to always have me turn to just the right one.

I'm sure I was probably just as shy as the other kids, but I was so used to having my preacher and pastor daddy leading meetings and church services and my mother teaching Sunday school and singing special music in front of everyone, that it came pretty natural to me. Our family history was comprised of many pastors, preachers, missionaries, deacons, Christian musicians and faithful church workers. My parents were also active in the PTA at my school and usually held offices that kept them speaking in front of all the other parents.

I'm chucklin' because I just remembered my mother's red dress. Daddy was our PTA President and she was the secretary. I would sit in the PTA meetings on the last row doing my homework. The regular monthly meeting had just been dismissed and the parents and teachers began to file out the crowded auditorium doorway. My dad was walking way up ahead of me and my Mother, who had hesitated by my chair while I gathered up my school books. We glanced up at Daddy, who was now climbing up the exit stairs in front of everyone and to our utter shock, had *his arm wrapped around a lady in a red dress,* the exact same color my mom was wearing that night! He was so busy greeting everyone he hadn't noticed it wasn't Mother by his side!

"Quick, Betty!" Mother said, "See if you can catch up and tell him!" I dropped everything and ran passed everyone to the stairs where I called out, "Daddy, that's not Mom!" He turned pure white before he turned as red as the dresses! Then he looked at the startled lady, and let go so abruptly, she staggered as she almost stumbled and had to clutch the handrail with both hands!

From that day forward we would tease my poor daddy by singing the popular song, "See the girl with the red dress on...." and he would inevitably blush. That was Ray Charles's "What'd I Say". We'd sing it or hum the tune whenever Mother wore a red dress or whenever anyone else in the room had one one, just to give my dear daddy a "heads up!" lol.

I had been named after my well known Aunt Betty Weakland (Bixby-Creighton), my mother's sister. We were both named Elizabeth, meaning "Consecrated to God", from which "Betty" is the commonly used nickname. She was famous from the age of eight when she began preaching to huge crowds and on the radio. She was and is listed in "Who's Who in America" as the childhood evangelist who drew thousands from across the country to hear her sing and preach.

All of this had made an impact in my life, but I can honestly tell you that I had my own close relationship with the Lord on a personal level as well. Later in life someone would wrongly accuse me of "being religious" *only* because of my "religious" upbringing. Of course you can imagine the positive influence of having been privilaged to hear at least three or more sermons a week since I was born, but I didn't just hear the messages, I remember *listening* intently to them.

Whenever the preacher gave a Bible reference, I loved looking it up and following along, underlining passages and writing notations in the margins. I can honestly tell you how blessed I am to have been raised in a devoutly Jesus-centered lifestyle, but that in spite of, and in addition to it, I experienced my *own* faith independantly (from parents and family). I was delighted to have a real relationship with our Lord, as my Savior, Friend, Messiah, Shepherd, King (of kings), Lord (of lords), and **my "Chief Jesus, the *Chief above all chiefs*".**

I accepted Jesus Christ into my heart at the age of six publicly and was baptized in the baptismal pool by my dad, Rev. Sherman Swan, at Midway Baptist Church, in Midway, Kentucky. This was on a Sunday morning around Easter time in the spring of 1949.

My favorite group I belonged to there was the "GA's" which stood for Girl's Auxilliary, the Southern Baptist club for girls to study missions and memorize scripture. I worked hard at it and rose up through the ranks of Princess, Lady-in-Waiting, and Queen during elementary and middle school. I was one of the youngest girls to do this but I was driven to do it by my strong love for Jesus and His Holy Word. To this day it is that experience of learning to memorize the verses that I have relied on my whole life and I praise the Lord for those years of preparation.

This brings me to share with you the Bible verse I start this book introduction with, Isaiah 57:13c (NIV). It was a favorite of mine and one I did a paper on in GA's. First of all, I had no idea in the second and third grade what a "refuge" was, but in life as we encounter fear, hurt, pain, disappointment, insecurity, danger and the unknown, we soon know the desire to have security and safety, and experience a longing for a place of refuge. So the verse says, "But whoever takes refuge *in Me, (in God Himself)*, will inherit the land, and......possess **My holy mountain!**"

Well that got my attention at that early age because I already had a love for, and a mysterious pull in my spirit, to the mountains. It would be knowing the shelter of love and safety of Jesus, that would make me find refuge *in Him only.* And when I read all the stories how Jesus went to the mountains, and how even in the Old Testament where it was up on the mountains where so many important events took place that would shape humanity and where God's divine manifistations would bring us into a supernatural understanding of Him and His Kingdom, I found myself longing for the mountains, and especially, for *His* holy mountain.

As a child I didn't know or have a full understanding if God's holy mountain meant a real mountain to climb and live on, or if it was a "Spiritual" mountain that you climb and live on even if your house is at the beach. I actually hoped it was both because I actively wanted both very badly. Now for me, in my lifetime, I now know it was to be *both.*

No, you dont need to have Indians in your family history, or a famous aunt, a strong Christian upbringing or a lot of encouragement, entitlement, or position in society. We need no one and nothing else, but Jesus, who is **everything.** Some time Google Alvin Slaughter's song "He's All I Need" and hear the *awesome* choir backing him up with "Jesus is everything to me, He satisfies, my need supplies, Jesus is all I need". When I hear the song I'm somehow projected gently high upon the mountain top, praising Jesus, Who is my everything! I dare you to listen to it soon or right now and it proves what I'm sayin'!

That reminds me of the person that asked someone, "What do I need to do to join your Southern Baptist church?" They answered, "Have just two things: Jesus, and a 9 by 13 inch casserole dish!"

Recently, John Swindell, a dear farmer and rancher friend, told us at a Bible study, that there is a good Christian book entitled, "Perfect Everything", that had been such a blessing when he read it in his youth. He said the Holy Spirit began a new beginning in him that enabled him to appreciate just exactly what that author was describing in life. It says when we allow *Jesus* to become everything, that He desires to bring to our lives…"perfect *everything*". I found the book and ordered it online. The author was Joel Rufus Moseley, written in 1952.

I, too, now have enjoyed reading it with an increased awareness of how God has been perfecting **us**, as saints, like the Bible says. But not only that, *He is able* to perfect *everything* in our lives, as Saints. He makes our lives exciting! Jesus said, "I am come that they might have life, and that they might have it more abundantly!" John 10:10 b (KJV)

There was once a popular, but, I thought a sad, secular song, "Is This all There is?" and the answer is "No, Miss Peggy Lee, there is so much more to life in **Christ,** *always!*"

Now the part about inheriting and obtaining, possessing things or land, even back then, held no interest on my part, in fact, it was only the simple things in life I ever wanted. Well I was still so very young. But I grew up at the edge a small rural town, at the city limits, in a modest house which was the church parsonage, mostly surrounded by Kentucky Blue Grass horse pasture. I had a wonderful dog a farmer gave me when I was six years old, a fullblooded newborn collie puppy that looked like Lassie, I named "Tucky". She followed me everywhere I went accept to the school.

Tucky and I would walk to the church on Sunday mornings together while my parents were still getting dressed for services. After church was over Tucky sat at the front door to the sanctuary next to my dad and as he shook hands with everyone exiting, Tucky would also shake hands with the congregation. I'm not sure we ever had a picture of that, but it was quite a sight. She would lift her paw, her tail happily swishing back and forth across the floor, and if you lingered, she'd probably even be licking the top of your hand. She was such a loving, friendly, "friend" to everyone, causing all the people to smile as they left the church house.

There was a huge tree in my front yard next to the road adjacent to a pasture gate that I would use to climb on to reach the lowest branch, then hoist myself up and onto higher limbs as far as they would allow me to climb. It was my hideout, I suppose, my high tower, lighthouse, watch tower, command post and look out.

I don't recall ever having taken food, drink, books or toys up there with me, but alone in my tree, I carried on conversations with God and I even felt like I had His attention, even with a sense of humor, mine and His, a warm presence, and a prayer time I still treasure with Him. It *was like being on a mountain with Jesus*. My parents always knew where I was because Tucky would be laying at the base of the tree trunk asleep in the dirt, patiently awaiting my descent.

I didn't have other kids to play with there, because none lived close enough. When I wasn't talking to God, I was saying a lot to my dog. Most of the neighbors on our street were elderly, but on Halloween, (something I renounced participating in later in life), they loved for me to stop and ring their doorbells, answering with things like, "Oh, hello Betty, no one will know who you are in that nice costume!" I never could figure out how they knew it was me and never realized it was because Tucky was at my side. She was already sort of a legend in our little town and most folks knew her by name.

That wonderful Collie was always with me and when I had just turned thirteen years of age, just before we moved to Florida, my parents would give her away without asking me or telling me. She had almost been my constant companion for seven years. Her loss gave me a shock I had never before known, an empty hole in my heart that could not find any solace except to live in the "refuge" of Jesus. I remember needing to, but refusing to cry, instead I held my head up high like an Indian I had seen in a movie once, giving it my best stoic look I could muster up, and then I breathed in a peace only the Holy Ghost can provide. That was how I discovered where my "refuge" was and Who He is!

In my heart I prayed for God to forgive my parents and to give me His forgiveness toward them. He did, and I forgave them. I was beyond broken hearted and felt betrayal for the first time in my life, but I never cried. Somehow, God used the experience to teach me how to take pain and disappointment and trade it in to Him for His forgiveness, His "forget-ableness", comfort and healing by His power to make my heart and spirit full of His joy, once more.

Their reasoning behind this event included how unkind it might be to subject a large, long haired dog to the hot, humid Florida weather. They were concerned that the new church parsonage in Florida might not be conducive to an outside dog with its intown neighborhood, the busy traffic, the lack of a fenced yard. And they dreaded telling me and breaking my heart so they let on like it was more of a "summer-vacation-months" temporary *arrangement* to give us time to settle into our new environment before school would be starting in the fall.

So I pretended to believe it, but I knew in my heart the truth and all I remember was that the pain of it could only be mended and healed by Jesus and He was faithful to calm and comfort me and cause me to look up and forward, and beyond the valley to my Spiritual mountain ahead. I asked God to remove my pain supernaturally and help me to become excited about our new life ahead of us, and He did.

Most of the members of our Kentucky church were farmers who frequently had us over after church for wonderful fried chicken dinners with big bowls of fluffy mashed potatoes, prepared in their warm cozy farmhouses in the country. There were several local businessmen in our church as well, and one very affluent man who kindly arranged for his personal limo driver to pick me up at least once a month to play with his daughter, who was my own age.

She also, did not have girls near their home to play with, so I was delighted to become friends and visit with her at her parent's grand estate, a colonial mansion surrounded by race horses, white wood and stone fences with iron gates and lush green landscaping. My dad was her father's pastor and her dad was well known and respected throughout the whole state.

For a little girl, (me), who probably by choice, only had little more than a couple of dolls, a Roy Roger's cap pistol and a little red record player, it was not her magnificent collection of children's toys, that would rival any toy store, that excited me. Neither was it the elaborate custom made dollhouse with real electrical lighting inside, but it was the chance to befriend her and make friends with their household staff also. I had somehow found favor with them and they seemed anamored with my love for the Jesus of the Bible and I found myself looking forward to my conversations with my new adult friends who were employed there.

It was fun to make them laugh and I would sometimes hear them later saying to another employee down a hall or outside near the porch, chuckling about what the "little preacher's girl" had said that day. It was one of my earliest recollections of testifying about the Lord to other people, and it felt really good to talk about Him. They were obviously surprised that a child that young would quote Scripture, talk about God and offer to pray with folks. Hey, I had my Aunt Betty's example in my life to follow, and she had a whole ministry going on at age eight!

This young girl was my first real friend and she later was married to the man who became the Governor of the State and she became the State's First Lady. I could recognize her leadership qualities when she was only still a preteen and she was destined for great things, sure enough. She would later be honored for her outstanding contributions to charity and her work with future agriculture and conservation planning. I was proud to have been her friend and playmate and I even named my first daughter after her.

I remember when three wonderful ladies from my grandfather's church in Jamestown, New York, the singers who formed the "Chapel Trio" and sang on his daily radio program, mailed me the most gorgeous pale pink satin dress with ruffles and ribbons to wear in Kentucky for Easter. I could see how special the dress was, but it was so dressy, there was no way I wanted to be seen in it and mother could hardly get me to even try it on.

I resisted by saying none of the other farm kids had anything so fancy to wear and I only agreed I'd wear it for some church function other than Easter Sunday, a special day when folks usually tried to either wear something new, or at least the finest thing they already had. I'm not sure I ever did wear it at all, aside from the day they had my picture made in the dress by a professional photographer, and I suspect it was made so they could mail a copy to the trio with their "thank you" letter.

It made me kind of sad to think I had disappointed my Mother so, about that dress, but I was somewhat relieved when I overheard her laughing about it in another room, as she told my chuckling daddy, "I guess our little 'Indian princess' doesn't wear pink satin!"

I kept my hair in braids and always prefered jeans and a plaid shirt with barefeet, sometimes a turquois ring or beads. (which incidently is exactly how I still look at this very moment, at age 79, lol). I even had a costume-type Indian feather headdress, a souvenir war bonnet I'd sometimes wear when I played, back when I was real little. Then I recall removing the feathers and putting them on my braids up in my tree when I got a little older. I embraced every Indian story my mother ever told me about the Iroquois ancestors in our family. Any books I'd ever check out from the library would also be Indian stories.

Every Saturday I got a quarter as a weekly allowance for always making my bed and keeping everything off the floor in my room, emptying all the waste baskets into the garbage can, and drying and putting away the dishes after every meal. I would take my quarter and walk to the Midway five and dime store with Tucky at my side. She would dutifully await my return by laying on the sidewalk next to the front entrance, a screened door which screeched when you opened and closed it, as a little bell attached would jingle. I can still hear it.

I would first routinely inspect everything in the entire store by strolling down every aisle, and then buy the same thing every week: 5 rolls of caps! I don't remember ever shooting them in the pistol except once. I would sit on the sidewalk with a hammer and roll out the little strips of dark red paper with the brownish black dots and pound them, one at a time, watching the sparks fly and the wonderful gun powder smoke fill my lungs, and the bang make my stomach jump! Tucky would leap up into the air and run go hide under the front porch until I was through.

Maybe it was the gun powder aroma that lured me to graduate later in life from the Palm Beach and Indian River Police Academies and then spend time annually qualifying at the gun ranges. I must confess though, that it was far more fun, than shooting, to be bustin' caps with daddy's old hammer on the stained and cracked sidewalk by the front steps! You might say I was a thrifty little girl who knew how to get more "bang for my buck", as the old saying goes.

Those years were some of my best years attending Sunday school and going to church, especially children's church, when services were held for just the kids in a separate building or room. There were several short illustrations I heard my dad tell that I liked to tell also, stories that helped explain in a more simple way, a picture of how Jesus came to save us. Sometimes in a children's class I would act them out so I'd have their full attention. The first one is the one about the King in his tower:

This old King loved to climb up high in his tower to play a beautiful handmade harp that played wonderful sounding music. While he played every day, the crowds would gather down below the tower of his castle and his kingdom would listen. It made them happy. It made him happy. But one day, the harp was broken and somehow quit playing music and the King was so sad, and so were the people.

One at a time, harp makers and musical instrument builders, would stop by the castle door, knocking, the guards would allow them to climb up the steps of the tower to the harp, but not one of them could repair or fix the harp. The finest and best harpists tried to get the harp to work right, but no one could. Now the harp never played, the people were sad, and the King was very sad.

Then one day, a poor looking man in raggety clothing knocked upon the castle door. Indignantly, the guards asked what he wanted. "I have come to repair the harp", he said. "Go away, old man!" they said, "The best harp makers in the world have tried to fix it and cannot!" and they tried to send him away, but the King asked who it was and the guards told the King.

The King looked hopeful and said, bring him on up, no one else could make it work, let him at least try!" So the guards led the old man up the tower stairway to the harp. He sat there for but a moment, and had the harp playing the most beautiful music once again! The King asked him, "How come is it that after all those harp experts could not fix my harp, why is it you were able to make it play again?" The old man in the ragged clothing said, "You see sir, I am the man *who made* this harp!" *It takes the One who made us, to put us back together again, when we need fixing!*

Another favorite illustration was the little poor boy who built a toy boat with his own wood, hammer and nails. When he finished, he painted it red and blue, and when the paint had dried, he took it down to the little creek to see it float. He was so excited to see it floating he turned loose of it, when low and behold, a wind came and filled the little white cloth he'd nailed on for a sail, and the little boat sailed away! It went down the creek too fast for him to catch up, and soon, it entered the lake and then the river and he never saw it again! He was heartbroken until one day he was passing by the toy store.

There in the store window was his boat for sale for ten dollars! He didn't have ten dollars, but he hurried inside to let the store owner know it was his boat. The owner said he had paid someone five dollars for it and he needed to at least get his money back and when he could bring him the money he could have the boat back. The poor little boy had never had five dollars in his whole life and went away sad, but determined to earn the money and save it, until be could buy his boat back.

The day finally came and he hurried into the toy store and emptied all his nichols, dimes, and pennies, out on the counter for the man to count. Then the man took the boat off of the shelf and handed him his little boat! The little boy was so happy, and smiling really big, he kissed his wooden boat, and hugging it tightly to his little chest, he said to it, "I made you, myself, little boat, now *you are twice mine*! First, I made you and then, I bought you back!" ***That's exactly what Jesus did, we are twice His, He made us, and then He bought us back....on the cross, when He paid for our sins!*** We are first born into this life and the Bible says that to enter the Kingdom of Heaven, to be saved, we must be born again!

My dad would tell about the farmer who had a barn he could see from his house. One day he was looking out the window toward the barn and called his wife to come look. He showed her a little bird out in the snow, alone, and shivering in the freezing cold! He told his wife he needed to rescue that little bird or it would certainly freeze to death. He first attempts to get the bird, but it was afraid and kept scooting out of reach. Then he tried putting out feed but the little bird was too cold and shaking to go to the feed. Then the farmer opened wide the door to his barn where it was warmer, and turned on the light, but the bird still didn't go in. Then he tried next making a pathway of the feed from close to the bird all the way to the barn for it to follow, but the little bird still did not move.

The farmer said to his wife, "I don't know what else I can do, I have tried getting the bird to come to me, to eat my feed, and to follow my pathway to go where it is warm and safe where he will have everything, but he won't do it!" And then the farmer said, *'IF ONLY I COULD tell him, or "BECOME "A LITTLE BIRD, MYSELF, and <u>show</u> him!"* and this was excatly what Jesus did for you and me! *Jesus became a baby, than be grew into a boy, then he became a man, a person like you and me, so He could show us the way!*

Once upon a time there was a poor little boy who lived on a mountain in an old house filled with glass windows. He would look out of his windows every morning at the house across the valley on the other mountain and see the house over there with all the golden windows! He would tell his family that someday when he was grown, he was going to cross the valley and climb the other mountain and go see the house over there that had windows made of gold and sparkling diamonds!

That day arrived and he said goodbye to his family and set out to finally do the thing he had always dreamed about doing. He was going to find the house with the golden windows that he had been watching his whole lifetime! He crossed the valley, he climbed the mountain, and as he got closer and closer to the house on the other mountain, why, there were no golden windows, at all! They were glass windows just like he had in his own house at home, and the house was old and in disrepair, not nearly as adequate as his own! The sad realization that there was no house with golden windows was about to settle in on him when someone at that house excitedly took him to the side of the hill to show the little boy the house he was looking for, that it was not the house he'd just traveled to see, it was a house across the valley that had the golden windows. The boy looked in shock, it was *his own house, IT WAS HIS own home, ACROSS THE VALLEY, REFLECTING THE EVENING SUN.*

There are several versions of this story and many of them leave it up to the reader or the story teller as to the "moral of the story" and some leave you NOT with a moral, but challenge you to apply it to your own life. It was rather meaningful for me, recalling all the thousands of "for sale" properties I had spent time on, using the internet real estate online resources....just to discover, I was already in my house, with the gold and diamond windows, on my own Jesus' Mountain. What is so neat about mine, is that from my house, I look across the valley to my churchhouse on the opposite mountain, and from the church, I look over to my house and guess what? Yes. Both of them are sparkling and dazzling as with the joy of the "windows of the Lord", filled with reflected light of happy peace and joy-filled sunshine!

Now I have painted for you a bit of the picture of my early years when I was first discovering seeking God in my life and learning to live for Him. I don't ever remember being sad or lonely, not for long, anyhow. Even alone in my tree I was not lonely because I was *not alone*, and I *knew it!*.

God was my refuge, my safe place. My tree was my high place, my mountain, my holy mountain, God's Holy Mountain. It would be the precious "place" I would frequent daily *in my mind* for the rest of my life *in my Spirit*, in my heart, resting in the refuge of my Heavenly Father's Sanctuary. It's that very place inside each of us where God is waiting to talk to us, spend time with us, and *find sanctuary....the Holy of Holies!*

The last thing I ever thought this book was to be, was an autobiography, a story of my life; however, in compiling each exploit, episode, miracle, and adventure, I became aware how impossible I thought it was going to be for anyone to believe the validity of what I was saying. I started to realize you would have to know me first, and how could you know who I am without finding out who I was and how it all started from the beginning. So here we go, *we are starting from the beginning because* it will help you to have the background, the foundation, the path the Lord led me on, getting me up here to the highest heights of His Holy mountain.

I will now tell you what else was going on in my young life, **because, "I was sitting with the Chiefs".**

"Wonder Johns, (1934-2012) Pastor Emeritus First Indian Baptist Church"

CHAPTER ONE

SEATED WITH THE INDIAN CHIEFS

---

*"But God, who is rich in mercy, because of His great love with which He loved us, even when we were dead in trespasses, **made us alive together with Christ** (by grace you have been saved), and raised us up together, and made us **to sit together in the Heavenly places in Christ Jesus!"***
-Ephesians 2:4-6 NKJV

One day my late "Papa" Weakland, my closest Grandfather, my mother's father, the Rev. Dr. Joseph Roy Weakland, showed me an awesome photograph in his study at the Betty Weakland Chapel, in Jamestown, New York, probably taken years before I was even born.

The picture was taken in one of his church services of Papa behind the pulpit, introducing the dignitaries seated in a row across the platform. The five or six Iroquois Chieftains sat in pulpit chairs in front of the stage lighting, that showed off their magnificent Indian headresses that were war bonnets boasting of multiple rows of authentic eagle feathers.

They wore fringed and leather clothing, suade looking moccasins, various necklaces with what appeared to be small animal trophies together with colorful beads. Papa also resembled the chiefs himself, actually, with his black eyes and hair, high cheekbones and inherited partial Indian bloodline. Papa appeared proud to have them visiting and the chiefs sat with stoic expression, sitting in their places of honor before a packed congregation of very interested and curious worshippers.

I could see how important it seemed to be, that he was showing me the picture, and he seemed pleased that I studied every detail in it so intently. He had looked me in the eyes like there was much he wanted to say but didn't. He probably thought I was too young to understand what he was thinking. That's funny, because now, all these years later, God tells me. He gives me those answers if I ask for them. The photo had served to paint a vivid picture in my mind and *in my Spirit,* of evangelism to Native Americans and to recognize God's plan for calling certain Christians to reach Indian people for Christ. Papa had answered that call...and now, I too, began to feel that I was going to answer that same or similar calling.

It would be many years later after Papa had passed away from bone cancer, that I would be visiting the new Betty Weakland Chapel sanctuary in Jamestown, when I saw the same photo in the reception area of the church, hanging on the wall, hung in a beautiful antique frame. My Aunt Betty Weakland had been giving us a tour and showing us her new church office and commented on the old picture.

She had said, "The Iroquois loved your Papa and could trust him, and he loved them. They were able to invite him to speak to their people and he led many to the Lord. This photo was made when Papa had invited them to one of his services and they came. The event was historical."

I never saw the picture again and it failed to emerge from all the boxes of books and old Chapel relics, but is still so vivid in my memory I think I could after all these years, draw it right down to it's most finite detail.

The first Chapel was an 1865 red brick Victorian building at the corner of Charles Street and 157 McKinley Street, in Jamestown, NY. It was originally the county school house "number five". My grandparents actually lived on the second floor, which also included Papa's grand study with his large desk surrounded by bookcase-lined walls and high ceilings. It was where I'd first been shown that life-altering photo. The new Chapel was at 35 Camp Street and is now renamed and belongs to a different congregation. But, I will forever remember the first one, though, and the smell of coffee perking in the church kitchen. My Grandma, Pearl Elizabeth Tabor Weakland, playing "red hot" revival-type piano, and the 1944 to 1960 crowds belting out the anointed songs that made me love church and where I had first learned to love Jesus and how to fight his enemy, Satan.

After I was grown, married with children, in fact, Sheri was in her mid to late teens, probably, my mother took us to visit the Seneca Indian reservation at Salamanca, not far from Jamestown, and we met the Ralph E. Bowen family who showed us around for the day. He was a direct descendant from the famous, Seneca "Chief Cornplanter", who was half brother to the Jesus-believing, Iroquois Prophet, "Handsome Lake". It was indeed an honor for us to be able to spend time with Brother Bowen, who was a tribal leader and Pastor of the Red House Memorial Chapel at the Alleghany Seneca Reservation.

We enjoyed the special festivities taking place that day, danced with the Seneca ladies in several of the traditional tribal dances in the gym, toured the fabulous museum, and Sheri was asked to sing the Star Spangled Banner at the opening of their softball game. I was so proud of her as she belted it out over the microphone and the crowds of tribal people clapped and cheered.

We spent time that day hearing some of Brother Ralph's war stories, as an honored and decorated veteran, member of our military's US Army Air Corp with active missions and war assignments in France and Italy. His wife, Delores, (Dee), who had shown us around, told us about the Christian ministry there and asked me to keep praying for Indian believers in leadership and the opposition they faced at tribal election time every year. I still remember her request and I still always pray for them. It almost felt as if we were leaving home, when it was time to get in my parent's van with them for the trip back to Jamestown. We made so many friends there that day, in only one day's time, and they felt more like family to me, instead of newly formed friendships.

Now we would be really honored when they accepted our invitation to visit us in Florida and stay in our home serveral days. It had been a special time for us we would never forget. Then something happened *a few years later* that was a bit of a shock to Sheri and myself when we got a call at midnight one evening at the ranch.

Sheri and I had been watching a television program that night that featured a segment on "shapeshifting", the metaphysically debatable transformation of a person changing shape into that of an animal, (at least by outsiders it would come into debate). It was common to hear among tribes that the medicine men and others could change from human form into a spirit animal, or is it a *real* animal, do exploits, returning back into their physical bodies once again. Sheri asked me, "You believe that Mom?" Before I could answer, Gary spoke up and said, "No, not me, I don't".

"Hmmmm...",I thought, "Well, I do believe that a person could meditate, and leaving his body sitting there on a chair, could *in his mind* think of himself as a cat or a bird or a dog, and believe he was in another location, I guessed, but to physically actually transform from human form into an animal and back, no, not really. Or even leave his body and his spirit man go on a journey, leaving his body in the chair, may be possible, but to change into a physical animal body and back, having left your chair empty because the real "you" had disappeared, "no." Sheri said she could possibly believe it. So, we asked the Holy Spirit for some assistance.

We left it at this: We would pray and ask God to show us the truth. We both believed strongly He doesn't want us in ignorance, and Jesus, being the Way, *The Truth,* and the Life, we needed to be aware of a truth here. That was at 11:45 PM.

It was probably a minute before 12 when my phone rang and Sheri hurried into my bedroom to see who was calling so late. It was a very elderly Seneca lady from Salamanca, New York. She said she was good friends with the Bowens and went to their church. She said she just simply wanted to thank me for hosting them in my home, years before. I looked at Sheri and we both looked at each otherde-eyed with bewilderment and curiousity. I think she said she was almost a hundred years of age and her shaky voice revealed as much; at any rate, it was an aged Indian lady who we had never met before.

She went on to say she had just been praising the Lord and **He told her to call me!** Now I was all ears. She said Dee had long ago given her my phone number, (probably in case of an emergency up at the rez while the Bowens were down in Florida staying with us). I told her if she was ever down this way she, too, was welcome to come see us and spend the night. We were just about to hang up when it hit me that Sheri and I had just prayed a special prayer just prior to her call, and that it was too coincidental there wasn't a connection.

I told her what an amazing thing it was she had called just then and I told her about our need for knowledge concerning shapeshifting and the prayer we had just prayed prior to her call. She did not sound surprised in the least and said, "Did Dee not share with you the strange happening they experienced when Dee was a young girl?" I said no.

She went on to say one night it was a cold winter night and there had been snow on the ground so several folks gathered around a bonfire when a stranger, an old man, walked in from no where and introduced himself. He had said he was from a neighboring town down the railroad track, declined someone's invitation for him to spend the night nearby, and that he'd just warm his hands before leaving to go back where he was from.

Soon he left headed toward the tracks and the teenagers all whispered together how could a man his age walk back that far in the black night in the cold. They decided to follow him. They hid along the way so he wouldn't see them. When he got to the railroad he stood up on the track and they could plainly see him transform into a dog on all fours, and race, *faster than a dog*, down the tracks and out of sight.

She said, "Yes, the practice is quite real, and most Indians know it to be so." We thanked her for calling us and we said good night. As soon as we'd hung up the phone, Sheri asked me what I thought. I said, "I think the Lord wants us to realize, that, as we minister to our brothers and sisters on the reservations, we are to understand that, *they* or *some* of them, firmly and seriously, ***do believe it.***"

I loved traveling with the elder Seminole people on brief daytime trips to other churches for revivals or overnight conferences, some with accommodations, or motels close by, and some rather memorable ones that didn't. Sometimes, I drove a group on the church bus, or in my vehicle, and we would leave the First Indian Baptist Church at Brighton frequently very, *very* early in the morning.

On one such bus ride we were being driven to the Florida State Baptist Convention by a chartered bus, where we were asked to bring a choir to sing Seminole hymns. It was quite an honor and it caused that audience we sang for, to wipe tears as they listened. Most of the time there's a heavy anointing on Indian hymns and songs, I think, because the singers are strong in faith and truly believe the words they're singing.

When we first left on the bus at the rez, everyone on the bus was

5

sitting silently, no one speaking, when one of the ladies asked, "Mrs. Luckey, glad you got up early to go with us. Sleep ok?"

"Well," I told her, "I sure didn't want to miss the trip for anything, even though I hadn't slept that good, since my back aches sometimes." Everyone on the bus was listening, so I added, "Anybody got a good old Seminole Indian remedy for that?"

Elder lay preacher, ordained minister, Howard Micco, always funny, didn't miss a beat, spoke up and said, *"Old Seminole Indian remedy.....Ben Gay!"* The choir howled.

One time in church the service was closing and Pastor Wonder Johns asked if anyone had an announcement or anything more before we closed in prayer. I stood up and said I had twenty free tickets to go to Benny Hinn later that day in Lakeland, if anyone was interested. To that, our great song leader, Sammy Gopher, excitedly jumped to his feet with his hand raised up! He glanced around as if wondering why he was the only one, and then he asked, *"Benihana's, right?"*

One night I was at another Florida reservation church where I had driven my new friend, at that time, Onnie Osceola, and her dear mother, Lena Gopher, with me for a two day assembly. I offered to get a room for us somewhere but Onnie said they were just planning to sleep in a back room in the church and I was welcome to do the same thing, so I did. I brought a blanket and a pillow like they had, and it was all I needed.

Onnie always spoke in English to me but her mother only spoke in her Indian dialect, but I somehow understood most everything she was saying, as if God was interpreting her words for me. On this one night, the evening service was over and the people had filed out the door to leave and the deacons had turned out most of the lights, so Onnie, Lena, and I carried our bedding with us as we located places along the floor in a backroom not far from the sanctuary.

I spread my blanket down saving half of it to put over me. I was happy we all had water with us and crackers and cookies because it was a perfect bedtime snack and we prayed over them first. Then it struck us so funny that we were all sitting on the floor in the dark, praying for God to bless the crackers and cookies, and that started the giggling. Then as we tried to get to sleep, one of us would start laughing all over again and then all three of us. We were not at all like three old ladies, we were young, giggly school girls again and the next thing I knew, I was sound asleep till morning. It was a very fun experience I would never forget, and it developed into a close friendship inspite of the language barrier.

There was something ever so comforting about sleeping on the floor in God's House. I'm not sure I ever even had a backache again, to speak of, after that night. No fears or apprehensions, no restlessness or discomfort even on a hard floor. I felt His presence and I think Onnie and Lena felt it also.

Lena, had sat directly behind me on the second row, for all the services up until the cracker night on the floor. The first Sunday we were back at our own church, she had poked me with her Bible on the back of my shoulder, which was, as if to ask me, to find the reference the preacher had just announced for his sermon. I would locate it and hand it back to her. I did this twice, two Sundays in a row. Then I began to just go sit next to her after leaving the piano where I'd just played for the song service. From then on when she handed me her dear little worn Bible, I not only continued to hold it, as she shared it with me, I would use my finger to follow along with each word the preacher was reading, as she watched attentively.

Onnie was the church treasurer and I became the church secretary later on and we became such good friends I cried having to leave her when we moved to the mountains. Every week we had counted the church offering monies together and done all the record keeping, and we never bagan any of it without praying over it together first. And talk about laughing, we sure would. That job was an awesome ministry experience and Onnie and I knew what it was like to know the Lord was right there with us, keeping it joyful.

One year I drove three of the elderly ladies from our church in my SUV for a week out west to "Falls Creek". I took Lillian Johns Bowers, Lois Johns Micco, and Goby Tiger to the Indian Baptist Christian assembly grounds in Davis Oklahoma, for the annual summer campmeeting. Now talk about laughing, only Lois spoke in English to me, but all of them carried snacks in their purses and they would offer me anything they happened to have with them as I drove. What they had, was something I had never acquired a taste for, but everytime they'd ask me anyway, knowing I was declining, and we all would laugh till we ached. What was in their purses? Saltines and sardines. What we did enjoy that we had in common was our love for hot coffee, so we shared plenty of that. Nice memories.

It was, and is, the largest gathering in the country of Native American Christian people from different tribes and reservations from all over the United States. I was looking forward to a week of attending Bible classes in the day and revival sevices by tribal evangelists at night, when an announcement notice was put out across the campground.

"Calling all law enforcement"! the posters, loud speaker announcements, and the flier said. So on day one, I started it out, not in a class, but attending a meeting. I was accepted into what I recognized as a pretty elite and interesting group of Indian men who were asked to volunteer all week as patrol officers, tending to law enforcement-related needs and services. They were Christian cops representing several different tribes who were employed in their police forces back home. It was led by an experienced, very capable man who was a police chief at his own rez. I was the only woman in the group.

There were several facts he presented to us as he explained our mission. He said he wanted all of us to meet early each evening as a group and share information. He said that already there had been a few minor crimes, such as thefts reported and since the camp was larger than it had ever been before, they predicted it would be helpful if our own people could help handle the cases or calls that would come up and ease the demand on the town's local Sheriff's department. He said every year that there was usually at least one person or small group of teenaagers who would attempt to challenge the leadership and authorities, while away from their homes, and we needed to be prepared for it in case it came up. He issued each of us our own walky-talkie radio/scanner.

Then he presented something different, that to me, made me remember Dee's friend who'd called at midnight that time. He said, "We may have shapeshifting this year. I'm told that the young people this year seem more tuned in spiritually (little "s"), some having experienced "the four winds", and may try to pull stuff on us, so keep it in mind. Pair up with a partner because I don't want any of you to have to work alone and camp rules require we deal with minors, especially, with a witness present." There was one young officer next to me who asked me if I had a pardner and introduced himself.

Now I was already used to being the only female in any particular group. I had been the only woman on the Sheriff's Posse in Martin County, I had been the only female at the Florida Marine Patrol besides the secretary, I was one of the few females in a large police academy class of menfolk, twice, and the only gal in countless specialized police training courses.

I was quite comfortable with that, but I also kept an open mind that the "guys" might try to fool me with something and when I got alone with my young Christian cop/brother, I came right out and asked him if the Chief was really serious about the shapeshifting and he assured me it was so, and that even he had seen some of it at his own reservation.

That week was busier with police service activity than I would have ever imagined, I mean we worked hard! Our patrol had ambulance calls, people to deliver messages to, missing items we located, suitcases misplaced, a purse disappeared, a few disabled vehicles, and folks in emergencies needing rides. There was a threat that a gang from town was going to descend upon a group of campers on the last night, and sometimes there was a need of a parent to discipline their kid with a good talking to. It still was just little stuff, so to speak, but it kept us hopping.

I was busier than most because I was the only officer with four wheel drive, and the only woman. Sometimes you need just need a female officer on a particular call. I was also the only one with her gun along, or at least who admitted to it. But it was my Bible on my dashboard and my readiness to pray with all the folks that made it successful. It was all good. The Falls Creek camp was run with the best administration, schedules, goals and successes of any camp I ever knew. I was very proud to feel a part of it. I really did feel the Lord's presence everywhere I rode or walked.

I was slightly thinking that the fellas might resent having a woman on their police "force" but after the first night, I was "in" like Billy Jack. Here's why, and what happened. One of the pastors was missing about six campers who'd made their beds appear as if they were in them, but they were not.

When we had a meeting of all our people on duty, I asked where the

9

highest altitude was located. I saw some of the officers kind of frown at my question. I was told about the higher elevation, usually only traveled on foot along rocky paths, but from up there you could observe everything happening below at the campground. I was told it was accessible only by 4 wheel drive, so I had all the officers on my shift pile in my new Isuzu Rodeo and I drove the squad up a rocky, bumpy hillside to the top with my lights off. Just as I thought, a campfire had just been snuffed out moments before, and under the dirt were red hot coals to prove it. In a circle on the ground around the smoky campfire, stood six icy cold, half drank beer cans. No teens. We poured out the beer on the remaining coals and drove back just in time to find six campers now sound asleep in their beds. Mission accomplished.

It made me feel pretty good when the chief asked me if I could come back the following year. I was also glad the Lord had downloaded some intel for me regarding the beliefs concerning shapeshifting, so that I didn't come across to the men as being quite so naive. I have to tell you though, I never quite felt the same again when I was approaching an animal that kept staring at me and it made me hug my handbag a little closer. Not because it had a gun in it, I just didn't want that "cat" or "dog" *stealing* my purse!

My Papa Weakland always carried a gun and had gone to California at one point in his life with my grandmother, rescuing young girls kidnapped into prostitution and human trafficing rings. Oh yeah, that stuff has been going on a long time. They would lead them to Jesus and relocate them into churches in California, who would minister to them, give them new identities, jobs, homes, and a church family to love them.

You have to know that Papa's great grandfather, John Weakland, was the pioneer man who single handedly faced an angry gang of men in Cambria County, PA once, who were going to kill the local Catholic priest. Because John confronted them with only a fence rail in his hand and a stern threat, they left the priest alone and my ancestor became the town hero with the whole story depicted in stained glass church windows that can still be seen today, even on line. You can look it up and see the color photos.

It was John who married the Indian daughter of the chief and the two of them were baptized at that same church and was even recorded in the historical records of the church. When they exhumed John's body to remove it to a place of more honor, his right arm had not deteriorated like the rest of his body. This was thought to be a sign of sainthood the Catholic church would have bestowed on ole John, and it was that strong supernatural arm that had also killed a bear single handedly, and threatened the angry mob. Even the muscular arm is shown illustrated in one of those stained glass windows near Carrolltown, PA and it even included the story about the bear.

You will notice the name was not "Mohawk"; but, it was one more difficult to pronounce so Mama never tried to. The Piscataway and Yoacomaco tribes settled right there in the area and at the time frame John Weakland was there. In fact, different articles record both tribes connected to my mother's great great grandfather, and it could well be that his bride was half from each tribe. Both tribes spoke the same language, Alagonquian. She'd always say "Iroquois", which took in several tribes officially, just as the Mohawk was included. But the name "Iroquois" described all the possibilities. All of them were related closely, who frequently and naturally, intermarried with the "Five Civilaized" tribes, like Mama's tribe.

Back to my Papa Weakland, he was worried that being raised in Kentucky in a small country farming town, I'd miss out on the cultural advantages that New York State had to offer, so when he knew we were coming on a vacation or on holidays, he would plan special trips to take me on, like to Chautauqua Institute on Lake Chautauqua, to hear the symphony orchastras, nationally known speakers, artists, musicians, ballets and operas.

Papa was well known from his daily radio program syndicated across the region, and was actively involved in many service organizations, who used his clergical gifts as Chaplain, for invocations, prayers, devotions, and public speaking at big public events. I remember how at the Hotel Jamestown Ballroom, I would sit beside him at the head table next to the Governor, Mayor, Police Chiefs, and dignitaries. He was training his little first grandchild, to be socially savvy and I was made to feel much like royalty, I think. I did have the sensation that it was as if, I was *"seated with the Indian Chiefs"* on his stage in the photo.

He was highly educated having studied at several universities, and graduated from a School of Divinity and others, including Moody Bible Institute in Chicago where he'd met my Grandma. She had studied music there as well as Christian Bible courses.

Papa had groomed my Aunt Betty, (Betty Weakland Bixby Creighton) for 'stardom' from the time she was eight. Well, not really, of course ; it was **not** for notoriety nor stardom, it was for something far better, a higher calling, *the ministry of Jesus,* he was coaching her in. The Holy Spirit had graced her with humility and poise, and had prepared her for the ministry ahead. God had called her from that early age to be a childhood evangelist who held huge revivals and healing services. She would preach regularly to a congregation of two thousand during the war years. We have the photos. When she was older she'd become the pastor, be listed in "Who's Who in America", and minister regular prayer meetings in Washington DC at the Pentagon in her later years, and be a missionary to missionaries, making trips abroad to minister to them in several countries.

In his younger years Papa had been a Shakespearian actor, in fact, had memorized, and could still quote all the lines in the Romeo and Juliet script. He had also done Vaudeville and could do softshoe dancing that was popular to watch performed on stage in those days. Once in a great while he'd surprise us and perform with a hat and cane, for all his little granddaughters, who would clap and giggle with delight.

Papa taught Aunt Betty, and also my mother, how to speak with proper diction and how to handle themselves on stage. He mentored them on how to dress, walk and sit properly, and how to always be gracious young ladies who would be sitting on platforms before large audiences and in the camera's eye. They would minister the Gospel with music and speaking, and help win this world for Jesus Christ, and he taught his young ladies to do it with dignity and poise.

Needless to say, lil' ole tomboy me would be on my best behavior as I accompanied him to his sophisticated events in the Chautauqua society. I mean, to this day, I do **know** how to walk, sit, and talk properly if I need to or want to, I just sometimes choose not to, maybe, and to just be me. lol

It was Aunt Betty who was once traveling in a Communistic country with a suitcase of brand new Bibles, that, if detected at the airport, would certainly mean jail time or worse. She was surrounded by military in uniform with automatic weapons, when they opened the suitcase, looked inside. All at once, and to her amazement, they promptly closed it, miraculously blinded to the contraband right before their noses! Thank You, Jesus. She would tell people the remainer of her life what a miracle the Lord had performed to get His Word to a country where it was forbidden.

She was very beautiful and had been offered a movie-making contract in Hollywood by the leading film producer of that day, but she declined the invitation to serve her Savior. She had her own invitations to give and it would be to invite the lost to come to Jesus.

Once when I had been sick for two days and now was in bed with a very high fever, Betty was visiting Florida from Washington DC. She came and placed her cool hand upon my forehead, proclaiming in her dramatically, magnificent voice, (reminiscent of the famous Katherine Kuhlman), "I command this fever to leave this instant in the name of JESUS!" And it did!

Aunt Betty could not only preach with such conviction thousands were saved, but she could also sing and minister in music like she did in words. It reminds me of the experience I told you when my own dad had, as a young man with his trumpet playing, and had chosen "The Old Rugged Cross" as the night club finale. He said, "What we had that evening in the city, was not a performance, we had church."

The last line in that song says, *"So I'll cling to the old rugged cross, and exchange it some day, for a crown!"* and when I'd think on that, it would remind me of the Chiefs on Papa's stage and how in Heaven they would gladly exchange their warbonnets for the crowns they'd lay at the feet of Jesus one day. That's in Revelation 4:10-11.

That also brings to my memory my favorite real life, spiritual Seminole Chief, Pastor Wonder Johns, in Florida, where at the First Indian Baptist Church I played piano, taught the adult Sunday school class, and had the privilage to serve as his secretary for several years. He had proved himself as a community leader and planner, an honorable member of the armed forces and Seminole military veteran. He was a true Pastor who loved the flock, and was highly respected by his Indian people, and had faithfully served them his entire life.

Just about two weeks prior to his "Glory Day" for Heaven, his family held an event at his home that was the day before his birthday. The house was packed with guests waiting, plates in hand in two long lines. They were standing before the most fabulous spread of delicious country cooking, prepared by Theresa and Cynthia, his daughters, their mother, Mary Louise, and their families, prepared as a celebration of his life. In the crowd I noted the presence of several men, lay preachers, a pastor, and tribal leaders.

It became quiet as Wonder welcomed everyone there and stood with us for the prayer, but to my utter shock, I heard him say these words, **"Betty Luckey, will you please ask the Lord to Bless the food?"**

I had to look at him to be sure I heard correctly and I saw that twinkle in his eye in spite of his serious demeanor. I tried not to allow my disbelief and amazement show, and I set my plate down and raised my hand unto the Lord, thanking God and asking his blessing not only on the feast before us, but on Wonder's faithful life of committed service and love to his God and to his Seminole people.

I was still stunned at the honor he had blessed me with that day. It was overwhelming and so unexpected. What I was thinking was, it had always seemed quite traditional that in mixed company, with other men present, especially, respected men of the Gospel, that certainly a woman would not be leading in the audible blessing of the meal. I mean, I had now been close to Indian folks for more than half my life, and I had never seen a woman be asked to lead an audible prayer in a situation like that. However, it was so like him, and it would be so like our Heavenly Father, and also to realize there was even *more* meaning behind the request than appeared on the surface. I knew the Lord would tell me just what it was. And he did.

God was about to take Wonder home. Wonder was appreciating me and his ministry I had helped to assist him with, and was giving me an honor, that of the highest magnitude he had available at that moment to give, and I knew it. I knew he was telling me to begin to conduct myself with a **new understanding for ministry** I would have ahead of me, but to *never again* feel in any situation *that I was inferior, unqualified, or second rated*. I was **to rise and shine**, share the Gospel **with a new boldness**, and always know that **God was with me** to help me do it! Right now I sense that God is giving someone reading this, the *same important message* and instruction.

When I visited him at his house the following day, he said as much. He had confined himself to his bedroom because he felt a lot weaker than the day before. I took Seminole elder and friend, Mabel Johns Haught, with me because it was also her birthday, as well as Wonder's, and I had homemade birthday cards to give them and a cake with a sparkler on top to light.

We stood by his bedside with his wife Mary and also a caregiver, we sang to them the "birthday song" and had a prayer, as I lit my match and then the fourth of July sparkler on the cake. All of a sudden we were shocked to have the sparkler burst into little flying, flaming, buzzing, tiny bits of dibris that flew and sprayed all over his bed, causing us ro run with the blazing "candle" into the bathroom, tossing it safely into the sink!

We all howled with laughter! Wonder chuckling so hard and wiping his eyes from the happy tears of joy, we scooted out the door, waving goodbye, and I said we were leaving before I burned his house down and we all laughed all over again! It was a fun moment none of us would ever forget.

I would stop by his house once more just before he left us for Heaven, and we both knew it was for the very last time. This time I prayed with him with tears flowing down my cheeks for the man who had been such an encouragement and mentor to me for so many years of my life. I thanked God for allowing me to know this incredible Pastor, and as I sat beside him on his bed, I knew that I was truly, ...*seated with a Chief.*

When my mother passed away she left a sum of money designated for us to use as a family for a special trip to take together or preferably, a ministerial project. It all started coming together the day I said that I would like to return to Wounded Knee, in South Dakota, at the Pine Ridge Lakota Sioux Indian Reservation and help do something special for those little kids. I had also said they had nothing at all to play with, just stones and sticks in the dirt, no toys at all. Sheri said, "Well, there's nothing stopping you right now!" And she was right, and we flew into action.

I had driven respected Seminole medicine woman, Alice Snow, there years before and was overwhelmed at that time by the apparent needs of the poverty stricken rez, where "Wounded Knee" was reported to be the poorest community on the poorest of all the reservations. Miss Alice and I had joined a group of Oklahoma Indian pastors and their wives to minister there, holding Vacation Bible School in the mornings and revival services at night. It was one of the highlights of my lifetime assisting her as we led little children who were so receptive, with Bible stories, music, crafts, and praying the prayers with each one to receive Jesus as their personal Savior.

Now I would attempt to connect with a church or a tribal pastor who could advise me where the greatest need might be. I phoned the preacher we had previously worked with, who said his ministry was all set up for the upcoming Christmas plans, however, he said there was a pastor there who had just asked him to pray for help he was badly needing.

I was soon on the phone with Pastor Stanley Hollow-Horn, at the Wounded Knee Church of God. He said there was no money that year to put on their traditional Christmas dinner, a meal that would feed their entire community. He said every year the Lakota Sioux people had looked forward to coming at Christmas for their traditional, hot, chili-type, nourishing soup their ladies liked to cook in huge pots with fried bread and hot drinks. He said it was the only really successful annual outreach they had, because the whole rez showed up. He said it had broken his heart the previous year to see the long lines that had come, but when the gifts ran out, so many children had to leave with nothing, looking very sad.

They had always tried to have one gift for every man, woman, and child. But this year it would be impossible for any such gifts. When I asked how many we should plan for, he said 500. I told him I wanted to do it. He also added that the greatest need was for warm winter coats and jackets for all ages. He said tribal men were going to work on jobs outside wearing nothing more than layers of shirts in the brutally bitter cold.

That was on December 3, 2007. My daughters and I called every newspaper, television and radio station, and church, leaving the announcement we needed warm winter coats, and new, or like new, children's toys. I had noticed for years the many yards at our own reservation that held so many very nice toys the kids no longer seemed to play with. I was sure we would get the donations. Boy, did we!

My daughters, Libby, Sheri, and her husband, Simon Bjorn and

I, manned a drop off location we had advertised would be located in Sebring, Florida, in a beautifully landscaped new large parking lot on US Highway 27, in front of a Circuit City store that had not yet opened. We would set up with trucks and trailers and we posted our dates and hours to collect donations every Saturday for three weeks, from 10 to 2:00, with plans to have a caravan leaving from Florida for South Dakota on December 20th. The Indian Christmas Party was planned for December 23, at 5PM. You have no idea how shocked we were at the tremendous outpouring of support!

Florida retirees in long lines, pulled up in their vehicles, bringing heavy winter coats, jackets and snow clothing including thermal boots, gloves and hats, items just stored in their closets, never worn in the tropics. Seminoles collected countless loads of new toys and even new clothing they had purchased. Some would also drive their own trucks and pulled at least four additional horse trailers packed full and drop their load at the party location located beside the church at the Pine Ridge reservation.

Seminole friend, late Alice Sweat, very active at our church, jumped into action opening her tribal office as a dropoff point and she and her crew packed everything in boxes and wrapped some of the toys. There were too many to keep wrapping and we ended up allowing hundreds maybe thousands of nice toys stacked on the floor by the Christmas tree in the community center at Wounded Knee. We had started out with a goal of a hundred to 500 coats...*We collected well over 1,000!*

When I was at Walmart purchasing supplies for the trip I included so many boxes of big black contractor bags someone asked me what they were for and I said that I didn't know, exactly, but God told me to.

I can't tell you the how joyful and emotional it was the night of the big event. In the afternoon when the pastor's wife, who was there with a multitude of ladies cooking, saw the enormous amount of toys there was, she asked me, as she was shaking her head, and said,"Mrs. Luckey, we don't see how in the world you expect all this can be given out?!" I admit that it did seem impossible there could be an orderly manner in which to do it! I breathed a prayer for the Lord's answer and I calmly replied, "Each child will be handed a big contractor bag at the door. They will approach the tree and pick out all they can haul away in their own bag".

She and several women gasped, and she blurted out, "You mean, like....a *free for all????*"

I smiled, nodding, and added, "Yes ma'am, a free for all", and assured her it would go along peacefully and in order. How did I know this? Because it just *had* to, (lol), and the Lord would only orchastrate it as such, because He had put it all together, the whole thing! It was only to HIS glory! Hallelujah! He'd handle every child and there would be no kids fighting over the bounty, which I knew, were the ladie's fears.

Sheri and Simon, who had a band and had produced Christian rock CD's, provided music at the Christmas program, much to the excitement of all the teens and youth there, especially. The nativity pageant we put on with help from another church from Tennessee, who had also come unexpectedly and unbeknown to us, brought a semi full of fruits, vegetables, candy, and gifts for the grown ups. God had it all "covered". It was all a miracle to behold.

There was another thing. The community was running out of heating fuel and the propane they depended on for heat in their homes. We were able to use up our remaining funds to be able to buy 60 propane gas and space heaters, one for each house. I sat down on a bench and watched with such thanksgiving to God for the sight in front of me. The Sioux had enjoyed a Christmas program and I'd watched the elders, all seated in the last rows, wiping tears from their eyes when we sang Seminole hymns for them. They had known no Indian Christian songs at all, and the Christmas carols we sang were anointed.

I watched as my grandsons, Justin Savacool and JT Luckey, helped little kids pulling their big bags of toys, all which went so smoothly, mostly because the kids were almost in shock they had never seen so many toys! This was truly the most magnificent celebration of the birth of Jesus they could ever imagine. Then there were those delicious bowls of their favorite red hot chili, and I watched my granddaughter, Tiffani Luckey, and my girls, Libby and Sheri, Simon and Gary, helping serve the appreciative crowd. Then Gary and I sat together on a bench watching in awe and with such happy hearts.

I felt someone sit down next to us to rest a moment, after shaking every hand there, while hosting this successful event that had drawn every member there of the community. It was Pastor Hollow Horn! I was *seated with a chief* of a man, and he could not thank us enough. He wiped his tears and told me, "Betty, thank you, I had prayed to God and He heard me crying out and He used you to help do it. It is so far above what I ever could have imagined, and you have no idea what a miracle this really is! *We were going to have nothing*, but *God gave us everything!*"

The following year and for many years afterwards, Mrs. Alice, her family, and others, picked up the annual Christmas party, holding fundraisers, collecting gifts to take, making trips with the church and tribal groups to keep the miracle going. Thank You, Lord, we praise and honor You for what You did!

There are signs, bumper stickers and teeshirts that say "Remember Wounded Knee" in reference to the original historical massacre a long time ago, and the more recent FBI conflict as well. In fact, the community center we had our music and Christmas pageant in, was the same room where some of the FBI shooting occurred during that confrontation, that eventually resulted in the well publicized incident with the jailing of Indian leader, Leonard Peltier. As I had watched our "Mary and Joseph" Nativity portrayed in the play, my eyes had wandered up along the walls and I looked at the still visible bullet holes in the plaster. I was so thankful that *Jesus came to heal all of the "wounds"* of this world, with His love, and to show His love for Wounded Knee that night, as *the Chief above all Chiefs!"*

"Author's parents Rev. Sherman and Dorothy Swan Palm Beach Gardens"

CHAPTER TWO

MY DAD SAID: "I WANT TO BE AN INDIAN"

———◆◆◆———

*"Who shall **ascend into the hill** of the Lord? Or who shall stand in His holy place? He that hath **clean hands,** and a **pure heart;** who hath not lifted up his soul unto vanity, nor sworn deceitfully. He shall receive the blessing from the Lord and righteousness from the God of his salvation."*
Psalm 24:3-5 KJV

My dad's parents were my pure blooded Swedish grandparents, Hulda and Lawrence Warner Swan, who used to love to tell us how when my dad was just a little boy, whenever people asked him what he wanted to be when he grew up? He would always say, "An Indian. I want to grow up to be an Indian!" It was obvious to them he had an early respect and admiration for tribal chiefs and warriors.

No wonder that when he met my mother, with the Iroquois ancestry in her bloodline, he may have recognized he had met the Indian princess God had planned for his life. When Papa Weakland introduced mother to him, he had been invited to the church office to make plans for dad to play a trumpet concert there for one of the church services. When Papa saw my mother bring to him the morning mail, he'd not yet opened, *for the second time that day,* he knew she had given him a secret signal to introduce them! When he did so, and it was love at first sight.

Grandpa Swan, my dad's Dad, had graduated from Jamestown Business College and was the head accountant for a large Jamestown tool Company, probably Jamestown's leading industrial employer in that day. He was also an officer in the predominately Swedish Zion Covenant Church where he taught Sunday School and served as a deacon and host for special events. He was a tall, dignified, courteous gentleman of whom my future husband would one day state, "He was the finest man I ever met, kind and congenial, always smiling, soft spoken, speaking with Psalms and Scripture in his conversations".

I never saw him wearing anything but a long sleeved white dress shirt and tie with dress pants (and with an additional sport coat for church, of course). And that included times he helped vacuum the livingroom carpet for Grandma. When we were visiting Jamestown I was so proud of him as we attended their church, to hear him begin every church service at the podium welcoming everyone in English and also in Swedish. He would serve as the interpreter for the pastor when needed.

Grandma Swan was an immaculate housekeeper who would have been proud of my daughter Sheri, as well as her sisters and brother, who are also skilled at keeping things very clean, neatly organized, and ready for company. Also like the kids, Grandma was gifted with God's special gift of hospitality. She was frequently in charge of hostessing at Zion's dinners and receptions. I will always remember how Grandma hummed happily while she cleaned and cooked, ever smiling, nodding sweetly at everyone she saw. She was known for her wonderful Swedish recipes and delicacies. Her home was always a big house, sometimes three stories, and beginning with the days of the great depression, she would sometimes open her lovely home as a bed and breakfast for taking in select tourists and guests for additional income.

Their house was an exciting and mysterious wonderland for my cousins and myself, who could play hide and seek for hours on end, running about whispering and giggling, while the adults were visiting in the large parlor and dining room. Grandma used candles, low lit lighting, and pretty, fresh flowers to make the atmosphere the epitome of ambiance, a quality I would try to emulate for the rest of my life. The home was filled with loving care and every event there began and ended with prayer. It always smelled of fresh perculating Swedish coffee.

My Dad grew up in their house, living there with his parents until the day he married, never having heard them ever raise their voises or act in anger. Once when my dad was about seven or eight years old, and he needed to ask his mother a question because of a situation he had, he found her kneeling beside her bed, her eyes closed, weeping in prayer. What happened next would shape his life, for the rest of his life. She had quietly, lovingly, said to him, "Shermy", (his name was Sherman), "Go tell it to Jesus."

Stunned, he said he went to his room where he also knelt and shared with God the crisis at hand, and to his amazement, the Lord assured him everything was good and that he had acted appropriately, and the peace that God gave him in that moment, would be a practice he would embrace for the rest of his life. God was really real! (God *IS* really real!) How true it is that we too frequently go share everything with everyone else before we realize we hadn't even run it passed God Himself, yet!

The long dining room table was large enough for the entire extended family beneath a lovely chandelier with lights that seemed to sparkle. Grandpa Swan always sat next to me, he said, to 'make sure I cleaned my plate', and he loved to gently tease me at any given opportunity to get me to laugh. Even as a child I realized that the Lord had provided Daddy's folks one of the finest homes in Jamestown and it was filled with His peace and a whole lot of love.

I also thought about how they always said that my daddy had longed to be an Indian, probably influenced by Native American teepees, campfires, and wooded lifestyles he'd seen in movies and read about in books. He had been a skilled Boy Scout who went camping, also played the trumpet marching in the school bands and playing taps at special events. It was an early beginning of a life of wearing uniforms, as he would later become a soldier in the United States Army Air Force, also a Chaplain for the Kentucky State Police. He was also the band commander at a Kentucky state detention center where he taught prisoners the Bible and how to play musical instruments while they marched, all these positions while pastoring Southern Baptist churches in Kentucky. I was used to seeing him in uniform throughout my life which probably had a strong influence on my tendency for doing the same thing.

I just realized for the first time something that had never dawned on me about how dressed up my dad was when he wasn't in a uniform. His "uniform" was his suit, dress shirt and tie, always looking like the preacher man. When I just remembered how my Grandpa, my dad's dad had always been more dressed up than other men, now I realize he got it from his daddy. And I probably after seeing my dad alwin uniform, at impressionable ages, made me want to do the same thing.

One day dad called me with a dilemna. He was having problems trying to fix the cross at the top of the steeple at his church on Alternate A1A in Palm Beach Gardens. There were no men around that day to help him. When I pulled up to the church there he was, already on top of the roof with a ladder! "OK, Betty, just let me know when I have the cross straight up like it should be!"

Oh, no, I was thinking, what if he falls, or the ladder collapses, or he starts to drop the cross and tries to catch it up there! He was dressed in his suit, tie, coat and all, going up the second ladder it took to get up that high to the top of the steeple where he could just barely secure it!

My heart was racing. "Is this good?" he called out, as he held the ladder with one hand and the cross with the other. "Yes! Yes! Yes! I yelled, "It's perfect!!" Now everyone will know why that cross was leaning for the following twenty five years!

I also wanted to be in law enforcement and wearing official uniforms may have been a prophetic sign of what was to come, that I would one day be in police work for 30 years. I had also been a Girl Scout, my mother being my scout leader, then later I had my own scout troops, Brownies, Cub Scouts and Girl Scouts and when I realized my kids' middle school didn't have a 4H club, I organized one. I would also graduate from two police academies and become certified in countless training classes throughout the years. The most fullfilling careers would be serving in the Indian communities where I could provide encouragement Spiritually as well as getting the cops, ambulances, and fire trucks when they were urgently needed. I loved working with kids because it was an opportunity while they were still youthful, to introduce them to Jesus.

One day one the young Indian fellas said he had a question for me. He said he really had a strong desire to be a police officer, but all his friends and relatives around him were involved in some illegal activities and he didn't want to lose their close friendship. He said if he joined a police department he would lose his friends. He asked me how was he supposed to handle it. I told him that he would have to keep in mind that a day would come in their lives when they desparately needed to call the cops for help and here he'd come, all prepared in every way to save their lives, and he would be their hero. He just nodded and said, "Thanks, Mrs. Luckey", and he became a good one.

I noticed that with my dad, and within myself, the wearing of a uniform was never to draw attention to ourselves or to excercize authority over other people, but it merely showed there were qualifications that had been met, training and experience to lend aid, when it was required. The role was always highly rewarding, but to serve others by inviting Jesus into their lives, became the most awesome and satisfying ministry I could ever imagine. I was proud of my dad in his Kentucky State Police uniform that included silver crosses on his shirt, showing his role as Chaplain.

I already felt a closeness, like family, to every Native American I'd ever come in contact with, and would immediately feel comfortable with Indians in a way I never quite had with other ethnic groups. Of course I have always loved **everyone.** I befriend every one I meet regardless of skin color or ethnic background because I feel we are all one, with no barriers and differences. We are all brothers and sisters on the planet. We are all God's Creation and we are all His children. It's not something I feel, but it is what I *know* to be true.

I could never stand to see anyone mistreated and after spending elementary school "buried" in Indian library books, it was no wonder there would be a greater understanding of just where my tribal friends were coming from. It would be Indians who I would embrace with an understanding that only God could have designed, I guess. Remember when I was a little girl it was the Indian feather headdress I liked to dress up in, and when my daddy was little, it was an Indian he would want to become. It was my mother who would instill in me respect and appreciation for our Indian heritage teaching me traditional ways and values. My ancestor John Weakland had married an Indian girl and he stood up and defended the famous priest who may have been killed by the angry town mob, so I guess its been "running in the family" to do this and its in our blood.

I used to see Gary watching a football game and I'd pass through the room asking, "who are you for?" Unless it was one of his beloved Florida teams, he always answered, "The underdog!" I think I have always known, in my own sense of the word, what it feels like to think of myself as an "underdog" at times, and it makes you want to defend all the other "underdogs," too.

What happens next when we move to Florida would be another chapter in this endeavor as we would actually be welcomed into the tribal reaches of the Everglades with open arms of friendship and fellowship with tribal Seminoles and Miccosukees through Jesus Christ.

Dad pastored at the Midway Kentucky Baptist Church until the First Baptist Church in West Palm Beach called him to move to Lake Park, Florida, and pastor their thriving mission church in the community just north of West Palm. It was exciting to be going to a different lifestyle in the tropics where everything was new to us. My baby brother had been born while we were in Kentucky and because my mother had a difficult pregnancy, I was the "nurse maid" who fixed his bottles, changed the diapers, bathed him and even cooked meals while mother had to stay in bed off her feet for at least three months. I was only eleven....and I loved every minute of it!

I felt like a grown up, taking care of Chip, (actually named after Grandpa Swan, he was officially, Lawrence Warner Swan, II) and who later would be called Lars, but he'd always be "Chip" to me forever. It was fun to be acting as a mom and I loved cooking and child care. It would give me the best preparation for the four children I would have of my own one day.

I was thrilled today when he had finished a new painting in New York City and had named it "Mountain Top". It perfectly portrayed what I was saying in this book and I was so excited this afternoon when he agreed to let me use it as the design for this cover. I had prayed for God to give me a little brother when I was eleven and He had done so. Chip would always be a blessing in my life from then, 68, years ago, including to this very moment!

I can honestly say that I was very excitedly looking forward to being a wife and mother, with children of my own. Had I been allowed to, I would have asked my parents permission to marry the boy I was about to meet, when I was only thirteen. In fact, Lela Luckey, Gary's mother, would often tell people that I was the most mature girl for my age she had ever met, probably because of my early responsibilities. Well, she had married at fourteen and her sister, (Nettie Pearl Stewart Howard,) at thirteen, not uncommon in the rural South. But God was with me and helped me with all of it. I felt His presence and guidance daily in everything from tending to a sick baby, to making homemade cookies for not just us, but for all the kids around.

This is probably an important side note about my cookie baking and cooking in general. I usually was using whatever ingredients I just happened to have on hand. I would begin by washing my hands in the kitchen and pray that the Lord would send me his cookie angels to help me measure and bake and I began my lifetime career in my kitchen never measuring a thing, just trusting God to guide me to create meals and desserts we would find "Heavenly" in deed! I do notice that I rely a lot on recipes now in my old age, though.

When people asked me for the recipes I would truthfully reply that I had none, just put in whatever the Holy Spirit told me to. I really don't think they believed me, but thought I was protecting our secret family dishes. Well, now you know the secret!

Chip was two when we moved into the parsonage in Lake Park, Florida. I had just turned thirteen and looking forward to our first church service when we would receive the "right hand of fellowship" down in front of the alter, meeting our new congregation. There appeared to be a large youth group of teenagers and the deacon, David Banks, introduced each one as we shook hands.

"Betty, this is our youth President and song leader, Gary Luckey", he had said as I turned to see a handsome boy with eyes twinkling at me in a way no one had ever looked into my eyes before! I remember saying to myself, "Hmmmm....Betty *Luckey*! I like it!"

He was fifteen and it was love at first sight. I was thinking what fine good looking children he would make some "lucky" woman. (See? I wasn't even a cattlewoman yet, but I already was thinkin' like one! Lol) We would begin talking on the phone every day, exchanging notes daily at the school bus stop, sitting together at every church meeting, and were inseperable from that time forward.

We would marry four and a half years later, and be divorced due to a midlife crisis over differences in our faith, for almost two years after thirty-six years of marriage. We would then be remarried (in Dr. Rev. Jess Moody's church office at First Baptist Church, West Palm Beach) for another 24 years, just 2 months short of making it to our 60th wedding celebration.

Gary would unexpectedly pass away from the coronavirus on Oct 15, 2020 at a hospital he'd been airlifted to in Gainesville, GA, while we lived in North Carolina. We would have three daughters and one son, six grand children and two great grandsons. Very handsome and beautiful kids, I must add. This family was out of "good stock", like the cowboys say, and the Lord had showed that to me, way ahead of time, when I was still only thirteen, down at the alter in the Lake Park church. He Blessed us.

What did we talk about when we met? Indians. He and I had both read all the same Indian books we'd ever seen in our libraries. Gary was a hunter who liked to camp way out in the woods and knew how to skin, clean, and prepare the meat because he was a butcher in his dad's meat market in his parents' grocery store on the same street as the church, Park Avenue. I was soon hunting and fishing with him when he turned sixteen and he got his driver's license in September that year.

I learned all the ways of the woods quickly, and to impress Gary, I showed no fear, even if I felt it at first. There were snakes and alligators everywhere but I would wade through the waters and tramp through bushes and palmettos, like he did, and soon I actually lost all fear. I would pray and trust God to be my protector....and He was, and He is! I was safe and I think I became more comfortable in the woods than I was around town.

Once when we got our car stuck way out in the Everglades, we had to work our way walking in the blackest dark to the closest highway with no flashlight. As I waded, sometimes in chest high swamp water, about a two hour treck through rough terrain, I thought about how terrified almost everyone I knew would be, if it had been them, faced with this dilemna.

Gary had said, "Betty, remember there's nothing out here gonna hurt you. All there is around you is grass and weeds, water, dirt, sand and trees. All the animals, snakes, gators and spiders will be more scared of you than you are of them and they will quickly back off to avoid you as they hear you approaching. Just keep moving at a steady pace without stopping. We're keeping our eyes on the horizon where the sunset was and the evening star is. Eventually we'll get to Beeline Highway, (State Road 710 in Palm Beach County) and we'll hitch a ride with somebody." From that night on, to this day, I was never afraid of the woods or the dark.

I had a strong Southern accent when I arrived in Florida after having been raised with Kentucky farmer's kids and some who had moved to Midway from the Appalachian Mountains. My parents had grown up in New York state hill country towns and cities and had more of a "public speaker's voice" than a regional accent. But Gary's parents and all of his relatives spoke pure Florida Cracker of the most "redneck", country-fied kind thar' ever could be!

They had both been raised in Labelle near Ft. Myers and the Luckey pioneer family was well documented and a familiar name in south Florida that even qualified us to be honored in the annual Swamp Cabbage Festival Parade in 1992 as the Pioneer Family of the Year. Gary was a direct descendant of Sam Luckey, and generations of farmers and cow men had who helped to forge the Everglades and woodlands in Hendry, Glades, Lee and Okeechobee Counties. We were very excited to be honored.

The parade made its way down the main street in LaBelle with horses, bands, dancing girls, majorettes, floats, law enforcement, you know, the usual small town parade where the streets were especially packed along both sides with alumni and former residents all making the annual treck to the old hometown and everyone was there. Our Luckey family included so many trucks, cars, and a float so full of Luckey family members that a man called out, "How come there's so many Luckeys!?" Everyone howled when my son Tifton stood up and waved to him and answered, "God said to be fruitful and multiply, so we did!"

Gary's voice reflected that extreme Southern drawl, but when he moved from LaBelle as a 10 year old, to Palm Beach County on the opposite coast, he was so intimidated by all the teasing he got about his accent, that he quickly improvised and could switch his speech around to suit the present company. Not me, though, I liked it, it felt natural, and I preferred talking like Gary's family, so I still do. Gary would always talk real Southern around us, but he definitely altered it when he was at Palm Beach High School and Palm Beach Junior College, just to survive.

When I was fourteen there was a disaster that was caused when a storm had come up through south Florida from Miami and the news was all about the urgency it created in the glades for food, clothing and supplies, especially among the tribal communities. Gary and I along with my dad, flew into action. I called all the newspapers and radio stations and soon had all we could handle, donated and brought to the Lake Park City Hall (also on Park Avenue), where the three of us loaded it up and headed for Brighton Seminole reservation located on the other side of Lake Okeechobee. Our contact would be with the Seminole Tribal Chief Billy Osceola, himself, who was also the pastor of First Indian Baptist Church of Brighton, still a mission at that time.

Now Billy, as well as being the tribal chief, was pastoring and preaching at the mission and would be instrumental in gaining autonomy for the congregation from the First Seminole Baptist Church, the mother church, located in Hollywood, Florida. It just so happened, my dad was doing the same thing in an identical situation, with being the pastor of the Lake Park Baptist mission, who's members wanted to be given autonomy (freedom) from the mother church in West Palm Beach. Both men would soon gain the release from the mother churches to make their congregation its own church, and no longer a mission. It would have its own bylaws, constitution, incorporation and title, etc.

My Dad and Billy hit it off immediately, the beginning of a wonderful relationship that would have us returning there, holding services where I played a really old piano, and where our Royal Ambassadors (the Southern Baptist boy's mission club) would meet with their RA's for meals, and touch football games one weekend. Then my dad hosted Chief Billy and his boys at our church in Palm Beach County, where they played touch football on the beach. A couple of the teenagers had never seen the Atlantic ocean before.

It was the start of "sitting with chiefs" in Florida where Jesus provided much fellowship, food, laughter, good times and many memories. My dad would also be introduced to other chiefs and Indian leaders at other reservations. He was able to renew his old friendship with a fellow alumni from the Southern Baptist Theoogical Seminary with the renowned missionary, Brother Genus Crenshaw. This man was loved by the Seminoles, and helped them creating new churches, and also, by helping several Indians receive their theological training at Bible schools, and by holding revivals.

Oh, a special word about that old piano! It was located in the little building that was the sanctuary at the time. Today the church building is used as the fellowship hall and kitchen. There is now a lovely big auditorium with awesome sound system, rest rooms and Sunday school rooms. But what I want to tell you is that as I played the first piano with the keys that were all stuck and that had never been tuned, this was around 1957, when I was maybe 14 or 15 years old when I had prayed, "Please Lord provide a new piano for them some day". I recall adding, "And Lord, please provide for them the very *best piano!*" because what I had tried to play had to have been the worst there ever was. Well, it was not only an old one, but back in those days there was no air conditioning and there was no way a musical instrument made of wood could survive the tropical heat and moisture in a building that close to the Everglades.

Over forty years later, one day Wonder Johns, then pastor of the First Indian Baptist Church, would call me up and say, "Heeeyyy, Betty", (that's how he always started out, sounding sort of like a rodeo announcer, lol), "Heeeyyy Betty, Come ride with me and Mary to West Palm Beach to Bob's Pianos and lets look at new pianos!" When we got there the huge selection of pianos in stock were hard to choose from but Mary and I both played every single one of them. After trying out the biggest, baddest, bestest, Grand piano of all, none of the others of course could measure up and I asked to talk to the owner. They said it wasn't possible but I persisted and I soon had him on the phone. It was a miracle when the man agreed to sell us that gorgeous shiney black exquisite *grand piano* at the price we were expecting to have to pay for a normal standard spinet piano.

When I heard Wonder tell the man, "Yes we will take that one!" I thought I'd fall off the piano bench! We were talking about an already sale price in the range of fifteen thousand dollars worth here, and that could have been half price! Why it seemed such an impossibility for such a small, agricultural community back before dividends were not like they are today at the rez. It would be set up with financing but the biggest miracle would happen that night at the prayer meeting where Wonder told the congregation about the piano that would be delivered!

That's when two ladies spoke up and said they would each give a thousand, then Holly Billie said she would take the existing piano and pay the church cash for it, then two other ladies each gave a thousand and then more and it was **paid for** before the meeting was over and miraculously paid *for in cash* before it ever got delivered! Thank you, Jesus. One of the widows said, "Betty, it means so much to us hearing you play, we wanted you to have the very best!" I wept. I wept because I had only wanted **them** to have the very best! Not *me*! And so did God! Wonder beamed with pride!

Wow, had the Lord answered prayer! My parents could hardly wait to come over from the east coast see it and hear it played. Wonder also asked my dad to come for that and preach and play his autoharp, ram's horn and shofar. When dad played one of Wonder's favorite hymns on his trumpet, at the service, there were tears in Wonder's eyes that rolled down his cheeks.

Driving home afterwards my daddy smiled at me and said, "Betty, I think *we're Indians* now!" (Something my daddy had always said he wanted to be). He could feel the love, the fellowship, and the acceptance by the Seminoles, and it made our family feel so blessed.

At one of those evening services something so funny happened I still laugh just remembering. The pastor announced that we didn't have a song leader that night and would anyone wish to volunteer. I saw a Seminole woman glance around, and seeing no one accepting the challenge, she raised her hand and walked with her hymn book up to the microphone.

She said, "Evenin' everybody, would you please take your song books and turn to CHANNEL 38?"

"Betty and Gary Luckey Wedding Dec. 10, 1960, Jupiter, Florida"

CHAPTER THREE

INDIAN LOVE CALL

▸────◆────◂

"Let thy fountain be Blessed; and rejoice with the wife of your youth!"
Proverbs 5:18 KJV

Gary attended Northboro Junior High in West Palm Beach and then Palm Beach High School, (before graduating from Palm Beach Junior College). He would ride the school bus from the bus stop in Lake Park where I would catch the bus to Riviera Beach Junior High School. Every day we exchanged love letters before and after school. He folded them ingeniously so tightly I could hardly open them. Same way he packaged meat in his dad's meat market. In the years to come I frequently kidded him that when he changed our babies' diapers, he bundled them so snuggly and especially in their blankets, he would wrap them with such precision they could hardly move, except to smile broadly, their little faces peering above the tightly folded baby blankets like little Indians tied onto papoose boards.

At church we sat together on the front row, during every service and one time got so embarrassed when my dad, in the middle of his sermon, stopped to reprimand us when he saw that I had wrapped my foot around Gary's foot. Right from the pulpit, he had said, "Betty, you need to sit up straight!" Well, I could not have been sitting up more straight, which prompted many folks after the service to express their sympathy, (because from where they were seated they couldn't see what mischief our *feet* were up to!)

We weren't allowed to hold hands at church and we quickly learned that the rule included feet, as well. At times, Gary even sat with me on the piano bench, causing all the people to smile at us. We used as an excuse that I needed help keeping my pages turned and in place. The truth was that we just loved sitting close together.

Our relationship began when we first met when I was thirteen and it was just before his sixteenth birthday. We were not allowed to date yet, but when he got his driver's license he was allowed finally to pick me up for church.

We saw an Indian movie, "Distant Drums" and later, "Drums Across the Mohawk" at the Riviera Theater when I was fourteen. We held hands and he kept his arm around me. I didn't want it to end. It was our first real dates, with Dairy Queen hot fudge sundaes afterwards, where we had walked just down the street. I was so proud to be his girlfriend that I kept hoping everyone I knew would ride by and see us eating our sundaes! I can still smell the Lake Park night blooming jasmine that filled the air.

I always rode close to Gary in his car as he drove and I would place my left hand on his right knee. Many years later when we were married, and my hands had still remained there even after all our children came, we were trying out a new Ford pickup model which no longer had the seat straight across. The salesman was showing us the new style console between the two front seats when Gary looked at me and said, "Are you sure you'll be ok with that?" I slowly and sadly nodded. I mentioned that event at Gary's funeral and how I will always remember my hand placed so lovingly on my husband who had, inspite of all the normal marital disasters, given me an extremely loving relationship as a gentle, tender and affectionate husband.

Throughout all the years I would sing my favorite song to him, "I Remember You", and every time when I would get to the lyrics, "When my life is through, and the angels ask me to recall, the greatest thrill of them all, I will tell them I remember....tell them I remember.....tell them I remember you!" I would sob. Still do. I still am. ("I Remember You" written by Johnny Mercer and Victor Schertzinger in 1941).

35

Gary didn't have much free time because his parents depended on him at their store, Luckey's Grocery and Meat Market, on Park Avenue by the railroad tracks. I used to ride my bike there to pick up food to cook for supper where I lingered at the meat market and he always gave me a coke and a candy bar. It was so hard not to kiss him goodbye each time, but it was strickly forbidden that I, the local minister's daughter, be seen doing such a thing in public.

Later in high school, we had moved to Jupiter where I attended school from the 10th grade till I was in my senior year. It was traditional that our friends would spend time up north of Jupiter near Tequesta at the resident camp of the legendary, Trapper Nelson, (over 800 acres on the Loxahatchee River), swimming, boating, picnicing on "skip days" with and sometimes without parental knowledge. Usually people reached his location by boat or by hiking lengthy distances through what would later become Tequesta, Florida.

Gary was an experienced hunter and fisherman who could traverse the Florida sand, muck and wetlands in any car he happen to have, long before the days and years when he would, from then on, only drive four wheel drive trucks and jeeps. He had figured out Trapper's unique strategies for making obscure gaps in barbed wire, locked gates, and palmetto scrub. Once when he watched us entering boldly through a hidden opening, we waved to him and he just looked the other way and never confronted us, so we knew we had, at least, somewhat of an approval.

I can't say he was ever friendly, but we figured Trapper liked us enough and that he allowed us to use his privately accessed pathways to get to his remote and "inaccessable" acreage for some unknown reason. Maybe he needed the snakes. He didn't charge us the normal entry fee if we would bring him a live snake, so we always did. We would bring venomous and nonpoisonous reptiles. Gary would slam on his brakes, leap out of the car and chase one into the thick palmettos, usually letting it loose in the car. I would ride with my feet up on the seat. I will have more to tell you about Trapper, so I will give him his own chapter later in this book, entitled,"Wild Man of the Loxahatchee", with my personal experiences about his faith...and his murder.

While Gary was busy working, I was busy with school projects. I was Vice President of the student council, editor of the school newspaper, assistant editor of the yearbook, sang in the school chorus, played clarinet in the band, and organized the Bible Club. When I was asked to plan the prom with only eleven in the graduating class, our small committee became responsible for the theme, decorating, food purchase and catering, music, programs, publicity and setting up the room.

Now, I was like many preacher's daughters probably, and had never attended a school dance before. When my parents saw how hard I was working to help make the prom happen, they told me I could go and that I could have Gary there as my date, in spite of the dilemna at church. The crisis there was the conflicting revival meeting, at which I was needed, for playing the piano that same night.

It became a matter of prayer and I shocked everyone when I left the prom just before it bagan, after seeing to all my arrangements first, I left the dance as students were arriving. I hurried to the church, and to the surprise of my very happy mother and dad, I sat down at the piano and began to play the opening music for the meeting.

There was a gasp from the audience and I heard someone say, "She missed her high school prom to be here!" But soon Gary arrived and I was quite relieved we were worshipping God together that night. That was far better than possibly being jealous that someone might have been dancing with my boyfriend, who I had been "going steady" with since seventh grade.

When Gary's parents sold the store in Lake Park, Gary was hired in Jupiter at the Piggly Wiggly meat market where he would be closer to my house. The day he picked up my engagement ring after having it sized, he called me from the store and asked me if I wanted to meet him on his break. I drove there on "Cloud Nine".

Gary placed a gorgeous solitaire on my finger, kissing me in the Piggly Wiggly parking lot, for the whole wide world to see, and we became engaged that day, on September 28th, 1960. We set the wedding date for Saturday, December 10th and it was the most beautiful church event I had ever seen. The sanctuary was decorated by a wealthy lady in our congregation who lived on the river. She used floral arrangements she made from her own plants and vines she grew in my wedding colors, shades of pinks and lavenders. The room was aglow with multiple sets of candlelabra.

My floor length wedding gown was white embroidered satin with sequins, a train, long sleeves, and a full veil attached to a sequined and beaded princess crown. Gary and his best man wore white dress coats with black trousers. My Maid of Honor, Sharon Smith (Perry), wore a long Southern Belle, floor-length, pastel mauve gown with long gloves to the elbows. The soloist sang our favorite song, "Friendly Persuasion" from the movie by the same name, about a young Quaker couple in love, and then the song we sang frequently to each other, "Indian Love Call".

Daddy gave me away by walking me down the aisle as we followed my little six year old brother, Lars (Chip), who was also in black pants and a white jacket carrying the wedding bands on a satin pillow. I carried my white bridal Bible with white roses and Baby's Breath. As we approached the alter Daddy stepped in front of us placing my hand in Gary's with a beautiful prayer.

When we said our vows, Gary and I both could not hold back the tears that rolled down our cheeks as we pledged a life together. It was such a sacred moment, truly *Holy* Matrimony. It would be a wonderful life with four precious children. We would have reached our sixtieth wedding anniversary had Gary not been called to Heaven during the Covid19 pandemic in 2020.

Back then in those days in my early teens up till the past maybe 20 years, folks almost never spoke about really personal subjects like sexual matters or women's time of the month, in mixed company, anyhow. But there was a miracle in my life I will share with you, because it was a profound moment that contributed greatly at the time, to my faith walk with the Lord. I mean, I had prayed about the matter many times before, but this time it was **real** *fervent!* (The Bible says the fervent prayer of a righteous man, well...woman, too, availeth much!)

My mother was also my Girl Scout leader and we had shown the popular movie for preteen girls, a delightful cartoon-like film about the female anatomy, at least once a year. I had also seen it in physical education in public school. After the film, we always received a sample sized box of sanitary napkins and the belt to go with it, from the Kotex Company who produced it. The movie revealed statistics, such as, the normal age for a young girl's monthly menstruation to first begin was age thirteen and four months on average. This was a fact I had somehow overlooked and had become extremely concerned about by the time I turned thirteen and still no monthly period.

Every one of my girlfriends had started in Kentucky and even also in Florida. When we moved there, the week summer vacation began, and the girls I met at church were complaining they couldn't go to the beach that week. It made me feel like such a "little girl" who had not yet matured. All of a sudden I became so self conscious and inhibited.

The girl that Gary had previously been calling his girlfriend was one of those. From the day he met me he never showed interest in her again, but it caused me to feel so concerned in my mind, that I was not yet a real "woman" and what if I never *did* get my periods?! *So,* I did what I always did when I didn't know what else to do: *I prayed.* It was June 11th, 1957, and I cried myself to sleep begging God, my Creator, to prompt my body to do what it was supposed to be doing and allow me to be, for lack of a better word, (I chuckle now), *promoted* to womanhood like everyone else. (I was actually only five days away from being "thirteen and four months" old.)

In the early morning, the hot Florida sunshine was already shining through my window and into my sleepy eyes and I hurried into the bathroom to discover the small crimson stain on my white pajamas. My parents heard me all the way to the kitchen where they sat drinking their coffee. "Thank You, Jesus! Thank You, Jesus! Thank You, Jesus!" I was shreiking! It was the happiest day in my young life! Mother said she knew instantly why there was such rejoicing and told Daddy that she, too, was relieved to know, I could at last, quit worrying about it.

When we told our very elderly lady friend privately at a WMU meeting later that day, she smiled shaking her gray head, and said, "Miss Betty, in all my years, you are the one and only woman, young or old, I have ever seen, so delighted with the monthly "curse"!

I suppose most people are probably much more Victorian than I and would never share such a personal and private story in my life, but I guess there is no one here to stop me anymore, lol, so there is something *else* I am going to tell you that occurred perhaps a year prior to our lovely candlelit wedding ceremony.

I was sixteen and I missed a menstrual period, and then another. I dreaded having to tell my parents but I prayed and the Lord gave me the boldness to plan to tell my Mother about it first. My Dad was busy preparing his Sunday morning sermon and I remember saying I wanted to take her for a ride out Indiantown Road to the orange groves to show her how beautiful the blossoms smelled in full bloom. (Uh...maybe you best not ask me how I knew where to go). I'll never forget the look on her face as she got inside the car, closed her door, and sighed with a long breath of "acceptance". Now, just what is a long breath or a "sigh of acceptance"? Well, I just made it up....when you don't know what's coming, but you know in your knower something is coming you will have to, by God's Grace, and somehow, *with* grace, accept it.

For the first time in my life I didn't feel like a kid, I was, instead, a full grown sixteen year old who was taking my mom out for a drive in the country. I felt like a young woman who needed to speak with another woman and was desparately needing her sympathy, knowledge, understanding and patience.

After a few miles riding along in the countryside passed green pastures full of little baby calves watching us passing by, as they stood close beside their mama cows, I was thinking to myself. My thoughts like, this is not a bad thing I have to tell my mother, this is the most healthy, normal and natural thing in the world and has been, since the beginning of time. Babies are from God.

I said, "Roll your window down, Mama, smell the orange blossoms," as I pulled into a little dirt road surrounded by fruit trees and parked.

All of a sudden a boldness came on me and I wasn't afraid, nervous, or shy. I was a grown lady with good news, no longer dreading my mission or ashamed. I felt the presence of God with me and I felt a measure of joy. I turned and looked into my Mother's eyes, which were now filling with tears. My Mother was perhaps the most intelligent, perceptive, intuitive, and Spiritually gifted lady I have ever known, dignified, wise, with poise and class. She was definitely already sensing the nature of our little "ride" and her warm tears reflected the tender heart I was coming terribly close to breaking.

I told her my situation and she scooted closer to me and hugged me tightly. I asked her to tell Daddy for me and she said she would. She explained to me that because it was perhaps, my first sexual experience, that it could be the cause and be just a temporary delay of my period and that we should pray and wait a few days. I agreed.

She held me as she prayed together, asking the Lord to delay motherhood, allowing a future season for an engagement and wedding, which she prayed in the name of Jesus. This prayer was answered and my period began the following day. It meant so much to me when my Dad held me in his arms assuring me of his love and support in all and every situation I would or could ever find myself, a very real unconditional love like Jesus has for us.

As we stood in the family dining room both my parents hugged me at the same time and prayed prayers of thanks to the Lord for the relief from the stress and worry and a prayer for Gary, and for God's continued Blessing and dedication and rededication of my life to His Glory. Then my mother made a "legendary" statement, causing us all to chuckle together, that would go down into the family memories of time and to tease me with for the rest of my life, when she said: *"My dear little Betty, you never could wait till Christmas to open your presents!!"*

"Betty and Gary Luckey, 2018, LaBelle, Florida"

CHAPTER FOUR

CHEER UP! I'M HERE! IT'S ME

Jesus said, "Cheer up, I'm here, it's Me, don't be afraid!"
Matthew 14:27 (WEB) Children's edition,World English Bible
Matthew 14:27 (WEB) "But imediately Jesus spoke to
them, saying, "Cheer up! I AM! Don't be afraid"

We were married on Saturday, December 10th, 1960, at the First Southern Baptist Church on Pennock Lane in Jupiter, one of seven churches my father, Rev. Sherman Winsom Swan would found, build and pastor in the state of Florida. It was packed with friends and relatives who threw rice and shouted well wishes as we drove away following the lovely reception in the Fellowship Hall for an overnight trip to Cypress Gardens.

Our brief honeymoon would be cut short because his new job at Pratt and Whitney Aircraft was unexpectedly scheduled to begin early Monday morning. We would be rushing home to our new/older trailer parked at Holshers trailer park on Federal Highway One in Jupiter near the Martin and Palm Beach County line. This exciting location was right on the sparkling Intracoastal Waterway with quite romantic ocean breezes, swaying palm trees, and amazing sunrises we would sometimes watch from the dock with our morning coffee.

My heart was so joyful with the anticipation of a happy life ahead and only one thing would jolt my world, that I will share with you in a moment and it occurred on our wedding night the night before.

Gary and I had been ecstatic about his new employment and that his application had been accepted at Pratt which meant awesome benefits and higher pay than cutting meat at Piggly Wiggly. It provided for the four children who God would bless us with and that all our maternity expenses would be fully paid for, as well, as any surgeries Gary would have in his future, not to mention the great retirement benefits they would provide one day. I am still thanking the Lord for those on a daily basis.

Two people were responsible for encouraging him to apply for their new training program at Pratt, my mother who worked in personnel and would be employed there for a total of 29 years before she retired, and Roy Roseberry, Gary's Sunday school teacher. I think Mr. Roseberry had moved to Florida from Tennessee to head up the Xray department and he had enjoyed having Gary in his class at the church and was a good friend of my Dad's.

Pratt Whitney was located thirty minutes from Jupiter and he would be working there faithfully for thirty eight years to come, in their Quality Control and Xray department. He would have security clearance required of the employees involved with governmental defense contracts and the space program. The jet engines they designed would be a vital part of our national security for military aircraft, as well as space craft exploration. Gary had regretted he'd not served in the armed forces but now would be playing an important role in respect to that and I was very proud of him.

On our wedding night I asked Gary if in the morning we could attend a little country church close to the motel I had seen as we drove into the parking lot. I said what a great way to start a marriage I thought it would be to visit there on our way home. That's when he asked me to come and sit back down on the bed beside him, (where we had just spent a happy and intimate time together), because he had something to tell me that he had been dreading to do.

"Betty", he said looking into my eyes as they slowly filled with tears, "I have not been a Christian believer for almost the past year, but I knew if I told you, that it would mean you wouldn't go through with our wedding plans. I knew it would mean you wouldn't marry me. I know you thought I would maybe be a preacher some day, but somewhere along the way I lost the faith."

He went on, "Maybe it was being on the debate team at the college, or being in the logic courses, or being influenced by my atheistic and agnostic professors, but somewhere along the way.... I now find myself with unbelief and *no* faith. *The only thing I do believe* is this, I cannot bear **to live without you** at my side. I won't have time in the morning to attend any church service and make it home in time to prepare for Monday morning. And besides that, I don't plan on attending any churches in the future and cause them to think I am someone I'm not, because I refuse to be a hypocrite!"

I could not have been more shocked or felt worse, if one of those central Florida sink holes had just opened up in the ground and swallowed me down into the depths of the earth!

When he fell asleep I wept openly and it never even woke him up. My pillow was soaked, as I had never even tried to put a stop to my uncontrollable sobbing. Then suddenly, all at once, and quite Supernaturally, a peace settled in on me *I had no control over*, like a cool breeze on a very hot summer day. That's when I heard in my Spirit a voice tell me ever so kindly, softly and sweetly, ***"Hey, Betty, it's Me, Jesus, don't be afraid, I am with you, I will always be with you, cheer up, it's going to be okay!!"*** My tears stopped. I *actually* **smiled**. Then I took a deep breath and fell quite soundly asleep.

Having a husband who believed like I did was almost the main requirement I had in a husband and he knew it. How many times had he heard me counsel others not to be, as the Bible warned, "unequally yoked". He had been the only young man in my youth who had ever even *said* he wanted to preach. He often was asked to lead in prayer by pastors in church services and at Palm Beach High school and Palm Beach Junior College he was frequently asked to audibly pray before meetings and concerts.

Gary was a member of the Phi Rho Pi speech fraternity at college along with the famous Burt Reynolds, (who they called "Buddy"). Gary was on the school debate team and always at ease when speaking publically. He was song leader in my dad's churches and president of the youth groups. He taught a Sunday night training union class for teenagers and was president of RA's, the Southern Baptist Royal Ambassador group for young men to learn Scripture, support missions and provide Christian fellowship. He sang in the high school and college choirs and served as their elected choir chaplain. He was active on our church visitation committees and I had personally witnessed him leading people to Christ. He could lead the choir and help deacons serving Communion to congregations, and he and I had prayed together on almost every date we ever had. There had always been plenty of evidence he was seemingly a man of faith, not to the contrary.

Incidently, Gary had never smoked a cigarette or drank a beer in the four and a half years we had dated, that I ever knew about, anyway. I had never heard him utter a curse word. We had often shared how we both were looking forward to having a family to take to Sunday school and having all of us sitting together in the same pew in church. I could only handle this awful news with hope that he would change. I prayed and fasted. I read every book in the Christian bookstores written to wives on how to minister to an unbelieving husband.

I broke the heartbreaking news to my startled parents who began to pray for him. Even when they traveled to Israel mother said they were weeping as they folded a tiny piece of paper with his name on it, leaving it prayerfully in a crevice in the famous Wailing Wall at Jerusalem. The kids and I would one day travel to the Upper Room available at the PTL (Praise the Lord Broadcasting Network's Charlotte, NC) compound and leave his name on the prayer request wall, there along with his picture.

I had given Gary's name to every church on television and had called men's Christian groups everywhere to add his name to their prayer lists. Things would seemingly get worse instead of better, though, and it became clear to me now that we had a real enemy named Satan who prevented us from so many things we had previously been desiring in our hearts. He was and is truly the master of deceit and the accuser of the brethren, always ready to trick and trap us!

Christian music on our radios, sermons on TV, Gospel CD's, discussions about scriptures we were excited about, church concerts, etc, all became forbidden in our home, taboo. If we forgot and made spiritual comments, Gary would get mad and would accuse us of "preaching to him". It would be the Country K country radio station that would become the norm in our household, sometimes playing from several radios all playing at one time, (I called it "redneck surround sound".)

In fact, that was my very effective method for getting all four children awake on early mornings before school, when they would hear Hank Williams, Willie Nelson, Waylon Jennnings, Charlie Daniels, Merle Haggart, and Johnny Cash, all calling them to their hot breakfast already dished out and "gonna-get-cold!"-country sausage, (usually our homemade venison I always mixed with wild hog), grits and scrambled eggs.

My church attendance now was very sporatic and Gary had given Tifton the choice of going hunting in the Corbett Wildlife Management Area or with me to church, when I could go. Tifton, who was a crack shot with any gun or bow and an unbelievable fisherman since he was six, always wanted to hug me goodbye and then run and pile in the truck next to his daddy, naturally.

He had actually been doing that since he was 18 months old. No car seats in those days, Gary, who always invited him, would brace him with his shoulder as he stood on the seat close to him. (Thanks, Lord, for always protecting my family). All my children were raised around guns, cowpens, and potentially dangerous woods and swamps, but there was never a day I hadn't covered them in prayer and the Blood of Jesus.

Gary became so involved in his career, as well as deer, hogs, gators, fishing and cows, and I was so busy with our four wonderful children plus working full schedules in law enforcement, the years fled swiftly by before we knew it. Where did they go? I now have the answer....they stay hidden deep within the heart and Spirit of their mother, wrapped tightly in sad and happy tears and prayers, in hope and faith, and in the precious Blood of Jesus Christ, who faithfully saves, heals, delivers, comforts, protects and holds us...in the center of the palms of His hands. (There's no other more awesome place to be, nor will there *ever* be, by the way!)

Our love for country music had me first in line at the West Palm Beach Auditorium every day tickets went on sale for Nashville concerts. My MO (method of operation) was to write a check for 50 center front row seats and then speed to the homes of close friends and collect their money for their two concert tickets and get all the money in the bank deposited the following day before the check bounced. That way, all our friends were guarenteed a front row seat shared with close friends and a fun evening ahead to look forward to.

I do want to add something important in defense of country music...the best part was that every concert closed with a Gospel song and usually brought tears to our eyes. Also, on the radio station the broadcasters and disc jockeys seemed, by their daily comments, to be Christian people.

The ticket plan always worked out, but the most challenging time was when the Country K radio station added a special deal: If you included an empty bag of Martha White flour with each ticket, it was worth I think, a couple of bucks off the ticket price. The cashiers at the Winn Dixie stores looked at me suspiciously, but never commented at the 50 bags I'd bought. Then it was even more of a challenge to help my friends empty them at home when they didn't have Tupperware or cannisters to hold their flour. We dumped flour in everything handy from tea glasses to cereal bowls. I probably looked like a cocaine dealer since there was no way to successfully get all the flour off my clothes after each delivery. Flour just sorta hangs on.

Of course when I tried to explain all the flour bags to Gary, he could only shake his head at me, moan, and say, he didn't even want to know. (lol) Well, probably it was Martha White who gained the most out of the deal. It was a lot of trouble to go to, but not all our friends had money for concerts, including us, but the concerts were worth saving for, and I had an old leather purse that got signed by so many famous Grand Ole Opry folks, that it would be a treasure to this day had it not disappeared. Oh, well, the names had been fading out and disappearing, as well, but the fun memories never would. It had been one of the fringe benefits of having a center stage front row seat.

Gary and I enjoyed doing this at least a couple of years, sitting in front row seats and watching our favorite singers, eating afterwards at Okeechobee Steakhouse and sometimes dancing somewhere nearby. Barbeques, holidays and hunting parties created a new social life we hadn't known before, but it would be a real open door for some pretty evil spirits to come and use, to take advantage of us. It became a time in our lives when there was so little Christian fellowship or worshipping happening, and if we could only have a "redo" of some of those "fun" times that weren't so fun after it was all over, because they were leading up to a fall. Thank You Jesus, that You pick us up when we fall.

Somewhere in time and space, maybe between Patsy Cline's "Faded Love" and "I Fall to Pieces"....and Dolly Pardon's "Here You Come Again" and "I Will Always Love You".....I think I swallowed a Black Beauty-type diet pill and discovered my orange juice had Vodka in it. Then the music took me off of my line dance routine and into an affluent cowboy's arms that didn't belong to me, and I remember cleaning my house from top to bottom till it glistened and sparkled and I had no recollection of doing it, well, not until I discovered I'd hung a broom (labeled with magic marker and masking tape, "broom") on a broom hook (I had labeled, "broom hook"), wearing a western shirt I didnt remember actually paying for, and telling an "insignificant" little white lie I may have told my mother, about where I'd been. Now I had never ever before, told a fib to her, in my whole life....and then there was a billboard on Military Trail staring down at me every day in town that read, **"Speed kills."** That's all it said.

To this day I'm not sure if it was sponsored by highway safety or an anti drug group, but I got the messages regarding both and more. God used that billboard to torture me with until I fell on my face before Him, repenting, as if I was in a pit too deep to escape. It was as if I had been speeding in the fast lane on such a treacherous downhill incline too fast to stop without sure enough collision and death. But God knows how to rescue us when we call on Him, and He pulls us out, and He did. Or maybe, He knew I was *about* to fall into that pit and He prevented it.

Once again I heard the voice of my Savior say, *"Cheer up, Betty! It's Me, Jesus! I am here, do not be afraid! Come back to Me!"* and I ran back into *HIS* *loving arms*, Hallelujah! When we feel dirty and ashamed and say we're sorry and we ask Him to, He cleans us up whiter than snow!

Even though my season of sin was extremely brief, (which is why I probably like to use run-on sentences to hurry up and try to get through telling it), you don't break God's laws, they break you. I was backslidden by having an affair, and broken, and because I was, and my Savior saved me and had rescued me, Jesus Christ became more real to me than He had ever been before, and *that's* sayin' somethin'!

Now for the first time, I had a hunger for the things of the Lord more than I had ever known a person could have. His cleansing and forgiveness are more incredibly awesome than I can describe! The Bible I had always cherished now really came alive to me! I would forever Praise and Honor Him. There were still some rough waters ahead, but He'd be with me all the way, and there was no doubt in my mind.

Another thing, I realized looking back, how the devil had set me up, deceived me so many ways, set up traps and had tricked me. I had unknowingly fallen for his schemes that he had so connivingly webbed around me. You know, when you're in the woods or on an unfamiliar mountain road, and you take a wrong turn, you turn around. I had run into a real landslide and Praise God, I turned my life around.

About this same time I attended a huge black funeral in a large Riviera Beach church and the amazing choir brought the roof down as they sang Edwin Hawkin's rendition of "O Happy Day", and I found myself crying uncontrollably in front of everyone. People handed me kleenexes probably thinking I must have really known the person well who had passed.

Truth was, the conviction for past guilt concerning prejudiced crowds I'd hung out with, and funny racial jokes on television I had laughed along with, hit me so hard for the first time in my life. "O Happy Day" became my favorite song and replaced all my country music from that day on. Listen to some of the words:

"O Happy Day, O happy Day, when Jesus washed, He washed my sins away. He taught me how to watch, fight, and pray, and live rejoicing every day, O Happy Day, O Happy Day, when Jesus washed, He washed my sins away!" (This song was written by Phillip Doddridge in 1755, recorded by the Edwin Hawkins Singers in 1967).

I can't leave out a very important lesson the Lord taught me one night when I was collecting tolls on the Florida Turnpike at the remote Jupiter Exit. It was the night I had to work, but oh, how I had tried so hard to get it off that night. Why? Because Edwin Hawkins was in concert in Miami and I had been longing for a concert close enough to actually see him live and in person. There was no one who wanted to trade shifts and work there at midnight, so I couldn't get off and besides, they had probably been sold out of tickets anyhow.

I was sort of feeling sorry for myself and while I stood there waiting for the next vehicle I kept thinking how disappointing it was for me.

The big tour bus that pulled into my lane slowed down and the driver rolled down the window and I said, "Thank you, God Bless you!" as I handed him his ticket. The smiling bus driver said, "God bless you, too!" As he drove away and I looked back because he looked so much like my favorite singer and song writer. On the back window was printed, "Edwin Hawkins Singers".

I think I let out a loud squeal and said, "Oh no, Lord! I had no traffic at all, I could have had a "private conversation" with Hawkins himself, all alone, something probably nobody at the big concert in Miami got to do tonight! I had him all to myself, my hero, my celebrity singer! Oh, how come I was so foolish to not recognize he was right here all the time!" Oh, oh, here's what He had to say to me,what God had to say yo me, talk about me being foolish!

"Betty, I am not your Edwin Hawkins or Andre Crouch, but I created them myself, to glorify Me. They are not here with you tonight, but I've been alone with you all night and this is the first moment you have talked to Me or recognized Me even being here with you. Who do you worship, the Lord your God, or His creations?"

Busted. Never again would I hold up any man or woman on a pedestal. The moment of shame that had brought to my emotion made me realize the truth about who my celebrities and heros are, and none are as great as our God. And He deserves all our praise and attention. Lesson learned. I repented and I think He got even with me anyway, having Edwin Hawkins driving his own bus and taking the Jupiter exit! I bet he actually got a big kick out of that! I can just see Jesus smiling.

I love that song, "He was There All the Time"! Google that one sometime and get blessed! It turned out to be an "O Happy Night" after all, because who the Lord loves, He chastises, and He made me feel very loved after all. Sometimes I just Google "O Happy Day" on my phone, just to hear it play.

If I don't go in the rapture first, y'all please sing it at my funeral, and I am thanking you ahead of time, lol.

That song told my story. I had just learned the hard way, that from then on I had to "*Watch, Fight, and Pray!*"........*and live Rejoicing!* Another thing I learned as a Jesus warrior, is we *can't let our guard down, we stay alert!*

I even joined the choir of a great black congregation in West Palm Beach and the Lord put such a love in me for all races and ethnic backgrounds of people everywhere, and I would later be used by the Lord on several mission trips to Haiti and Dominican Republic.

Here is something even my children don't know because no one ever asked me what happened to my original diamond engagement ring, my next one we replaced that one with, then the one after the affair, and the next one after the divorce? Well, I will tell you. I sold all of them to pay for all those mission trips. Gary was always consulted first, and had gladly agreed to it.

Then one day Gary had me go to Palm Beach for an outragous diamond ring sale that everyone at Pratt Whitney was abuzz about. The men Gary worked with "shamed him" (his words), into realizing that after all he had put me through, my whole lifetime, he needed to take advantage of a sale of a lifetime by such a prominant jeweler, and bless me with one that would "knock my eyes out" and I would never ever want to sell it for anything, was the way they'd said it. (After you work with the same men every day for thirty eight years, you pretty much have formed more of a "family" with them, than just fellow workers, so Gary was their "buddy").

It would be a diamond cluster with a stone representing each of my children, grandchildren, and great-grandchildren and their spouses and left room for even more babies to come. It will be my forever family ring, I would like to keep wearing, even if the day comes when I remarry, if the Lord is willing.

While singing in that choir, we were once honored to have been selected to travel to Miami to sing in the Orange Bowl for the grand half time show. Our choir had a magnificent choir conductor who God used to perfect every anointed song, note, and message we were prepared to perform. We practiced at the big dress rehearsal a few days prior to the event. It was amazingly the best we'd ever sung. We were so excited!

It should have been a major disappointment when the leader broke the news to us: Following serious discussions with the choreography personnel *who were dictating a few changes*, he had prayerfully **withdrawn** our participation in the event, that was to have been covered, telecast, all over the world.

Wow! When he turned them down because they were in some way, attempting to alter our presentation into a more secular portrayal, a possible move to mess with God's heavy anointing He had going on, through the music, **I was jubilant *with agreement*!** We were praise and worshippers. We were not the world's entertainers. Remember in the Bible when the Jews are in captivity and have hung their harps upon the willows, when their captors required of them to perform, to sing songs of Zion? Yep, we weren't gonna stoop down for nobody. We would serve only God Almighty and sing for Him and for His Glory only, *and where* He ordained it.

Why, NOT singing in the Orange Bowl, became better than *singing* in the Orange Bowl. Maybe many might disagree, that we had missed an opportunity to minister to the whole world that day; however, I'm sure other Gospel choirs were more than delighted to take our place. But we would only be placed where the Lord wanted us to be. I learned almost as much from that incident as I did in all the pastor's dynamic preaching there. What I mean is, it really taught me who we are, and who I am, and it stayed with me as one of the greatest sermons I ever experienced.

Of course, when I broke the news to my Miami football fan husband, he cringed, and then said, "Uh...is that sorta like y'all ain't gonna cast yer pearls before the swine?" I laughed and said, "Yeah, *somethin'* like that!"

My favorite songs now were "Spirit in the Sky", the "Hallelujah Song", "No One Ever Cared for Me like Jesus" and "Softly and Tenderly Jesus is Calling", "Power in the Blood" and "He Looked Beyond My Faults and Saw My Need (Dotty Rambo's lyrics to the old familiar tune, "O Danny Boy"), and that secular hit song, "Amen". Oh! and Jimmy Swaggert's "Come Home, Come Home, its Suppertime"!

So, you can see now that for years I had been torn. Half of me was the most excitedly fulfilled mom with my great kids and a husband I was devoted to inspite of the faith crisis. The other half of me was devastated, lonely, crushed, discouraged, heartbroken and depleted not to have the Spiritual fellowship with my husband I had so longed for, and for so long. I never wanted anyone else but him. He was the only man I had ever really loved. We had an active and satisfying sexual life inspite of our differences. Even throughout the years when he would be angry or maladjusted, we always made love. Well, the Bible does has some instruction regarding that.

Along with Gary's unbelief were changes in his personality especially if he was drinking. He never became alcoholic but just after a couple of beers his manner toward me became more tough acting and harsh talking at times. He almost hit me when I asked him if I could tithe at church, but when I went and added to it, how the Lord would bless all our money, our 90%, if we gave Him His ten per cent, and *he'd never again have to complain* about my mishandling our money, he was outraged. He hit me so hard on my head it caught me off balance, causing me to fall into the back screen door onto the ground outside. When he never came outside to comfort me or apologize or see if I was ok, I knew for sure, for the first time, that he actually, was no longer, a real believer.

As I sat on the grass I looked up into the stars in the night sky and cried, *"Jesus"*! I heard Him say to me, **"I'm here Betty, its Me! Don't be afraid. Cheer up!"** Why, I could just picture Jesus standing there smiling at me giving me a hand up off the ground. Remember, He always sees the *big picture* while we're still just reeling in at the present circumstance.

What an anomaly! (opposite response) Right when you are most full of fear and terrified, God tells you to "Be not afraid!" When you are heartbroken and can't get the tears to stop or the sadness to leave, He says to "Cheer up!" But I have to say to you, it works! I have lived it! When we ask Him to be with us, *He is,* and truly does come and He cheers, comforts, and He also provides an escape when we need one. We have to trust and obey Him. He's our Commander in Chief which means as His soldiers we obey His commands. Its not optional. Also, we need to see our situation through His eyes, not ours.

When my Seminole friends sew their Indian skirts they make intricately designed patterns out of tiny little pieces of cloth which are too perfectly beautiful for words, but if you turn the material over and look at the underside, you see what appears to be uneven seams, unruly threads, and a maze of ravelled patchwork with no pretty design at all. God is looking at our lives much like that, He sees the upper side of the skirts and jackets with the perfect design, and we are seeing the underside with no visable pattern making sense. In Heaven one day He will show us

His magnificent plan and pattern He made with our lives. Like another of my favorite songs these days, "We Will Understand it Better By and By!"

Gary would shout five words in anger and he meant them, and, that he meant for them to be obeyed, and I knew they were fighin' words and I obeyed. They were: "DO NOT PREACH TO ME!" So I didn't. He had already heard all my sermons anyhow, complete with their corresponding Bible verses, songs and illustrations. So it wasn't really necessary.

Only Sheri, I think, could get away with it, and the two of them could sometimes be heard respectfully arguing all through the night at times. Yep, I had my own debate team in the house. I overheard from other rooms, Sheri preach to Gary the most effective and profound sermons as she countered his interpretation and confusion. Sheri could help him understand what a preacher was saying or what a Scripture meant. She could get away with arguing with him, in a good way, though, that he never allowed for me to even attempt.

She was like the Bible says our children would be, an arrow in our quiver to protect the Gospel against intruding enemy invasion. They frequently brought the debates to a happy closure when he would be seen patting her on the shoulder, and lovingly saying goodnight, usually when he'd been brought to a standstill point that he found no effective reply for. (lol) The Lord seemed to always give her the perfect Scriptures when she needed them. You know what I discovered that follows "perfect" Scriptures? *Impossible rebuttal*, that's what!

Sheri had and has an anointing on her and her music. She not only left home once and joined and graduated from the Army Reserve, (and I'm so proud to have a Vet in our immediate family), but left for Bible College at Southeastern Bible College in Lakeland, FL, for another year or two, as well. I often tell her she should probably have been a lawyer and she is someone you may never want to tangle with over theological matters unless you do your homework and prepare yourself pretty good. (lol) Even into 2020 before Gary passed away, she would spend countless hours confirming or expounding on sermon outlines he was listening to during Covid, by his favorite, Brother Jentezen Franklin, and others on television.

Now you want to know why God knew He could tell me to 'cheer up' that, things would get better? Because, yes, He knew things *were about* to get much better. Well, for one, He knew that Gary would allow me to spend 50 years without him at my side in church, *but, that the day was coming* when our "wonderful" Pastor "Wonder" Johns, at First Indian Baptist Church at the Brighton Reservation, was going to have to be away out of town. Brother Joe Bishop, (Chaplain at the Okeechobee Sheriff's Department and dear friend of the tribal congregation), filled in, and after his first sermon I went home excitedly telling Gary all about him.

I told Gary that Joe's sermons were actually a little over my head at times, intellectually and philosophically; but, I knew that he would probably like his preaching a whole lot. Now, understand this, of course I *loved* Joe's preaching too, but I was trying to think of a way to entice Gary to attend the services, since he had not gone to any church for all those years. I also wanted to help build up the crowd I thought might fall off, like they sometimes do, when a pastor has to be away.

Well, I think maybe it touched Gary's heart that I'd humbled myself into knowing this and expressing it, and that he was going to enjoy listening to someone *smarter than I was*, lol. In other words, Gary took it as a compliment for both Joe and himself and he not only went back that night, he attended every service on Sundays and Wednesday nights from then on. Brother Bishop preached on a level Gary understood and God used him to reach my husband.

When Wonder got back, (Gary had waited to walk the aisle for after our pastor had returned), and when the invitation was given he rededicated his life to Jesus! When I joined them at the alter Gary and I both wept for joy and hugged each other. After that night he then became the church song leader and never missed church again, ever, until Covid, anyhow. Wonder took Gary under his wing and frequently spent time with him in his pasture or fishing, and would sometimes call us and our grandson Justin, to come join him and Mary for dinner somewhere.

Gary remained faithful to his faith in Jesus and when we moved to the North Carolina mountains we joined Notla Baptist Church and the choir. Pastor Jerry Morrow and Gary hit it off immediately, both men who owned cows and enjoyed a comraderie over their agriculture interests as well as the Bible.

Up until that time it had been crucial that I stood by his side all those years and even following a divorce at one point in 1996 and remarriage in

1998, all of that had lent itself to bringing us not just closer to each other but closer to the Lord big time! We both had learned this: we had once fallen for the deceptive bait orchastrated by our common enemy Satan. We had both committed sin, in different ways, before God and found His overwhelmingly awesome unconditional love and forgiveness. Gary had become so humbled, remourseful, apologetic, and sincerely begging for my forgiveness, (and we both had), so thankful that He had pulled us out of the miry clay and set us free....and now we forgave each other so readily, filling our hearts with the greatest joy we had ever known.

Jesus was and is truly alive, and with us, and He had replaced our fears and sadnesses with **His cheerfulness!**

In my first book I spent more time going into the midlife crisis back when I was fifty three, we had experienced, that had caused Gary to want a divorce. When we were sitting before his attorney he asked Gary why he would be divorcing a woman who loved him and didn't want a divorce and he told him, "irreconcilable *religion*," was all. The lawyer had replied, "Well, that's the first time I ever heard *that* one!"

One of Gary's fellow workers at Pratt once asked Gary, "How come your wife is *always* so happy and smiling?" And Gary, who disagreed with me on every Biblical argument, answered, "Because **ignorance is bliss!**" lol

During the next two years, until we would remarry in 1998, Gary never found a wife and I never even thought about looking for a husband. But you know what? God used those two years for me to learn and grow spiritually. I moved to Nashville. I worked security for TBN (Trinity Broadcast Network), and lived with two outstanding Christian celebrities while I was there.

I stayed at Pastor Bob Beeman's lovely home, where I had my own room and helped fix big country suppers for him and several young men who lived there who were in Christian music and ministry. I didn't have to clean, just sort of be a house "Mom" to the guys, and help Bob with evening meals and grocery shopping. I worked at TBN.

It was through Pastor Bob, I was introduced to Lulu Roman, my favorite "Heehaw" comedianne and singer. For a year I lived nearby in the upper floor of her log home, that overlooked Nashville, not far from Pastor Bob's. I would drive her to a few concerts, recording studios, and trips to the airport, keeping watch over her home while she was away.

What a blessing to be the first to hear songs she'd just written that were so anointed we'd have to cry right there in her living room. Just knowing how the dynamic music she wrote was going to help save souls and give them eternal life, was overwhelming.

I patroled the grounds on a midnight shift, for two years at what used to be the old Conway Twitty's, "Twitty City," until it was purchased by Paul Crouch and it became TBN's *"Trinity* City". What a blessing walking through the gardens with the waterfalls, all lit up with colored floodlights, beautiful, softly-playing Christian instrumental music that was played 24/7. At Christmas time it was transformed into glorious *"Christmas* City" with millions of little twinkling lights.

In the evenings before my security schedule began, I sang in their large "Revival Explosion Choir" under the dynamic leadership of Bill Morris. I literally had a front row seat listening to all the best preachers, Bible teachers, and the greatest musicians of the day, just a few feet away. Frequently, I would join them in local restaurants following services, and it was like I'd done died and gone to Heaven!

It was named the explosion choir, and I thought the place *had* exploded the night Prophet Kim Clement was ministering one night and had smashed glass purposely on the stage to illustrate an event in Bible Scripture he was preaching on. Moments later he was praying for Jan Crouch, who was slain in the Spirit, landing right on top of the broken glass! Now, that was a scene to put a security guard on full alert, and now twice that night I would rest my hand at my waist where my robe concealed my Smith & Wesson 357 Magnum, as I quickly assessed the situation. What I immediately discovered, though, was that the Power of the Holy Ghost operating through the Blood of Jesus, is **greater** than weapons, demons, *shards of glass, or explosions!*

"Author's log home rooftop in the mountains, Cherokee County, NC"

That evening I learned something else and it was about how valuable a treasure the anointing is, and the prophetic, and how beyond comprehension it is ever so exciting and fulfilling to be living **with Jesus on His "mountain"**.

CHAPTER FIVE

SIGNS UNTO YOU

"And this shall be a sign unto you, ye shall find the Baby (Jesus)
wrapped in swaddling clothes and lying in a manger"
Luke 2:12 KJV

A new star had lit the sky and angels proclaimed the birth of Jesus to the Shepherds in the fields. It was a sign that Jesus was there and I liked having Christmas cards portraying the big event. The shepherds would find him in a barn the Holy parents would be dwelling in.

I would also like painting signs in my lifetime that announced our house was there and also saying in some way that Jesus was also there with us. In fact, on my gates I always post Deuteronomy 6:1-9, that includes some instructions that we are to share the laws and love of God every day to all we see, tell about Him in town and to our children, write His statutes on our hearts, foreheads, door frames of our home and on the gates, and share the love and grace of Jesus Christ at every opportunity.

I always had enjoyed writing Christmas cards every year and they were usually Leanin' Tree cards with an Indian cowboy Christian theme. Mostly they were Nativity scenes pictured around a "teepee" inn with a baby Jesus in fringed swaddling clothes, his Holy parents dressed in Navajo blankets with feathers and beads. Sometimes they said things like "from our tribe to yours" and always included a Bible verse. I loved writing "Mr. and Mrs Gary W. Luckey", but when I could afford it I would have it printed on the cards and some included the names of each child and the name of the present ranch where we were living.

Our first one was sent from our first home we built in Palm Beach Gardens on Square Lake Drive. We had a sign there with our cow brand on it reading, "Luckey Cattle Company." After all, that's how our official cattle brand was registered in Tallahassee. The homes and ranches that followed through the years would be houses and land we bought and had mortgages on and sometimes pastures that we leased. Gary cut all our fence posts by hand and I don't remember ever buying any till we moved to the mountains.

Starting out, Gary and his dad leased a section of pasture at the corner of Donald Ross Road and Military Trail in Palm Beach Gardens, FL from local real estate magnate and friend, John D. MacArthur. (Luckey's Grocery Store and Meat Market, were located below the upstairs office complex of Mr. MacArthur's on Park Avenue, next to the railroad track.) Years ago I could still see cowpens they'd built there from a distance, but when I saw Gary's heavy corner posts he'd cut by hand with some barbed wire still stapled so securely to it, I couldn't hold back some tears, and I still can't.

The sight of it brought back all those many years I'd watched Gary build miles of good fenceline and each post served to me, as a memorial to him and all our happy young years together, riding through the pastures, checking cattle, and eating picnic dinners in the cowpens.

The next pasture they would lease was on Hood road, a ranch where we lived for a year in a trailer we named "Lucky 7 Ranch". What I remember best about it was the garden Pa Luckey had growing there of big red tomatoes fertilized by the cow manure, and healthy, dark green collards, the best I ever cooked! (About the only things I canned with any regularity would be fresh blackeyed peas and snaps, and guava jelly.) Now they would refer to the first one as the "Old Luckey 7 Ranch" and Hood Road pasture as "Luckey 7 Ranch".

Two more locations, one ranch at Military Trail close to Northlake Boulevard and the other which included both sides of Blue Heron boulevard along the east side of I-95 were simply "Luckey's (Blue Heron)

Ranch" and "Luckey's (Military Trail) Ranch". And that's what my signs said.

I had to laugh once when Gary looked at me with paint dripping off my forefinger, and said, "You sure like signs, *don't* cha?!". I never used a brush because it was easier for me just to dip my finger in the paint can, and a lot easier to clean off my finger instead of a messy paintbrush. I accumilated and saved quite a stack of old signs I'd made through the years for souveniers, but I think I eventually forgot them on a barn somewhere....fond memories.

Oh, and speaking of signs, I once felt so inspired to paint signs that just said, *"JOHN 3:16"* that I painted about twenty-five or more and drove to major intersections and unique places on country roads, some in town and some out of town, standing in the bed of my pickup, I reached up high as I possibly could, and nailed them to whatever looked appropriate, a post, a tree, or a utility pole, usually ones that already had nails or signs in it. It took me a whole weekend to get the last one posted in place. Want to know what happened next? I noticed one missing the following day, so I began to check on each one, and they had all disappeared! To this day, I have no idea who removed all those signs. They almost had to have taken them down as soon as I was putting them up!?

Now that reminds me of a very funny day when Gary, armed with a burn permit, issued from the state forestry office, had spent an entire day, starting fires in his grasses in the 2,000 acres of Lucky Buck Ranch, that would bring fresh green, healthy and nourishing new growth soon, days afterwards, for cattle and the deer. The legal permit assured the public and local residents that the fire was being monitored by the landowner as well as the fire departments who would be notified, with weather conditions, such as winds, all having been taken into consideration.

What Gary's dad, Pa Luckey, did not know, was that Gary was hard at work setting all the fires that were causing all the billowing smoke for three miles in two directions. Pa was accompanying a local volunteer fire truck through the pasture, desparately putting out the fires in the opposite side of the ranch property. Pa Luckey arrived to our house first, face sunburnt and shirt wet with sweat, when up drove Gary, face sunburnt, shirt wet with sweat.

Pa said impatiently to Gary, "Well, I'd sure like to know just where *you have been all day long while I've been putting out all your pasture fires!?"* Gary answered, trying his best not to have to smile, *"Dad, I've been all day long, working really hard at setting them!"* It would be a perfect example of lack of communication, and it would always make Gary laugh to tell about it, but Pa would never crack a smile, and never did. "Some things just ain't funny!" he once said.

While we had still been living at Square Lake on Square Lake Drive, we began leasing two sections of land (1,280 acres), way out Beeline Highway known as the "Old Box F Ranch". We were able to purchase 10 acres to build on, adjacent to it, so we had named the whole thing, "Lucky Buck Ranch". We killed so many deer there Gary said the bucks were lucky that got away and he was lucky for the ones he shot, so it earned its name" Lucky Buck". Of course the main reason for the name was Gary's determination to try to become millionaire one day and he hoped the "buck" stood not just for deer but for the money.

Lucky Buck Ranch would eventually be 10 acres we owned and over 2,000 acres we leased along C-18 canal in Hungryland Slough, in Palm Beach County. We built a long ranch house with a separate bedroom for each of the children. We lived there in a trailer before building the house with no electric power or running water for almost a year. Powerlines were yet to be brought that far from town in those days. We bathed in the ponds and cooked over a campfire in the yard. We developed close friendships with the very few others who, also were roughing it in the area, like the Primm family.

Sylvia Primm, (Rogers Primm Sr's wife and Rogers Jr, Piper, Sugar, and Chris's mom), our neighbors at "Far Out Farm", about a mile from us, had asked me what we did *that* for, (go build ourselves a five bedroom house), didn't I know that all four kids would end up in our kingsize bed? I chuckle because she was right. Every night all six of us would pile in the bed for a late night discussion before a prayer and so many times they'd fall asleep before they could leave for their own bedrooms.

Oh well, Tifton used his room to store all his guns, ammo and hunting parapharnalia, Libby used hers for her clothes, Sheri, her stage costumes and makeup, and Niki her dolls and games. At sometime during the night they would get uncomfortable and retreat to their own bedrooms. Ah, fond memories, the kingsize bed, where it was usually Tifton who always kept us laughing. In fact, when I think about it, from the time he was born, he was never *not* funny.

We would have the cattle lease for 25 years next to the house and raise our family there. It was like owning our own private park. We really enjoyed being there but decided to sell the house when John D. MacArthur gave away, (donated), or sold our adjacent pasture to Palm Beach County for an actual county equestrian park. Some of the county maps still say "Lucky Buck Ranch" across those three sections, 23, 24, and 19.

We sold the house to the parents of Venus and Serena Williams, the world's best tennis players, we could hear practicing under flood lights at night because their Southern colonial home was secluded on the 10 acres in the trees next to ours. The girls had even invited our grandsons, Justin and Sean Savacool, to come over and teach them to play at least a set or two once or twice or more. The boys were probably no older than 8 or 9 maybe, (I've lost track). It was a very happy memory all those kids would have and so kind of the girls to give our guys the impromtu tennis lessons.

When we decided to put our house up for sale I had called their mother, Oracene Price Williams, whose cell phone I had kept in my wallet. However, I was surprised when she actually answered it. I said, "Mrs. Williams, this is Betty, your neighbor next door just letting you know we're selling the house in case you're interested in having it as a security buffer for your home." To my utter shock, she simply replied, "Ok, Ms. Luckey, I'll cut you a check Thursday". And she did, when Gary and I met her that Thursday with husband, Richard, at their lawyer's office.

Funny story: we all arrived at the attorney's very nice, upscale office before Richard got there, and when he did, he was *barefooted*. Oracene was appalled and made him return to his vehicle for some shoes. It made us all laugh as we watched the world's most popular and famous Nike shoe commercial spokesman, sit on the plush office chair, reluctantly putting on his shoes just for us. I liked Richard immediately. He was not only independant, confident, bold and friendly; but very funny, making us laugh repeatedly while we were there.

Our entire family will all agree the favorite idyllic ranch with the historic Fisheating Creek meandering throughout the 100 acres, at Venus

63

FL, (speaking of "Venuses"), in Highlands County, was the best place we ever owned. There would be electric power issues for the area that would prevent building there at that time, and that we decided not to pursue. We owned a home in town and lived there; but we really enjoyed driving out to Venus for the next 25 years hunting, fishing, camping, raising cattle, and telling real stories and playing music around campfires. We named it "Two Creeks Ranch" because you could spot it immediately on any satellite map where Fisheating Creek and Bootheel Gulley Creeks intercepted at the very center of the one hundred acres tract, then flowed as one creek, as that historic Fisheating Creek, southward into Glades County. It would be the ranch we always simply referred to as, "the Creek".

There were hundreds of huge old Granddaddy Oaks with Spanish moss, bass, specks, talapia and catfish, plenty of whitetail deer, and we can prove it by all the deer racks we accumilated. Turkeys and wild hogs were so abundant there, it kept Gary, his daddy, our son Tifton, our grandsons, JT Luckey and late Justin Savacool, camping there often and their freezers full of wild game. There were all kinds of critters like raccoons, fox squirrels, foxes, and a weasel or two, alligators, otters, soft shell, box turtles, as well as big gopher turtles, of great value to the older Seminoles.

In 1998 we bought a house in Okeechobee at 1903 SW 3rd Ave within walking distance to Walmart, sold that house after maybe five years there, and in 2006 bought a large home up on the Lake Wales Ridge near Lake Placid, at 1385 State Road 70. It was nestled between orange groves, with an ancient flowing spring well known to the Seminole Tribe with the awesome pure spring water that we had piped up the hill into the house.

There were bears in the area, one I almost hit once, on the highway in front of our house, and there were also panthers. I watched one running behind our house in the adjoining orange grove. The outstanding view from the ridge would give you glimpses of Lake Istokpoga several miles away. I named the house Luckey's "Seminole Spring Ranch" where Gary had a few cows and Justin had sheep. It would be a home large enough to bring my aging parents to, in their final years where I could help care for them. After my parents passed away we sold the house and we sold Two

Creeks Ranch and bought a ranch house on 40 acres along Jack's Branch in Glades County near LaBelle.

Gary's family had helped pioneer Ft Myers and LaBelle. Our family in 1993 had been honored to be celebrated as the Pioneer Family of the Year and ride in the annual Swamp Cabbage Festival parade. The Luckeys were already included in several books and tons of official records, and Gary and I joined the LaBelle Oldtimer's and the Historical Museum groups. It was lots of fun to feel part of the community and its history. We named the LaBelle ranch, "Luckey Island Ranch" where we lived from 2014 until 2019.

The first "Luckey Island "was the land up along Fisheating Creek south of Venus that was originally named Tasmania, Florida, at Rainey Slough. It was ten miles north of the ranch on Jack's Branch and was homesteaded by Gary's great grandpa Sam Luckey in the 1800's. Granny had lived out there too as a little girl and went to first grade in her original old one room schoolhouse still standing on Farabee Road in one of the pastures. Pictures can still be seen when googled Luckey School House. The farm lands were swampy in places and Granny's family and Pa Luckey's family had raised cattle and farmed the high grounds that when flooded appeared as actual islands.

We took an exciting day trip once when we drove Granny to see her actual grade school she had later when it was moved from Castallia, Florida, to the Tampa State Fairgrounds. It was set up renovated back to to its original condition for people to see an authentic early century schoolhouse. When we let the people staffing the pioneer section of the fairgrounds know she was there, they hustled around and interviewed Granny. Her full name was Lela Stewart Luckey, and her video interview is on display in their historical video library at Tampa. The LaBelle Historical Museum also has an interview of Granny's sister, Nettie Pearl Stewart Howard, and both videos are really good and very informative about early pioneer life and how it was during the Depression, along the Everglades.

Talk about signs...the Lord had told me things would be changing, and *His* "signs" were everywhere. The government, society, economy, many Bible prophecies were fulfilled, national security, the environment, and the nation's spiritual status, to name a few. I can honestly say I saw that we were about to experience something very bad in the very close future and told everyone I could feel it just ahead but didn't know yet what it was.

What it was, was time for everyone to return to God and get close to Jesus and hang on tight. Now we know: There was coming a pandemic and I never would have believed it was about to change my life forever. I was seeking the Lord in prayer because He was telling me to flee to the mountains, begin the reality of survival preparation, and settle down somewhere with preferably, altitude, fresh natural spring drinking water, a food supply, and privacy.

I knew my whole life that at some time in my future I would move to the mountains. One year at Christmas I had even surprised everyone and amused them, I'm sure, by making them a robe, each made out of an army blanket, I labeled, "Mountain Fleer"! That would be taken from Bible references to "Flee to the Mountains!" It was meant to be an all-purpose survival garment/blanket, robe, survival sleeping bag and duffle bag, all rolled into one in case of unexpected doom and gloom.

I guess maybe people thought of me as a survivalist and prepper and I had even put together a little red pamphlet once predicting difficult years ahead and how to prepare. It was my Gospel tract with warnings to turn one's life over to Jesus before it was too late. He was telling me that now it was time. The Gospel tract included emergency supply lists, the plan of Salvation, and the sinner's prayer.

When we found the house in the Smoky Mountains in 2019 in Cherokee County NC, near Murphy, at 144 Hawks View Terrace, I named the 11 acre ranch "Winterhawk" after my favorite Indian movie. It would be the first place I ever lived that would sparkle in seasonal snow flakes and have a view in North Carolina of mountain ranges as far away as in Georgia and Tennessee. When the mountains are covered with snow, which is rare, but it is unforgetable, as they glisten in the distance, like gold, in the sunshine.

Since Gary was the son of James Luckey (Pa), and the grandson of Pa's dad, Sam Luckey, who was the son of the first Samuel Antony (not Anthony, Pa always would remind us) Luckey, all Florida cattlemen, Gary was bound and determined to never leave his Florida homeland. He liked to study ranches for sale in far away states but I don't think he would have ever actually moved there and leave the land of his roots. He was an avid hunter, fisherman, and cowboy who enjoyed the simplicity of having rich green grass available for cows all year long, without having to farm for it.

Gary always believed in buying and selling property to keep increasing holdings that might someday give the remaining family a nest egg to divvy up between the four children after we were gone. He often lectured us about saving money and not spending it, so any money we could ever accummilate was quickly reinvested in land or cattle so we couldn't!

It made us chuckle every time we'd hear someone begin a statement with, "If I had old man Luckey's money...". That statement probably had started ever since the first Sam Luckey was reported to have over a thousand head of cattle, but that was way back in open range days of raising cows before fences, when Sam's herd stretched across the everglades from the Devil's Garden swamps to Ft. Myers.

We were land poor just as Gary planned it, and had given up using credit cards soon after they were invented. It was a real tribute to him to keep a tight budget and to the Luckey men before him who were all known as very frugal, hard working ranchers with stamina. In fact, an article appeared in Ft. Myers once, and a historical book chapter entitled, "The Luckeys had Stamina!" I still have a copy.

It was Gary's grandpa Sam who built what was called, "The Luckey Fence". It was the first fence stretched across the Devil's Garden for 15 miles made solely from Sam's hand hewn liter pine fence posts and handmade rails put together with his own hammered nails, being also a blacksmith by trade. Sam was also a well respected saw mill owner in Orlando before also owning one near Fort Myers. This fence was commissioned for Sam Luckey by Jake Summerlin, the man with the largest south Florida herd at the time. This was putting an end to open range grazing, and moving cattle around on horseback, using leather cow whips, campfires and branding irons, something Gary's dad had done throughout his youth.

His dad, James Franklin Luckey, would frequently remind us, that he actually didn't *have a* youth, because his dad had him living in the woods to cowhunt as soon as he finished eighth grade in LaBelle. His sisters would stay in town with their mother and get to remain in school, and maybe his brothers, too, because, I think it was only Pa that stayed mostly with his dad living in camps in the woods, and on horseback. I asked Pa one time to come out and camp one night with us and he just looked at me and slowly shook his head. Oh, yeah, then I remembered, he had said he'd already had enough of it to last a lifetime.

That fence was not far from the Big Cypress Seminole Indian Reservation, and pieces of it could be seen and were photographed many, many years later. I was truly proud to have married into the Luckey family to a Florida Cracker, *a **real** Florida Cracker*, whose leather, hand-braided whip still hangs by my fireplace.

Gary could stretch the tightest barbwire fence lines, so tight, I had to use a crowbar I kept under the truck seat, just to get the gaps open at times. He cut his liter pine posts with an axe, not a chainsaw, and always had an eye peeled to the woodlands for those tall bare trees standing high above the others, weathered and petrified and he would comment, "Hey, looky thar over yonder at that one! Thar's a good 3 to 4!" That meant he could cut that many posts out of it. And he would cut and haul the heaviest posts I ever saw! Much of the time all by himself.

When our son Tifton wasn't able to be there with him, or our grandsons, JT Luckey or late Justin Savacool, or son in law, Simon Bjorn, and usually, Sheri, too, he managed completely alone and would get the job done.

When the kids were young they would also be enlisted to help Gary way out in the wood's pastures, long days in the hot Florida sun, even little Niki helping to carry the buckets of heavy staples and nails. When the four children would remind him how long they had been helping him, he would usually start winding things up, to their relief, and look forward to the hot suppers waiting in the house when they returned, browned from the sun and very hungry!

All four kids knew what it was like to spend a day in the pasture or the woods with their daddy helping him do all kinds of things other kids probably never had the opportunity to experience. Helping drive a truck, tractor or swamp buggy, when they were too little to even reach the peddles, pulling or towing everything with ropes and chains, from huge heavy fence posts, to cattle, to alligators.

The kids were needed when he would have a vehicle stuck in swampy muck or water, and he would come home bragging about how tough and brave they all had been and were always obeying him and making him so proud of them, the *grandkids, too*. Sometimes he would get back to the house with JT or Justin, who'd be covered with dirt, mud, sweat, and sometimes animal blood, but smiling! Gary was stretching fence right up until he was 80 and his daddy *did* fence well into his 80's, helping at Gary's side.

When God told me it was time to move to the mountains I had no idea Gary would ever hear of such a thing, but I knew the Lord was in it for sure when I told Gary and he replied with, "Well, lets go look and see if there's somethin' near my brother Glyn's place near Murphy". I could have fainted!

Several things were leading up to this which included signs the Great Spirit would sometimes allow to urge me in the direction He needed me to go. It seemed as though Glyn was having increased visits with his North Carolina cardiologists and I knew it weighed heavily on Gary's mind. Also, Gary had begun telling me that he, himself, was going to probably "kick the bucket", as he put it, well before I did, and he wanted me prepared for it. I think I spent a lot of years mourning ahead of time, for when that day was going to come. I remember tears I cried as I'd sing some of our old love songs from years ago. Gary and I loved singing together and harmonizing and sometimes I still can hear our voices praising the Lord with the old hymns.

My favorite secular song was "I Remember You" and my favorite line was ...."When my life is through, and the Angels ask me to recall, the thrill of them all, I will tell them I remember, tell them I remember, ...*tell them I remember you!" (Written in 1941 by Johnny Mercer and Victor Schertzinger).*

Our most memorable times would be around the campfires singing with Granny and Pa, and the whole family. Granny had an old guitar she played chords on and a harmonica Sheri and Simon had bought her for a birthday. When she tried to play it in the firelight, she made all the grandkids laugh when she told them she would *at least try to play it, that* she could never remember whether you were supposed to blow it in or out. But when she played, it really sounded good and we all joined her in singing "Amazing Grace," "I'll Fly Away", and "In the Sweet By and By". Another favorite we had fun with was, "The Circle Won't be Broken" and how we'd sing our solo parts when the words said, "Daddy sang bass", "Mama sang tenor", "Me and little brother would join right in there!"

We had been living in LaBelle and had endured a horrific Hurricane Irma which caused our family in several trucks and vehicles to flee the swampland pastures for higher ground. Everyone piling in with clothes and supplies, we traveled on crowded Florida interstate highways with thousands of other evacuees. All of us on our cell phones, they began to ask as we passed all the "no vacancy" signs and gas stations starting to close, "Hey Mom, where are we headed?"

As God is my judge I had no idea, so I prayed, "Ok Lord, where *are* we headed?" In my Spirit I heard Him say loud and clear, "Monteagle"! As I relayed the message, everyone started typing in the name on their GPS when someone asked, what is Monteagle?

I had made several trips from Florida in the past to Nashville, TN along Hwy 24 between there and Chattanooga. Every time I'd begin the assent up the mountain I would just know in my knower that the Cherokee and Indians before them, had called it Eagle Mountain. Later when I researched the history I found it to be actually so. It was a safe haven high above rising waters with protected pockets and valleys buffeted from high winds, and from which the views were spectacular and inspirational.

I had heard and read in magazines folks describe the route there as one of the most dangerous drives in the country and they dreaded it especially in rain or snow, but not me! Every time I traveled through the area I always had a supernatural surge of safety and well-being. Sometimes I'd roll down my windows and just take in the fresh mountain air, breathing it all in, along with prayers of thanksgiving to the mighty Creator Who'd thought it all up and designed an awesome masterpiece of mountain views and natural beauty.

The few days spent there at the Smokehouse retreat cabin where we slept like babies and enjoyed sumptous Southern cooking, were addictive and I would always want to return. It reminded me of the safe nests perched securely along the cliffs there, made by Golden Eagles for centuries who historically had originally given the mountain its name, later shortened to Monteagle.

The Cherokee were not the only people to first discover its vantage point that overlooked other states and mountain ranges, it was stated in tourist brochures that there was evidence in area caves of inhabitants for thousands of years. At Sewannee, another close community, the University of the South emerged since the 1800's with historical cathedral styled architecture comparable to Notre Dame and other European landmarks. It would be home to the fine arts college sponsored by Episcopalians in Great Brittain who were responsible for its founding, and their magnificent church cathedral building there, "All Saint's Chapel". In other words, I had not by any means been the only person who recognized a mysterious awareness of the area's sanctuary for safety, praise and worship and a closeness to God.

When we left Eagle Mountain some of us continued over to Cherokee County in North Carolina where Glyn and Pam lived at Brasstown. While we were there we began looking online for local houses for sale in the event we would sell the LaBelle ranch soon. The rest is almost a blur it happened so quickly.

The tragic loss of Sheri and Simon's beloved stallion once belonging to our Seminole friend, late Weems Buck, which had been given to them, and the deaths also, of our two Bloodhounds, Bo and Belle, all occurred mysteriously within close proximity to each other. It left us with a new desire to leave our 40 acres of lush green pasture land along Jack's Branch.

Well, that in addition to, especially the way Hurricane Irma had brought four foot high flood water within an inch of the threshold at the front door and cloudy flooded creek waters with twelve foot long alligators. Sheri always reminds us how we waded through the property in chest high water to get to the house, carrying loaded shotguns up out of the water, held high above our heads!

Sale of the ranch occurred quickly and as we packed up into trucks and trailers and headed north on I-75, the new house in North Carolina on Hawks View Terrace was posted online. Miraculously, when we had stopped at the Macon bypass rest stop, Sheri and Simon, who had his parents, Conny and Agneta Bjorn riding with them, saw it pop up as "just listed"! They called about it and we arranged to see it the next day.

The following day would be my 77th birthday on March 16, 2019. The realtor, met us to show the house and we signed the contract right there on the spot. It would be the most awesome piece of property I had ever seen. It had everything I always looked for in a piece of property, privacy, high ground, pure, natural water source, and room enough for cattle or wildlife, in other words, a food source as well.

The house was a three story log home on almost 11 acres with a mountain view to inspire my book writing and Sheri and Simon's song writing. There were fruit trees, walnuts, blueberry, blackberry bushes and grapevines, flowers of every color, and I could see mountain views from there in GA and TN. It had a pond, a creek with pure fresh water always flowing, two barns and several small pastures, enough for a few head of cattle. When Gary looked at my lit up countenance, he, too, had a big grin on his face and I knew we were home.

The Lord had told me I would know it was the right house when I'd see a little stone country mountain church from our bedroom windows. Sure enough, historic Notla Baptist Church would be our new home church located on the mountain across a little valley, clearly visable with its white steeple, stained glass windows and well kept lawn. I would look at it every day whether from the porch rocking chairs or my desk up on the loft. It would be clearly visible from my bed without even lifting my head from my pillow.

Gary and I loved Pastor Jerry Morrow and his wife Trudy right away and we became members of the church and joined the choir. Pastor Jerry had cattle like Gary did and they had great comraderie over their agricutural interests as well as in the Bible. We would attend together faithfully as long as the pandemic allowed us to, right up until Gary passed away from the virus on October 15, 2020.

Brother Morrow officiated at his funeral along with (Gary's brother) Glyn's Pastor Aud Brown of Little Brasstown Baptist Church, also located not far from our house. His brother Glyn had taught their senior adult Sunday school class and been an active member of their choir, known and loved for solo parts sung in his rich tenor voice.

Gary would be buried that week at the Greenlawn Memorial Cemetery at Peachtree close to Brasstown next to Glyn and his wife, Pam. I was heartbroken along with the entire family. It was a traumatic shock that would require some time before we could even begin to accept it.

Losing Gary, my true love since I was 13 years of age, left me clinging to the Cross of Jesus and the Holy Spirit was and is faithful to comfort and stay with me night and day. Sad days and long nights, I became glued to Christian television up on my loft with the peaceful mountain views. I would spend time writing my book when I wasn't worshipping and praising God with my television church families especially since the virus quarentines prevented me from attending both Notla Baptist and Little Brasstown Baptist churches.

I was so thankful to Pastors Morrow and Pastor Brown for helping minister to Gary the months before his passing and for helping him prepare to enter Heaven's gates. I had always enjoyed several television preachers like TD Jakes, Jack Van Impe, Oral Roberts, John Hagee, Ken Copeland, Reinhart Bonnke, Adrian Rogers, (Adrian was a personal old friend of my Dad's), Pat Robertson, Hal Lindsey, Charles Stanley, Jimmy Swaggert, and Billy Graham.

Now I spend my Sundays watching Perry Stone (pastor in Cleveland TN), Rabbi Jonathan Cahn (Messianic Rabbi in NJ), and my favorite Prophet, Robin Dale Bullock (Pastor in Warrior, AL), Kat Kerr, and Gary's favorite, Pastor Jentezen Franklin (in Gainesville, GA).

The last thing Gary and I did before we were sent to separate hospitals with Covid in 2020 was to enjoy one of Jentezen's great sermons together. He had patted the couch beside him where he always sat and smiled at me and said "Come sit here beside me, its time for church to start!"

Well, the truth is that the *very* last thing we did was later that night sleeping together in our log canopy bed high up on the Smoky Mountain where touches of Autumn were already felt in the air. Beautiful colors were painting the leaves outside the windows, and where romance was always on the agenda for us ever since we were young'uns. My life's adventures with that man will always be with happy memories....and if there was ever anything unpleasant, it was forgiven and forgotten and permanantly left under the Blood of Jesus at the cross. Our romantic experience that night had left us giggly and flirty, like we were kids.

Speaking of which, I am reminded of two conversations I once had, one with my mother and one with a friend. My (preacher's wife) mother said that her generation was too Victorian to speak much concerning sexual matters and it had left her curious when she was young, about elderly couples and at what point they no longer shared those intimacies. She said, "Just so you and the kids will know, (and I now share with the whole entire world, lol), Betty, your dad and I are 86 and 88 and we still enjoy each other in those ways!" Well, that was already obvious to everyone the way they still held hands, lit candles in the evening and always on their dining tables. He frequently walked with his hand around her waist even in public, and I never knew a day they weren't talking softly, sweetly, and laughing together, about everything.

I have known very few couples with such an expressive relationship in their marriages, but my daughter Sheri and her husband Simon are a prime example, like my parents. Even when one of them leaves the room for a few minutes, they pause and kiss and say I love you, and I know, because we share the same house, and they've been married over fifteen years!

Then there was a young and beautiful police officer I was dispatching for, who once asked if she could confide in me a question that had been greatly troubling her mind. "Luckey, (the cops always called me), at what age do seniors give up having sex? I mean there comes a time when we are no longer appealing to each other, I'm sure, right? We get too fat or too skinny and wrinkled and maybe failing health issues....I guess what I'm trying to ask is, when do old people quit 'doing it'?"

First, I expained it is erroneous to think you would ever have to stop. Sex is a God-designed gift that enables marriages to become closer than ever before, and may continue growing even more enjoyable the older we are. Then I whispered a prayer to God that surely there was a better way to tell her, *some Divine, simple example*....and then the Lord gave me an answer for her that evoked a huge smile and a loud outburst as she shouted for joy, "MRS. LUCKEY!!! Thank you!!!!" when I said:

"Always remember this, regardless of how you look or feel, all you need to do is simply reach over and just *turn out the light,* and you both are suddenly young teenagers once again!"

"Sheri and Simon Bjorn, Smoky Mountains, North Carolina, 2022"

CHAPTER SIX

THE SPIRIT OF THE LORD IS UPON ME

❖

"The Spirit of the Lord is upon Me because He has anointed Me to preach the Gospel to the poor, He has sent Me to heal the broken hearted, to preach liberty to the captives and recovery of sight to the blind, and to set at liberty them that are oppressed"
Luke 4:18 NKJV

"Preaching the Gospel to the Poor"

I was sure enjoying a beautiful day off from work, (in training at the Florida Turnpike at the Jupiter Exit on Indiantown Road), and in spite of a cold snap we were experiencing, I sat out in the sunshine on the front steps to our trailer we would live in until our new house would be built later that year. The trailer was placed on the same ten acres where the house foundation would soon begin.

I watched the cattle grazing along the palmettos nearby and listened to a brightly colored Cardinal as he sat singing to me from a Myrtle bush. I commenced to continue praying just as I had earlier that morning when I was inside drinking my coffee. And then I casually asked God if there was anything He needed me to do for Him that day and unexpectantly, and to my astonishment, I heard him speak!

He asked me to go get 100 Spanish Bibles. I asked Him twice if that was what He had just asked, and He said "yes" twice! I was electrified with excitement and ran into the trailer to get my purse and find some shoes. I drove to town and using my parents' house phone and phonebook I jotted down numbers for the local Christian Bookstore, Noah's Ark, Gideon's International, Inspiration House, American Bible Society and their stories were all the same. Bibles everywhere were backordered and no supplies like that quantity seemed to be available anywhere.

I was determined to not give up. I called back the owner of the store closest to me and asked him if there was anyone in the area he knew who might have a personal quantity of Bibles. He said he had heard of a man in West Palm Beach named Elmer Anderson, who might be able to advise me, if I could locate him.

In the phone book was listed, "Anderson, E." It looked like my only hope. A cheerful lady answered the phone and when I told her my name and that I was trying to locate an Elmer Anderson, she asked me to hold and she would get him. I don't think I actually expected to find him! When I told him I was looking for 100 Spanish Bibles he said he might have them if I could meet him downtown in his office near Clematis Street within the hour. It would take me that long to drive there, and I did.

When I drove there his office was located in a very old building on the second floor up a steep stairway behind the building next to the small parking lot. When he opened the door for me I was amazed at all the boxes of Bibles stacked on the floor against every wall. There appeared to be a collection of every kind of Bible you could think of.

I waited as he walked around checking each stack and from the huge bare windows was the most spectacular view! I could see the Intracoastal Waterway in the distance with its dazzling blue water sparkling, as was the Atlantic Ocean across the horizon beyond it. You have to remember these were back in the days before all the high rise construction when no tall buildings were allowed to prevent the public view of the ocean.

"I have them!" he called to me and picked up the heaviest looking huge box as he asked me to please open the door. Now let me tell you, this dear man was no young whippersnapper, as people say, he was tall and thin with white hair and glasses, and maybe 75 or 80? Why, he whisked right through that door and bounded down those frightful steps effortlessly! He reminded me to hurry to grab the tailgate and get it lowered and the second I did, he dumped that big heavy box in the bed of my truck and with a big grin, he nodded and said "The Lord bless you!" as he started back up the stairs.

"Wait!" I cried out after him...I told him he hadn't asked a thing about me and we had not discussed the cost or where the Bibles were going, or anything! He kept climbing as he smiled and said, "No need! You're just doing the Lord's work and so am I!" He waved without looking back and disappeared into his "office".

Stunned, I was reflecting at his age, agility and strength and thought on the verse that God is saying in Isaiah 40:31 (KJV), " But they that wait upon the Lord shall renew their strength; they shall mount up with wings like as eagles; they shall run and not be weary; and they shall walk and not faint!" Why, it would not surprise me if God had not already told him I'd be coming before I'd ever called him.

I sat in my truck a few moments, actually dazed. I was glad he hadn't asked me where the Bibles were headed because I had no idea either. In fact, I was aware I had no gas to speak of, and no money for gas; but, Hallelujah I had a hundred Bibles in Spanish! I needed to stop and think where I *was* supposed to go next.

As I began heading north in city traffic I prayed desparately for God to tell me what to do. I asked, should I drive home and He said "no". I was glad to hear His voice again. When I asked should I go to my dad's church, or head toward my parent's house, to get some gas money for instance, He again said no. When I asked Him if He wanted me to keep heading north on I-95 toward Jupiter He said "yes."

I was soon passing cattle pastures and orange groves along the north county countryside when I felt lead to pull into an area on Indiantown Road where I had frequently watched Spanish speaking migrants loading up into buses as I worked across the highway at the Jupiter toll exit in training on the Florida Turnpike. Should I park here by the road? The Lord said yes.

There was a kind black man working there who came up to my truck to see if I needed help. When I told him I needed to speak to one of the Hispanic workers he explained that no one was there due to freezing temperatures that week. A little boy who was there with him came up to my window staring at the colorful "Good News" paperback edition of the Bible I had on my dashboard. When I asked the man if I could give it to him he said I could.

I have never seen anyone so excited to have a new Bible! He hugged it tightly in his arms dancing around skipping and jumping with the biggest smile on his face! I thought to myself, "Lord, please forgive me if there is ever a time I am not that excited to have Your Word! The little boy was expressing exactly how I felt about my Bibles, and always had.

If anyone had stopped to asked me why I was waiting there I would have truthfully had to say that I was "waiting on the Lord". Then I felt a sensation that the person I was about to give the box of Bibles to was a half a mile away, and then a quarter of a mile, and when I asked God if that person was about to come around the curve in the road, he said yes.

All at once an old school bus painted pale blue came around the curve and began slowing down! Over the windshield written in Magic Marker type lettering it said, "Dedicatio al Christo" or something similar. Dedicated to Christ! I just thought for certain the bus would pull over into this loading area to the vegetable fields where I was waiting but, to my surprise, instead it turned into the entrance across the street and entered the turnpike!

I started the engine and sped across the road getting a ticket from the exit manager who was working the ticket booth. He distracted me though, when he began questioning me if I knew if they had assigned me yet to this exit or the one at Palm Beach Gardens. I failed to see if the bus went north or south, it was out of sight, but when I asked the lord, He said "south"! I followed south and caught up with the bus. I was disappointed when it passed the next two Palm Beach Gardens exits and was worried when it missed the next one.

Finally it left the turnpike at the Lake Worth exit where I was sure I'd need to fill out a form allowing me to mail in the toll money. Of course I was also praying the gas would last. As I began explaining it to the toll collector, I saw in my console the exact amount of change for the toll. Maybe I had just overlooked it before and it had been there all along, I'm not really sure. The bus was still in sight and was now pulled over to allow someone to get off. I flew up to the bus, got out, and stood at the open door and looked at the surprised bus driver.

The Hispanic driver looked at me and about fifty migrants seated behind him all stretched and leaned to see who was standing there. I said "Hi! My name is Betty Luckey.....(I paused, not positive how to begin!).... Are you a Christian?" He said "Si". I said, "Do you need Bibles?" His voice became weak and he answered softly, "Si". Then I breathed a big breath and said, "Do you need one hundred Spanish Bibles?" His arms went up, He looked to the Heavens, and cried, "Si!" as tears rolled down his cheeks. He was too overcome with emotion to speak and I asked if someone would help me get them out of the back of my truck. All the people responded in hushed whispers and then loud voices, "Eeesa-Mee-ree-cal!" over and over again, "It's a miracle!"

Two strong looking young men followed me to the back of my truck where I put down the tailgate and the two of them together carried the heavy box dropping it carefully onto the floor of the bus. It looked and sounded as if the Bibles were so heavy the bus bounced! I instantly thought about Elmer Anderson and how he had handled the box all by himself with such ease.

I could hear Hispanic voices all excitedly speaking at once, clapping and waving as I drove away. I may have never known the story behind this Divine assignment, had I not been surprised by visitors two weeks later at my home way out in the woods. I was alone in the trailer when I heard a car coming down the dirt road and up our driveway.

It was a shiney and long older car with two men inside, each wearing dress shirts and maybe ties. The passenger was that bus driver, the one I gave the Bibles to! The driver was his pastor and they were on their way to a church service in Indiantown on Highway 710, (the Beeline Highway) in Palm Beach County. They had seen the little sign I had painted once, that simply read, "LUCKY" with an arrow. I had nailed it to a power pole down on the roadway so that the cattle truck from the Okeechobee Livestock Market could locate our ranch, the Lucky Buck Ranch.

The English speaking Pastor said the Lord told both of them at the same time that it was the Mrs. Luckey who dropped off the Bibles! So they turned around, followed the dirt road where the sign was, and somehow made their way another three mile maze to my house. We had good friends and relatives who used to get lost looking for that house, but they had no problem, the Lord was leading them.

As they sat having coffee with me the Pastor served as our interpreter as he told how the night before I brought the Bibles, the bus driver had been on his knees before God about the crucial decision he had to make as to whether God was really calling him to become a missionary in Mexico. He told the Lord, "How can I go to Mexico to preach the Gospel if I have no Bibles for the people? I am too poor. They are too poor. Please give me a sign that it is Your will I go to Mexico to preach. Please give me a sign I would somehow have Bibles. Please I need a sign very soon!"

Tears again rolled down his cheeks as he told the story and his Pastor relayed the message. Then the man said he told the Lord that there was no way he could start a new work in Mexico without Bibles, and that since He created the whole world it should be an easy thing for the Creator to provide these needs....and that, why, tomorrow would be good! Why that should not be impossible for the One who made everything and had created the whole world!" But then he stopped and thought a moment, and then added to his prayer, "Oh, and Heavenly Father, if You provided one hundred Spanish Bibles tomorrow, *then I will know!*" He figured he needed a miracle so impossible, that it would be an unmistakable sign of God's will.

He was telling the Lord that if He provided the Bibles the following day, he would have the confirmation he needed to accept His calling, become a missionary and go to Mexico. Then the very next day as he was dropping off the workers at the migrant camps, a lady stops to give him one hundred Spanish Bibles for free and all he could remember was she said her name was Luckey. Then when they passed my sign that day (which was maybe 35 miles or more from where I'd met him), the Lord said to both men, "that's the lady"!

They were so amazed they had to follow the roads and trails to find out! They said they had come to tell me "the rest of the story". You may be too young to remember the broadcaster, Paul Harvey, who ended his commentary each day with, "And now you know the *rest* of the story!"

We had a wonderful prayer together blessing the man and his new ministry, and then off they drove in what had been a very shiney car at least until they found my roads. I watched as they drove away in a cloud of dust and I rejoiced with thanksgiving at what the Lord had done and thanked Him for allowing me to have a part in His miracle!

It was an example of the Lord's provisions He gifts all of us with, to accomplish His Kingdom work. It was a poor bus driver about to minister to an impoverished people, and with a treasure he needed supplied by a rich Heavenly Father using a poor believer in a trailer (me) in the wilderness with no running water or power. And remember I never even ran out of gas when the tank I'm sure, was empty, and money was there I was sure had not been there before to pay my toll. God answers prayer! The Holy Spirit anoints us to preach the Gospel to the poor, just like the Scripture says.

"Healing the Broken Hearted"

When my daughter Sheri, (Sheryl Luckey Bjorn), felt led of the Lord and traveled to Sweden, she found more than musicians she was scouting for as possible band members, she met the man of her dreams. Their gorgeous wedding was in Sweden over fifteen years ago. Simon Bjorn is not only a gifted songwriter like she is, but plays many musical instruments. He is even able to maintain several bands at a time, in fact, that have a musical range of categories from melodies my great grandparents loved, the Irish, Scottish, Swedish, and German, to the Holy Ghost anointed praise and worship, Gothic, and the heavy metal my grandchildren do.

Their band "Wedding Party" amazes me and I am provilaged to be privy to outstanding song writing sessions and anointed rehearsals. Simon is an awesome drummer whose workouts have me marching around my upstairs loft and dancing when nobody's looking. Their duets bring tears to your eyes and smiles. Their songs range from gentle close and moving harmony to dynamic, strong, war-like anthems to stir the soul and prepare for battle!

They have always been a blessing to me and Gary, and whenever they could be with us, they were helping at our home with everything needing to be done and keeping everything ship shape. Both of them always becoming cowboys when it was called for, helping Gary out in the mud, storms, cowpens, hot burning sun, to work cows, build fences and cut grass and weed the yard and pastures.

These days in my widowhood, it is their daily company that keeps me laughing and feeling very special. They are both the hardest workers who seem to never have time to stop. They have raised and have bred our Bloodhounds, repaired anything, excelled with all the technology and home management, well I could go on forever, but let me share with you the best part. Sheri and Simon really love people and know how to pray and counsel with them, and boy, do they.

They make every day on my mountain, one filled with peace, joy, and fun surprises. They have the whole house clean and decorated in little white twinkling lights. Inside and outside, and the yard mowed and trimmed with solar torches and lanterns and have turned the log cabin into an exciting spectacle that has the mountainside lit up at night with sparkling ambiance and wonderment. And its not even Christmas yet!

Sheri was born with a clear voice with a perfect pitch for being right on key. She had been a local hometown rock star with band rehearsals in my garage that still have my ears ringing. (Well that and all the 28 years of law enforcement gun range shooting). But the start of my hearing loss was the heavy metal version of Sheri's Christian music she wrote and sang. It was really quite good and there was never a day she clumbed up into the Palm Beach Gardens school bus out there in Hungyland Slough, she didn't look dazzling as if climbing up onto a concert stage.

Sheri had and has a heart for hurting people and has always spent time ministering and praying for friends or strangers. Years later she and her sister, (another "dazzler"!), Libby (Luckey Fraund), would do concerts together, Libby singing back-up, playing bass, or Spiritual dancing on stage to the music. At out of state festivals they were known to stay up all night sometimes, praying with people following their concerts, prayers of salvation, deliverance, rededication, and healing for broken lives and relationships. They would lead them to Jesus, the Healer of the broken hearted and the Holy Spirit Comforter.

Sheri agreed to do a concert at the Lake Worth bandshell and told me she wanted to have about a hundred paperback Bibles to toss out into the audience at the close of their music just prior to leaving the stage. She said they were readily available for a dollar each at local stores, if she could raise the money. I told her not to worry about it, that I would take care of it, after all it was three weeks away and she had hugged me and thanked me.

Then I completely forgot all about my committment until the very night before the concert. Sheri had to be there early that next morning to help set up the stage and do a sound check.

Before falling asleep I was laying in bed praying when I suddenly remembered that I had promised 100 Bibles and there would not be time enough to drive all around finding enough of them and I also had no money to get them with! I fell asleep by leaving the dilemna to the Lord. I asked Him to please help me find a solution in the morning. Evidently as soon as I prayed that prayer, an amazing plan was set into motion.

I had just fallen asleep when the phone rang.

It was Roger Primm, a close friend and neighbor who lived at Far Out Farm, a mile away from us. He was calling from his hospital room in Jupiter where he was recuperating from a horrific automobile accident. This had happened on a hunting trip in Central Florida when he had stopped in heavy fog at the scene of a wreck in the middle of the road. When he got out to help, another vehicle who could not see them, plowed right into Roger's truck pinning him against it and could easily have severed his body in half, the doctors had said. Both of his parents had recently passed away and his only brother, Chris, who was engaged to my daughter Libby, when he had died in a different wreck as he was driving my truck in 1980. Roger was broken hearted from all this loss but at the moment, his voice was filled with great excitement!

"Mrs. Luckey! Mrs. Luckey! Listen up! I'm calling from my hospital room! I was watching Wheel of Fortune on channel 12 and they drew a card like they do from the thousands of people who mailed them in for a chance to win a hundred and twelve dollars. They announced that Sylvia Primm had won if she would call them at the station within twelve minutes! I yelled to all the nurses, 'THAT'S MY MOM!', who said quick, call her... and then I told them she died, I can't! So I called the station to see if I could collect it in her place and they said yes, as long they are called from the phone number on the card within the next now...10 minutes! Mrs. Luckey there's no one at the house and there's nobody but you who could possibly do this!"

Roger explained I would have to drive faster than I ever had, and when I got to his gate, jump out of the truck, and because the gate was locked, climb over the wood board fence and run like I'd never run before, down the long driveway with their horses chasing along side me in the pitch black dark. I should go break open the back door, cross over the kitchen toward the right, where the phone was, and dial the number. He said the dogs will bark so hard they'll sound like they're going to devour you, but just ignore them because they never bite women! (I suppose that was meant to be somehow reassuring).

He had said, "Mrs. Luckey I will understand if you can't do it, but if you do the money is yours." I told him no way did I want the money but I was already in the truck and would try to pull it off.

I drove faster than I ever had taken those roads, I even left the engine running as I jumped out and climbed the fence, the horses snorted and stomped as they galloped close by my side as I ran down the driveway that seemed ten times longer than I ever remembered it. I broke into the back door per his instructions, closing the door before the snarling, howling dogs could get out, and dialed channel 12!

Although they could barely hear or understand me over the ferocious barking, they congratulated me and thanked me for calling.

Driving home through the woods, the isolated trails, and the yet undeveloped remote countryside, I felt an amazing peace to have been able to bring any measure of happiness to our dear friend Roger. We had done three funerals together in the past recent years and had spent hours praying he would recover from many surgeries yet scheduled ahead. I again prayed for God to heal not only Roger's broken body, but his broken heart, as well.

When I returned to the house I called the hospital and I had never heard Roger so excited! "Mrs. Luckey! You called in time, you did it! They announced on television Sylvia Primm's family gets the prize! I have cash on me so please come by and get it, they're mailing me a check."

Of course I tried refusing to no avail, and then I remembered the Bibles when he asked me how the kids were. I told him about the concert and he said to come get the money, and then go buy all the Bibles available from Jupiter to Lake Worth, and take them to Sheri's concert and it would be a gift from his mama!" HalleluJah! I did and Gary helped me take the Bibles the next day to the bandshell where Sheri was busy with a sound check and preparing the stage set.

When she saw her daddy delivering all the boxes she said "Oh good, you remembered! Thank you! They will go out tonight to *heal* a lot of hurting and *broken hearted* people!"

I could hardly wait to tell her all about how *I* had forgotten, but Sylvia Primm's *angels* had "remembered" and had helped to make the miracle happen! Thank you, Roger, your mom, and especially, thank You, Lord!

A couple of years later a pretty, young woman stopped me and said, "You're Sheri Luckey's mom! She threw out Bibles once at a concert! I thought that was just so cool.....and it changed my life!"

"Preaching Deliverance to the Captives"

When I wrote my first book, "Operation: Devil's Garden", I began with chapter one, "I've Come for the Haitians". I will have to share it with you this time, too, because it was a significant event in my life in that God's voice was as loud and crystal clear in my Spirit, as another person's voice who is speaking to me out loud if they were standing right next to me. It would be the first time He had ever instructed me to do something so radical on pure faith and it would require a boldness and bravery I had never depended on in such away before.....I will begin.

I was home alone one day at Lucky Buck Ranch enjoying a rare day off at home with the truck. The children were all at school and I had dropped Gary off at work. How I loved having some time of solitude to really read the Bible and pray. I remember how intense my praying was that morning and after having coffee at the table, continued with praises and thankfulness to God and sat on the couch, then I was soon sitting on the floor with my head bowed. I remember praying everything I could think of on my mind, but still felt like I wasn't through. That's when I stretched out face down on the floor.

Soon I found myself really seeking the Lord as if I felt that He wanted to say something to me. I had already said everything I could think of to Him. I lay down on my Navajo rug on the floor and let my tears flow. I wasn't sad, but sometimes I think we have times when the Holy Spirit is perhaps cleansing us and we have tears, it humbles us, or maybe He is just so close by us His holiness causes that reaction, I really don't have an explanation. But it probably prepared me in some way for what was about to happen next.

I felt prompted to ask God something so I did. "Lord, are You trying to tell me something?" That's when I heard Him say, "Yes. Go to the West Palm Beach jail and I want you to say, 'My name is Betty Luckey, I've come for the Haitians'!" I asked Him to repeat it and then I heard myself agree to do it!

You have to realize I actually had no idea much what a Haitian was. I presumed a person from Haiti but I had absolutely no knowledge about Haitians, or information about anyone incarcerated. I knew where the Palm Beach County jail was, but had no idea where the city jail was located. We were living at the time in a trailer thirty miles away from West Palm. We would not be able to start building our house until power was installed from the Beeline Highway to our area and I didn't have any radio or television news or newspapers, and if any Haitians had been in the news of late, I certainly didn't know anything about it.

However, the excitement of hearing the Lord's audible voice energized me and I grabbed my purse and jumped in the truck. The Lord led me right to the crowded parking lot at the West Palm Beach city jail and there was not one open place to park when suddenly at the very moment I needed it, a vehicle pulled away right in front of the front door to the reception area.

I was probably a bit shaken, however a peace came over me and a boldness, and I walked right up to the woman at the window as if I came there every day. God had given me such a limited message to say, and with no explanation about what I was doing, that I just trusted He would help me and so it was with a lot of faith, I spoke out the only words He had given me to say.

The receptionist wasn't very friendly but simply raised an eyebrow at me and said, "Yes?" I said, "My name is Betty Luckey, I've come for the Haitians". She had me go take a seat in the room filled with people seated in rows of chairs.

A uniformed police officer with a clipboard in his hand, entered a door and standing in front of me said, simply, "Yes ma'am, what can I do for you?" in front of everyone. "My name is Betty Luckey, I've come for the Haitians," I said still seated. He looked at me intently and told me to wait there. I felt my heart beating faster and I thought if they decided to haul me off to the mental facility I would just graciously accept my fate.

The Lord had not given me a single thing to say other than what He had, so I just kept praying silently and hoped no one would ask me questions I had no answers for. Several minutes passed when the door opened and a higher ranked officer in dress shirt and a tie, stood in the doorway holding it open and spoke over to me almost as if he knew me, "Ms. Luckey, What can I do for you?" "I've come for the Haitians". I said calmly. He told me to remain in my seat and he let the door slam shut as he left.

To my surprise, the door soon opened once again and a corrections officer held it open as he called my name and I followed him up stairs and down hallways and then he instructed me to take a seat beside a tall counter.

Moments later a different officer asked me to come sign a paper on the counter. To this day I have no idea what I signed, all I know is the shock I felt at what happened next!

The door behind the counter opened abruptly and eleven Haitian men walked in single file behind an officer who asked me where I was parked. I followed them outside into the glorious sunlight as we gathered next to my pickup truck and I put down the tailgate.

They spoke no English and I spoke no French Creole. They were well dressed and friendly and in spite of the language barrier I knew exactly what they were asking as they all spoke at once, as we all shook hands, and I motioned for them to get in the back. Who was I? Where were we going? How did I get them out? I wanted to know the same answers, too! Finally I just said sort of shrugged my shoulders and said, "Jesus!"

Wow! Boy did they know who He is! Now they all jumped back down out of the truck and we shook hands all over again and hugged this time! I was their sister in Christ. Now they knew who I was.

In all the excitement I didn't notice the dark clouds that were rolling in and the rain drops starting to fall. A driver sitting in a large nearby van with the words "Community Action Council" on it asked if he could take the men in his van and follow me. That's when I knew we weren't going way out to my ranch, we would go to my dad's church in Palm Beach

Gardens next to where the mall is now. The driver knew where it was and said he'd meet me there.

I had a front door key and I enjoyed showing the men where the restrooms were, and the kitchen, that had eleven cans of soup miraculously, and a stack of eleven warm blankets. Not two weeks prior to this I had begun a campaign to start emergency supplies at the church and so far had only gotten eleven cans of soup and eleven blankets! But when I showed them there were eleven pews they were welcome to sleep on, and I pointed to them, counting the pews, the soup and the blankets and we all laughed! If only they could realize as I did, how miraculous it all was, miraculous provisions for eleven men. As we were looking inside the sanctuary there was a commotion at the front door.

As my dad always used to say, "Lo and behold!" there was a caravan arriving out in the parking lot of reporters, photographers, television cameramen and news broadcasters. I recognized newsmen from Channel 5 and Channel 12, the Palm Beach Post and Miami Herald. They had seen on the police blotter that Betty Luckey had eleven Haitian prisoners released to her custody and their investigative reporters had done a fine job of tracking me down in record time.

One of the newswomen could speak French fluently so she had all the men line up on the platform in a row for a press conference. They beamed happily with great big smiles as the flood lights lit up their faces. The reporters all sat on the pews, as the lady interviewed them with the shocking revelation: ....all eleven of them were Haitian *Pastors!*

These men pastored churches in Haiti and had been arrested by the Communistic regime with charges they had spoken out against the government in their sermons. They were given a choice. They could face execution or be allowed to leave in an empty boat set on the ocean seas with no supplies so they chose the boat. Their story would also include an attempt to be allowed entry in a Bahamian port but were told they could not stay there. Ocean currents carried them into the Palm Beach Inlet and onto the western shore whose jurisdiction was the West Palm Beach Police Department. They would fast and pray with no identification, no immigration papers, and no advovate, they knew only God could get them released and it would take a miracle.

Here is an interesting point that may have been overlooked in some way by the entourage of media. I had said to them several times that day what a miracle it had been that the Lord had me go get them. It wasn't until I heard on one of the television broadcasts, the reporter say, "Mrs. Luckey, *who had been working for their release,.....*" That had never been stated in the entire interview and it could not have been farther from the truth. I knew nothing about the men or their plight, but probably people would not believe...and perhaps even the reporters would not be able to believe there could be such a thing, as such a miracle. God and I know differently! Praise the Lord!

My parents and my preacher-evangelist, missionary Aunt Betty who was visiting from out of town, cooked them a big hot breakfast with bacon and eggs the next morning at their home. I made each man a "Betty Luckey Immigration" card with 3x5 index cards with their names on it which I signed and stapled a copy of the news article to it, with my phone number in case they were questioned by authorities anywhere.

The Immigration folks in Miami sent a bus to get them that very day, but not before we all held hands making a big circle out in my parent's front yard on Holly Drive, and dad prayed the Lord bless their ministries and thanks to God for sparing them and giving them favor.

To this day I probably don't know all the details or the legal predicament they were in or the police officials either, for that matter, but all I do know is that they cried out to God for help and He told a little ol' housewife way out near the everglades to go to the West Palm Beach Jail and say," My name is Betty Luckey, I've come for the Haitians"...and I did.

"Recovering Sight to the Blind"

I was a member of the First Indian Baptist Church at the Brighton Seminole Indian Reservation west of Okeechobee, Florida, for about thirty years. Most of that time I played the piano for all the services, taught the adult Sunday school class, directed Vacation Bible School once, and was a substitute teacher in the Christian school they sponsored one time for high school kids at the rez.

I would also dispatch for the Seminole Tribe Police Department for five years and be co-owner with my husband Gary, of two restaurants on the rez., (Alice's Restaurant and the Windmill Cafe). I think between all our family members we probably knew the name of every tribal member, where their homes were, and how they liked their coffee fixed and their eggs cooked. Gary always prided himself remembering each one and what their preferences were. I loved to watch him laugh and talk with all the Seminole cowboys who liked swapping hunting and fishing stories with him as well as cattle tales.

I played piano for so many weddings, funerals, and even tribal meetings and services through the years I felt like I was part of the Seminole family. I loved everyone at the reservation and our whole family felt the same way. I was honored to be the secretary for Pastor Wonder Johns for several years, and my daughter Libby was his secretary before I was. Her son Justin worked for "Alice's", and delivered all the to-go orders, soon getting to know everyone and how to get to their homes. Libby and Sheri cooked and waitressed and considered the clientele not as customers, but good friends.

My friend Eugene Tommie was a young man who had recovered in the hospital after having fallen from a pickup on the highway but still had an arm that never completely healed back to its full use. He had been in a coma for days and his sister Leoma, a close friend, had asked for prayer for him at church. I had even sent word with her to please tell him to remember the scent of the myrtle bushes as he rode through them in the woods, and know we were all trusting God to heal him so he could return once again to the countryside he loved to ride his four wheeler through. She went to see him in ICU at the Tampa hospital where he had been airlifted.

Eugene was miraculously healed and was released to go home and right away became a dear friend who would come see us at the restaurant to eat and would ride up to the police station where I was dispatching on the night shift. We would read our Bibles together and pray.

One day he told me that he heard that Benny Hinn was going to be in Lakeland at a big meeting and could I take him. I told him I would like to have prayer also for my eyes which had just been diagnosed both with glaucoma, in fact, I was due an operation the day following the healing service. He told me that maybe the evangelist could pray for his arm because it hadn't gotten any better. Right away I planned to do so and I promised to pick him up. He rode with me and Sheri and we sat in a huge auditorium packed with people.

After Brother Hinn had preached awhile he said that the Lord wanted to especially pray for eyes that night. That was unexpected, I thought. He asked that everyone with eye problems or blindness to stand up. Then he asked us to place our hands covering our eyes, which I did, while he prayed. I remember Sheri coming close to me and placing her hand gently over my own hand. I could hear her praying along with Benny Hinn that all the glaucoma be gone and good eyesight returned.

It must have been the tremendous crowd that night prevented the long lines of people who usually formed for individual prayer, but for some reason there was presented no opportunity for Eugene to be in a lineup for folks needing special prayer.

After the service I told him I was so sorry that he hadn't been able to receive a personal prayer, but Eugene said, "Oh no, its all good, I'm ok. I don't need him to pray because the Lord *did give* me my miracle! My arm is still the same, but now I don't care! God showed me that if it was working good, then people would say I was happy because my arm was better. Now they will know I am only happy because God is so good and so Holy, and that He loves me and I love Him... even if I'm *not* healed!" I thought, that is heavy, and so precious!

Wow, what a testimony! And then on top of that, what a testimony I had the following day when my eye doctor kept re-examining my xrays and records, and then announced: "No surgery for you, today, young lady, not a sign of glaucoma, no longer in either of your eyes!"

"Setting Free Those Who are Bruised"

The Scripture there in this verse says that God sends us anointed to preach the Gospel, to heal the brokenhearted, to set captives free, to bring sight to the blind, and to "set at liberty", or "free those", who are bruised, downhearted, or oppressed. A good example of this is sometimes depression which is running rampant in our society today. I had two such young men I was concerned for that I share in my first book.

Jimmy Best lived with his father at their home way out in the woods not too far from where we did at Lucky Buck Ranch. Jim became good friends with our kids and frequently came over to sit with my teenagers around the nightly campfire before we had power available or running water. He was probably a few years older than Libby and Sheri. He would walk over through the woods, about a mile away. He was a tall lean Mohawk tribal member with straight long black hair past his shoulders.

I would sometimes cook enough supper on an open fire for everyone which once in a while included three other families living nearby. We all had a special bond. We were all part of a society or a spoiled generation of people who had previously been living lives of comparitive luxury and in the land of plenty, but who had, at the same time, chosen to embrace the pioneer lifestyle of the old timers who had settled those swamps and Everglades initially and were learning how to "rough" it, at least temporarily.

Few families would have attempted doing what we were. Going into town to school everyday, employed at places like Pratt and Whitney Aircraft, nearby, or jobs in town, but we were still having to take baths in the creeks and ponds, and cook over a campfire. Actually, we loved it. But sometimes Gary would come outside early in the morning when it was still dark, and get his coffee I was boiling for him, and grin at me. Thats when I knew I had black all over my face from the bottoms of my pots and pans blackened from liter pine I'd used to start quick fires, sometimes because I was cooking in a light rain.

That was probably a tough time for young people stuck out there living in the middle of no where especially if your old car wouldn't start and it was too far away to have a regular job especially if you're still in school. Well, Jim was through with school but his Jeep was sitting in the back of their property and even though it wouldn't start, he remembered it still had a little gas in the tank.

He was on my mind, as well as another neighbor boy who also had probably never gone to church that I knew of. So I put both boys on my prayer list, Jim and Pete. I had never actually asked either one if they were saved, or if they believed the Bible or knew Jesus. I knew I had to fix that somehow, or sometime or someday...meanwhile I'd start praying for them...today.

Now you may find this strange or a weird thing to do, but sometimes

I'd just write little notes to God, fold them up, and put them in my Bible. It could be special things I was praying about. I didn't throw them away till they would become a praise report instead of a prayer request. They usually started out, "Dear God, This is Betty".

On this one particular day it was especially sunny and hot and I had all the windows open since the air conditioners don't run if there's no electric power. I decided to make one of those little notes because something was making me pray over the two teenage boys near me and their discouraging situation, probably that of not being in town where they could work and have transportation.

Sometimes the teens nearby looked so discouraged and depressed and boys that age have the conflict of transfering from boyhood to manhood especially around the age of 17. I think they were both 17. At any rate, I prayed my neighbor boys would be happy and find Jesus. When I remembered something.

I recalled hearing that a new Billy Graham movie was opening that very day in Lake Worth at the Dolphin Theater about two 17 year old boys who were struggling with their fathers and they end up at a crusade meeting and it turns their lives around. How better to be able to witness to my friends than to take them to Rev. Billy Graham himself, and have *him* minister to them through the Christian drama film! Except, I had no gas in my truck (as usual), and no movie ticket money, either. I put all that in my letter to the Lord. I let Him know that if He wanted us to go, I was available to be used for Him to provide a miracle if that was His will. Boy was that an understatement! I put the letter in my Bible and placed it high on a shelf in the livingroom.

The wind picked up, no wonder it had been so hot, dark gray clouds were rolling in and I began to hear thunder in the distance getting closer by the minute. Soon a gust of wind knocked my curtain rods down and blew my curtains across the room, rain poured down so hard that the pounding noise on the metal roof almost prevented me from hearing Jimmy banging on my door.

"Jimmy!" I exclaimed as he came in with soaked shirt and jeans, his long black Indian hair dripping wet, I handed him a kitchen towel and said, "What on earth are you doing out here in this mess? " He explained that he heard on his transister radio we were getting a really bad storm with tornadoes possible. He said he missed his mother and grandmother who lived on a reservation in Canada and that he would have run through a storm to check on them, too.

I told him about the note I had written that had his name in it. I took it down from the shelf and out of my Bible, handing it to him to read. He said he knew how we could go. He said the rain was letting up and he would leave in a few minutes, walk over to Pete's house and tell him to get ready, then I was to go to Pete's and pick him up and then go over to Jimmy's where he would siphon gas from the old Jeep into an empty milk jug, put it in my gas tank and we'd be off to the movies! Sounded like a plan......one of God's plans because already there were miracles going on....a letter in faith, a storm, a boy running in the rain and lightning for a mile, and in just enough time to make it possible, possibly. lol

I was shocked to see what looked like a standing room only, sold out crowd lined up in front of the theater. We waited in that line a long time getting closer and closer to the ticket booth. Finally, Jimmy spoke up and said "We don't have any money, do you?" I smiled and maybe a little bit weakly-voiced said, "No, I don't either but I think I'm just going to ask the ticket lady if we can see the movie now and pay later". Then the three of us all bent over laughing at how rediculous that sounded!

I thought that at the worst all that could happen is we'd be turned away, but God had orchastrated this whole thing and I had a strong feeling of happy anticipation at whatever the outcome was going to be. Now there was only one person ahead of me in the line so I began to clear my throat to speak when something happened.

As I approached the window a man in a white dress shirt and a name tag that read, "Manager" said, "Ma'am, how many are in your party? He was holding three movie tickets in his hand spread apart, in his fingers. I told him three. He handed them to us and said that the theater had mailed free tickets to local church pastors and those had been returned and we were welcome to use them.

Well, I constrained myself from hugging the dear man, as I thanked him, and I glanced at Pete and Jim whose eyes were big as saucers staring at the tickets and they were pale as ghosts.

We had experienced a true miracle of God and I have to tell you that all three of us could not have been more blessed from the movie.

The fellas could identify with the whole plot and liked Billy Graham's preaching because they both had tears in their eyes. When the movie ended the lights came on, and an invitation was given by a local pastor who asked anyone who wanted prayer or to receive Jesus as their personal Savior to come forward afterwards or just raise their hands and pray along the sinner's prayer. During the prayer, I peeked and both boys raised their hands and then prayed the prayer!

We drove to my parents house on the way home, where my mother fed us sandwiches and chips and brownies and slipped a twenty dollar bill in my hand for gas.

When I got back home after returning the two happy boys to their houses, I took the note back down out of my Bible and wrote, "Thanks, God, this is Betty. I just want to say thank You, and that today..*You sure did good!*" God had set free, from some sadness, loneliness and depression, the boys who didn't just hear about some miracle, nope, they got to be a part of a real one they'd never forget!

"Author wearing her Florida Turnpike toll collector uniform 1977"

CHAPTER SEVEN

SEE YA' LATER, ALLIGATOR!

---◆◆◆---

*"Therefore, if any man be in Christ he is a new creature: old
things are passed away; behold, all things are become new!"*
2 Corinthians 5:17 KJV

T he kids were saying that to each other, "See ya later, alligator!" way
back in Kentucky when I was in grade school. By the time we'd moved
to Florida where there actually were a lotta gators, the middle school
students were still saying it and replying with, "After awhile, crocodile!"
And sometimes when we had company come from out of state, my
parents would find time to drive them somewhere to see the real deal
at a waterfront park or a canal close by. All you needed at night was a
flashlight and they'd surface with their brilliantly lit up eyes glowing
orange from the water or the shore.

Now my husband, Gary, was fourth generation Floridian and had
always reflected an attitude from the old pioneer spirit that believed the
Lord had created a world to meet man's needs and his family's needs and
placed him in dominion over the wild animals, the fish, the birds and
every creeping thing that creeps on the face of the earth, (from Genesis
1:26). "And God said, Let us make man in our image, after our likeness:
and let them have dominion over the fish of the sea, and over the fowl of

the air, and over the cattle, and over all the earth, and over every creeping thing that creepeth upon the earth." Genesis 1:26 KJV.

Originally, it was not against the laws to kill alligators but when the law went into effect it was rigid and to be arrested meant jail time, lawyer fees, and lots of bail money. I guess a lot of Florida Cracker folks ate gator tail during the Great Depression, but I don't seem to gather from the conversations I recall, that the elder Luckey's were saying they did it very much. I think they'd tried frying almost anything else in those desparate times, but pretty much avoided eating gators. It just didn't appeal to them, I guess. Gary was the same way. His ancestors sold the hides and made enough money to buy groceries, though, I know for a fact. Some of the relatives were known for making moonshine, as well.

Gator tail has been a delicacy to most folks, though, and I have a son who cooks it better than any I ever knew. I'll bet his secret recipe could provide him a financial future to put him on easy street the rest of his life. The first time I ever watched him cook his first fried gator tail, was the first gator he'd killed all by himself. He might have been nine or ten years old.

We had company with us that day so Gary and his friend rode in the front with all the shotguns and rifles standing on the floorboard between them leaning on the seat. I was in the back with the man's wife and all our kids, when Tifton announced, "Hey dad, there's about a five up ahead in the water". Gary stopped the truck and handed Tifton a gun out the window saying, "Go ahead Son, if ya want him". I frowned but didn't say anything as eagle eye Tifton stood up in the bed of the truck and gave the gator a perfect shot to the side of its head before it could submerge. We were all amazed at the precision of a shot by a younster that age and the kids actually clapped.

"Aren't you gonna get him, daddy?" I heard Tifton ask. "Nope" he replied. "You shot him, you gotta go get him!" Oh, NO, I thought, the gator was already out of sight in that deep canal and even though the shot was accurate, no one could be sure if it was dead or alive! We all watched in frozen silence as Tifton stripped down to his swim trunks beside the truck and dove in after it!

I prayed silently and out loud both for God's protection. Was I relieved when they both hit the surface and he swam with it to the shore. It was still flipping and flopping but Tifton hung on and Gary helped pull it on shore. I was bursting with pride at his accomplishment but still too overcome with my emotions to even speak. I didn't know whether to be fightin' mad or to celebrate.

When we got to the house Gary said that "whoever" kills one, has to go get it, then they gotta skin it, and then they gotta cook it! Oh poor Tifton, I thought, but I looked at our son, shoulders back, head held high, a mature look on his face I never saw before. The group stood around him in the yard and watched him cut off the tail and skin it. All the kids followed him watching him take the post hole diggers and bury the carcas in a deep hole. Then they stood around in the kitchen as we all watched him fry our supper.

Gary explained to our guests we had quit selling hides but that we only killed one occasionally now to feed folks. The little squabble I had planned for Gary when we would finally be alone later, my anger about making a child do such dangerous things....had subsided. When everyone had eaten their fill of the delicious supper that night, and the company had gone home, I could hardly wait to squeeze my son Tifton, tightly and smile at him when I said good night. He knew what was on my mind, too, and he knew I was proud of him. I said, "That tasted really good, Son!" and he returned a big smile and with a naughty twinkle in his eye, teased me by saying, "Well, it tastes a lot better if you marinate it in beer!" I yelled "**TIFTON!**"

Now, how and when and where he'd had that or done that, I had no idea, he was now a man of his own who was his daddy's buddy in crime, and he was only ten or so, and I was becoming more and more a prayin' mama for sure!

There is a story I read once in a book, that Gary's great grandpa Sam Luckey, had so many hides he'd skinned wrapped up and ready to deliver that his boat couldn't hold them all. Well, I have seen in gator poachers' photo albums evidence of so many gator hides that had just been skinned you couldn't count them in the picture, and that's for real. Hides have always brought good money, just consider how much one pair of western alligator boots cost, for instance.

Without going into much detail, all I'll say is, we had access to dead gators, hides and teeth throughout my early marriage when it was tough at times to meet heavy land and house payments and insurance premiums. When you are raising a family on a very tight budget, you naturally keep thinking up possible ways to make money every way possible, especially if you're a mother far out in the woods with no way as yet, to have transportation for employment in town, some twenty-five miles away.

The Indian blood in me would come up with some pretty striking items from time to time such as jewelry, head bands and hat bands. Before I could ever have time to mass produce any of them, though, they usually became gifts for family members who had begged me for them. I would utilize any natural substances I had or found and make something useful with it or nail it up in my rustic house as a wall hanging. I could probably make a chapter just out of some ingenious creations I thanked God for, that I did sell.

Probably my most unique and practical item was making a strip of hide about an inch and a half wide utilizing the rugged top of the gator's back on a small 3 footer. I would tan it and soften it to bend easily by rubbing it on a piece of wood while I watched Rev. Rex Humbard, Oral Roberts, HeeHaw and Grand Ole Opry. Then I sewed the ends together with thick black thread, the perfect size to slip onto a cowboy hat or wear on your head to keep your hair back as a hair band, or around your head Indian-headband style.

But who always wanted it, was my children. There was no better teething tool ever made. I remember Libby handing one to Sheri when she was a baby and Tifton to keep them happy, but it was Niki who relished it to the point I never took it away from her. She'd hold it in her little hand and just rub it gently on her gums, along the hard little leather bumps, as if that's why God created them there in the first place! And, I think it really did help their teeth come in faster and relieve the soreness on their gums. I don't remember any of my kids having teething problems. Many a stranger in a store asked, "Is that a strip of gator hide she's chewing on?" I'd just nod and smile. I can't remember when our family just wasn't a little different than other folks!

I'm reminded of something funny. A hairdresser was trimming my coarse Mohawk-like hair and commented on the texture. She said a dental hygienist was cleaning a tribal lady's teeth and asked her if she was using the dental floss she'd given her and she admitted, no. "Why not?", she'd asked. The Indian lady said, "Well, because my hair works much better to clean my teeth with, and the floss is what I use to string the beads I sell!"

Sometimes I would experiment stringing Indian beads on leather with a real gator tooth hanging in the center. Why, I could make the necklace for small change and sell it for twenty dollars each back then. Once when I needed emergency funds I passed a shoe store and the owner had thrown together boxes of cowboy boots with only right footed boots, no boots for the left foot, they were only boots for display that were being closed out. I asked about them and he gave all of them to me.

I took all those boots I got for free, took wild weeds and flowers I'd picked in our pasture and hung upside down to dry, made an arrangement for each boot, drove them to the Texas steakhouse on Military Trail in West Palm Beach and sold all of them to the owner for thirty-five dollars each for table decorations. God supplies our every need! Hallelujah!

One day we were out of our dry dog food and had several hungry hunting dogs and no money till the weekend. Much to Gary's dismay, since he had never heard of such a thing, (well, neither had I, but you gotta do whatcha gotta do, right?) I took a six foot alligator that had been just hit on C-18 canal road and hauled it to the house. I built a red hot liter knot fire way out in the yard away from the house and I let that carcass sit in that fire burning all day. You never saw such a sight! There was billowing smoke just a pouring out both ends, looking like an industrial plant with multiple smoke stacks a goin'. Even the dogs were fascinated and lay around encircling the fire with obvious interest and maybe anticipation.

To speed things up I took a sharp pointed tip of a machete and poked a hole in the stomach that made it sound like a loud whistle, like a tea kettle or maybe the whistle at the" industrial plant". Three hound dogs all jumped backwards at the same time and hid in the palmettos. But before the rising sun, and the cool night breeze across the everglades had cooled it off for many hours, I looked out at an amazing sight I bet few have ever seen.

It was the first canine all-you-can-eat reptillian buffet, good to last a couple of days, at least till Gary would remove it into the pasture before the buzzards discovered the bounty. The dogs were lined up in a row just gnawing away at the hot gourmet delight. I grinned at Gary who did not look pleased at all and said firmly, "Please Betty, don't ever do that again". "Okay, I won't", said I, but you know what? We never ran out of dry dog food ever again!

We lived on the edges of the Florida Everglades where the pine woodlands begin and the dryer land is located that produced the miles of palmetto plants beneath the pine trees, frequented by diamond back rattlesnakes. Sometimes, when friends killed one they would drop it off to me and I'd always kill the ones I saw, making the property safer for my children. Usually they only wanted to keep the rattles and I would always skin the snake, salt the backside, rolling it up tightly if it was going in the freezer, or spead it out and tacked down and salted and nailed on a piece of plywood to dry.

Oh my, I am reminded of the large six foot rattlesnake that came to Vacation Bible School one day where my dad pastored the First Baptist Church in Palm Beach Gardens, on highway Alternate A1A, right next door to where the Gardens Mall would be built near PGA Boulevard.

My dad, Rev. Sherman Swan, played the trumpet every morning and all the kids, about one hundred of them or more, every day would march behind him in single file behind students carrying the American and the Christian flags and someone carrying the Bible. He would loudly play "Onward Christian Soldiers" as we marched. I was in the rear marching with all the teachers when we heard his trumpet abruptly stop!

"Everyone **HALT!**" his loud voice commanded. Cornered in front of my dad right where we were going to be making a sharp right hand turn down the very narrow corridor along the outside of the sanctuary building. We were wedged between the building wall and a bench-like wooden border supported by cement blocks and palms, and no way of retreat possible without someone being bitten! Especially my dad. Now daddy was no light weight, he was six foot four inches tall and a little overweight, but he had one second to decide how to handle the coiled up viper with his tail rattling loudly and it was only two feet in front of him! The hissing sound was unmistakenly meaning serious business! He had a hundred school kids to protect standing immediately behind him! With trumpet still in his hands, daddy JUMPED right on top of the hissing rattlesnake! He yelled, "Betty! the shovel behind the church!" I never delivered a shovel so fast in my life! He gave me his trumpet and grabbed the shovel, pushing it deeply into the snake's neck along the side of his shoe, down hard against the cement sidewalk, and with the point of the shovel perfectly centered, severed its angry head!

Afterwards I rushed to the piano, my heart still pounding, and as I played the most inspired rendition ever of "Onward Christian Soldiers," the kids took their seats in the sanctuary and daddy took his place at the pulpit. He gave a special thanks to God for protecting everyone that day. Then he commenced to tell the children how Jesus, when He died on the cross for our sins, crushed the devil, Satan's head for us. He explained clearly how we now are given authority over Satan who is "under our feet"! He turned to me at the piano and asked me if I could bring the skinned snake to the church the next morning as a visual aid, and he would use it to help illustrate and explain our defeated foe.

That piece of plywood with the rattlesnake skin was displayed in front the next morning and the church had the largest crowd we'd ever had. That was a relief when I realized parents and kids might not wish to return there with rattlesnakes attending. Later I shellacked it and he had it in his study for years. It would be an illustration (and a souvenier) of the power of God against Satan, sin, death, and the grave.

The marching soldiers would now sing along that song, understanding the words as never before! Now they understood we were Christian soldiers marching into battle against a real enemy, but God was with us to win it! Well, because He won it at the cross, now we can win the battles in our individual lives. It became more real to me, also.

The most frightened I have ever seen my late mother-in-law, Granny Lela Luckey, was the day I forgot and left a headless freshly killed snake in my kitchen sink. I would do that because the snakes move around awhile after they're dead from just a normal muscle response. You can't skin them with a super sharp knife, which it requires to make the straight lines, until they settle down. I wouldn't do this outside because I was trying to keep them clean and free from sand. I'm explaining this to you now because Granny never gave me time to ever tell her, she ran off so fast and right out the door to her car. She never let me tell it all through the years because even the thought of it was too terrifying to her. It was an accident on my part that it happened because I would never have wanted her to see it, knowing her fear of just pictures of snakes, even.

Well, I didn't *like* snakes either, which was one reason I didn't mind shooting them. I was just pretty sure I could handle the dead ones without being grossed out, at least long enough to see if I could make the popularly sought after hat bands. The local cowboys and hunters were looking for them and they were rare *and* I knew they'd pay good money for them.

Of course I always threw the carcasses away in the campfire we kept in the front yard at night, or I'd bury them along with the head. Only once did Gary come up with a "double dog dare" that I slice a 7 footer up and fry it for him to take to serve at Pratt and Whitney Aircraft for their annual Christmas party. He wanted to take something unusual or at least some fried venison or swamp cabbage and just didn't happen to have anything else available that day. I mean everyone was taking the usual finger foods and salads. Finger foods just didn't even sound like us.

The snake was sliced into one inch wide pieces resembling chicken back. There was little meat on each backbone, hardly more than a piece of regular chicken back, and when it was salted, peppered, sprinkled with Everglades Seasoning, floured and fried in Crisco, you actually would not know if it was diamond back rattlesnake, (DBR) or KFC. I arranged two trays of it on Christmas paper with red doilies, garnished with sprigs of fake Christmas holly, a colorful festive toothpick stuck in each piece. It was not only very attractive but it smelled and looked quite delicious, if you didn't know the truth.

To this day, all those employees talk about the day ol' Gary Luckey in the Xray department brought rattlesnake to the Christmas party! Their stories about how Northerners tried it, how they used it to bamboozle the innocent, or treat the brave ones to a once in a lifetime experience, or make them taste it to try to guess what it was, spread throughout the plant and Gary was never forgotten, well, he was actually a legend there anyhow already. I don't think we ever told Granny.

There would be many times I would prepare gator tail though, and even though I was never fond of it, we got through lots of meals with it. The only time I ever really thought it was good was when Tifton made it and it *was* good! I was reluctant to try it at first but when he assured me I wouldn't taste the beer in it, and he was right, it was outrageously fine.

There was one such time a Florida Highway Patrolman on duty at the Florida Turnpike, flew into my toll booth parking lot about three o'clock in the morning and ran up to me. He said, "Betty, there's no traffic tonight hardly at all. I just had to shoot a six footer crossing the highway so it wouldn't cause a wreck, its in the median strip! I can watch your booth if you will jump in your truck, go to the mile marker where I left it, and cut off the tail, I'll take fried gatortail to all the officers and toll collectors on the turnpike tomorrow night!" I believe that, too, was the week of Christmas.

I guess that when you work the midnight shift you get a little spacey. For some reason both of us thought it was a great idea, after all, what a waste, six feet of free holiday hors'doevres! He watched the booth, I flew away in my pickup, and spotted the gator in the center of the road up on the median.

Our turnpike station at the Jupiter exit had a janitor and maintainance man, a friendly, loving older black preacher-man we all thought a lot of, named Martin. He always had his Bible with him. One day he had told me I was disobeying God because women weren't supposed to wear pants, but skirts. Then he had me read it out loud for myself from his old, worn out Bible.

That day I ordered the skirt that went with our official police-looking uniform. All the other collectors hated the skirts and I would be the only employee for five years in the official suit. The employee manual specified that with the skirt you were required to wear nylon stockings and black closed in shoes with a dressy (short to medium) high heel. The skirt matched the gray sport jacket that had our Florida Turnpike patches on the sholder sleeves, and the gold badge on the front with name tags and collar brass.

That's what I was wearing when I crossed the desolate highway with my opened pocketknife and knelt down on the grass cutting on the tail of the very large gator. He was bigger than a six so it was taking longer. Even dead gators won't be still for that and the only way I could do it was to sit on him while I did it. I was just thanking God there was no traffic when I saw on the horizen headlights headed my way. I was relieved to see it was a semi because I knew most all of the semi drivers to be very down to earth and would find it funny.

I sawed away faster than ever as I heard the breaks of the semi truck slowing down behind me. I glanced back at the driver who had rolled down his window, and even though his voice was barely audible above the loud engine, I clearly heard him say, *"NOW, I've seen everything!"*

The tail was so heavy I was afraid the driver would try to get out to help me and I didn't want him involved, so I quickly snapped the last bit of tough black leather and putting my closed knife in my pocket, I tossed the heavy tail without expressing or showing the immense pain and strain of its weight as I threw it into my truck whose tailgate I had already left opened when I first got there.

Well, it worked, the trooper was beyond himself thrilled we'd pulled it off and he had not had one single customer while I was gone, thankfully. Had he gotten a call I would have heard it on my hand held radio I had with me and I'd have aborted the mission and returned back to my booth, which was probably only two minutes away. I prepared the fried gator tail much as I had the rattlesnake, and the next night the happy trooper treated everyone with something special the turnpike would probably never see again. That semi truck driver was certainly treated with something he, too, would never see again, that's for sure!

When it was time for me to pick a topic for my English thesis at Palm Beach Junior College I didn't like any of the topics suggested. It had some strict criteria to follow and it seemed to me that if I did it on "Alligator Poaching" I could navigate the subject in such a way as to fit the rules. I actually got the permission from the professor and was pleased that it would make it easy for me to do a subject I was already pretty knowledgeable about. Of course I would manage to write it in such a way without revealing any identities or provide any evidence that would be incriminating to me or anyone else.

I had so many friends whose families hunted illegally, that once when I applied to be a game warden and made perfect scores on every test and even in the final interview, I coerced a board member to tell me why they wouldn't take me. He reluctantly said, that off the record, could they ever be sure just which side I was on? They had actually decided it might place me in a compromising position sometimes so they turned me down for their academy. I would later graduate from two other state police academies. I think that because of all my experience with people in and outside the law, they knew that I could be an asset to their department and wanted to hire me.

Well, the truth is this: there has never been a time I didn't behave with integrity and loyalty on the job because of what Jesus had done in my heart. He was always with me, protecting me and keeping me honest, well pretty honest. I always answered to a "Higher Authority". And besides, Jesus knew that I didn't really want to be a game warden, anyhow; but now, dispatching was a different story. I *loved* dispatching.

That's what I was cut out for and spent at least twenty five years doing. Being a 911 operator had a spiritual calling to it and a challenge to be accurate, brief and clear (the ABC's of law enforcement radio and communications). Knowing that I could get a cop, ambulance, fireman, or a wrecker faster than anyone, was a daily rush you never forget. It's in your blood.

Even though I spent time employed as a certified police officer, security guard, and served as a special deputy, it was emergency radio that I loved and would still be doing if I could still hear good. Gun ranges and loud music had done some damage.

There is a strong correlation between 911 operators and the body of Christ. I loved it when I was out on the road or in the field employed in law enforcement. You are prepared and trained and equipped to be there. On your belt you have lined up every tool required, gun, ammo, radio, lazer, flashlight, multi-tool, etc, all at your fingertips, and your patrol car stocked with emergency supplies of every kind. As a Christian, God needs for us to be ready in the same way with the Spiritual gifts He gives us to help Him rescuing a lost and dying world without Him.

One year it was on my birthday and I prayed in a cheerful, fun and maybe silly sort of mood, "Good Morning, Holy Spirit, I bet You wonder what I want for my birthday today?!" And then I said something that I had actually wished sometimes, that we had a little gator out in our pond behind the house that I could see out my kitchen window every day as I washed my dishes. We had a dishwasher but I liked keeping them done up as soon as possible without all the noise they make and all the extra water they used. So, because I stood there working so much gazing out the window, there was nothing to look at but an occasional cow walking passed, pine trees and the pond.

I heard Him gently saying something softly in my Spirit, "Betty, go look out that window". I flew from the living room into the kitchen and peered out the window above the sink. "Hallelujah, Praise You Lord! Thank you", I said, and it even brought tears down my cheeks.

There in the pond, splashing in the water, as if to show off for me, a little black three footer played in the center of the pond. She would swim to one side of the shore and then to the other, she made circles and sometimes just rested taking in her new surroundings. There had never been an alligator there since we dug the hole for drinking water for cattle as well as a pad for the construction of our house.

When the girls came in we all watched from the windows so as to not spook the gator, but she was obviously hiding below the surface. I told them all about my funny prayer and then the miracle, and how it was not getting a little "pet" and a birthday present, what was so shockingly awesome was that God was with us listening to us all the time and He had just confirmed it! Well the girls didn't get very excited probably thinking maybe I'd imagined the whole thing until Gary and Tifton came in at dark.

All excited, I repeated the whole miracle. Tifton, who was barefooted, as we all always were, reached over and strapped his headlight around his head, removed his jeans, and in his boxer shorts said, "Ok, everyone, step outside real quiet like!" and we did. As he shined the pond, up popped two beady bright orange eyes looking at us as if it had just become invited to a birthday party! Gary and the kids shouted for glee *in whispers*! lol Not everybody knows how to do that, I bet.

Then Tifton told us to stand still and not move and he disappeared. Gary had to remind us not to talk at all. Tifton had turned the spotlight off and it was pitch black in the backyard. We waited. Moments later there was a huge splash when the light shone by the pond! I will never forget the sight we beheld! Tifton emerged with the light lit on his head, his underwear dripping wet, and with a little alligator he held in his hand by the back of its neck! We all oohed and ahhed and touched it and she would swing her tail!

"How did mom know it was a girl?", Libby, Sheri, and Niki all asked at once. Gary said, "Your mama knows these things." and I replied, "Yep, and I named her "Heidi" today, but no one's gonna touch her little hide!" Everyone laughed and Tifton placed her gently back into the water.

We never saw her again but proof the living God Almighty, the Creator of Heaven and Earth and all within it, was and is alive and well and ready to be a part of our lives, which was why He made us.

Well, there would come a day when I would not care to think about alligators ever again, that I'll share next, and then you'll see why I will probably never touch one again. It will be why I would now say, "See ya later alligator!" and be given new revelation, perception, and discernment from the Holy Spirit. It involves that thesis on poaching.

Word had spread about my paper I'd written, probably because of the sensational sounding topic. It was not your normal academic suggestion the English teachers offered and maybe because my name was known to so many groups in the county, from law enforcement, the colleges, churches, hunters, and news media.

For some reason a high ranking official got my phone number and wanted a copy of the thesis and called me three times. Gary was always sitting right there listening to the brief conversations and heard me decline the man's request to allow him to read it. Gary was a witness to my conversations with him and could attest to the fact that neither of us were what you would call, in any form, flirting.

I told him that because it was of no use to anyone and contained no sensitive information or material in it that folks might think would implicate the criminal elements in our area, I didn't understand why he was so interested. I would find out a few days later. His answer he had given me was that it would be a good resource to include in multi-state law enforcement libraries, Florida wildlife literature and collections of data for the southeastern United States regarding alligators. Well, I decided that even though the A-minus grade I'd gotten was something I was proud of, I'd best burn it in my campfire and eliminate any "interest".

When he called the second time I told him there was no longer a college thesis that existed and it had gone up in smoke. He sounded satisfied with my answer, but before hanging up the phone, he said that I would probably like to see something few people had ever been privilaged to witness and that was the swampy wetland where confiscated live gators were released, such as nuisance gators. He said it was a pond teeming with thousands of alligators and it was too bad information regarding that and photos of it could not have been included in my paper. The thought crossed my mind that perhaps there were literary opportunities in the future for me to be actually documenting interesting stories like that, but I failed to indicate to him any such interest.

A few days later, I was quite surprised when he called to say he would be in the area the following day and would have just enough time to make a quick trip to show me the phenomenal collection of reptiles. I asked Gary if he wanted to come take the ride and he frowned, shaking his head, but said I was welcome to go, so I did. It never dawned on me that this elderly man had any agenda other than appreciation for wildlife, or the law, or just for journalism and public awareness.

It took every bit of energy and combat training I had ever had to struggle with the man for fifteen minutes once we had driven far into a secluded wooded domain. His strong theory he was determined to prove, was that all women want sex regardless of any excuse they might give.

No amount of theological debate, no argument, no threat, nothing I tried, would avoid the wrestling match I was entangled with, which had started when he asked for a kiss. Evidently he didn't take no for an answer. Well, he never got the kiss, and I never saw the first alligator, but I fought him with everything I had when suddenly I felt my strength giving out.

At last thankfully, I finally remembered *to pray!* I cried out *audibly,* actually demanding with a loud voice, *"JESUS! TELL ME WHAT TO DO!"* I heard the Lord in my Spirit, answer firmly, "Tell him these words: *'This is going to cost you your career!'* " As soon as I spoke those eight words he let me go as if I was a red hot coal! It was as if a switch had been turned from on to off. We had been fighting inside the car and outside, but I was not about to allow him to force me into the hunting cabin he had driven up to.

He started the engine and we didn't speak until we got back to town. The smell of his cologne, that I hadn't noticed before, now turned my stomach. He mumbled something about he didn't know what came over him, and included the word 'apology'. I told him to never call me again. I closed the door of his unmarked car and said, "You need to get right with God, not me!"

I learned a lot from the humiliating experience. First of all to never be that naive again, and that such an assault can happen without any even hint of flirtacious manner or behavior. I learned not to ever be alone or go into any man's car for any reason alone. I also learned the value of *always* carrying weapons, not just *most* always.

Here was a person who had impressive credentials and position, that as a rule, I *thought*, meant he had a measure of integrity. I had not known him personally, but he held a prestigious position of authority. I was quickly reminded we have an enemy who is doing all he can to hurt us. Satan's demonic forces operate in deception, and they, too, use every method and scheme to bring us harm, and bring us down.

It had been a close call, but God rescues us when we call on Him and will show us how to flee the enemy by resisting him. The Bible teaches us to resist Satan and he will flee from us. You know, I would never have thought of those particular words to say, that the Lord showed me would be my weapon. It was a miracle and it was my ammo.

The man retired not long after that and passed away, but apparently, it was not just a promiscuous older man I was dealing with, I felt, but a spirit that was inside him. I was completely innocent of any wrong, but what I want to convey to you is that it left me feeling so yucky. His demonic darkness was now shadowing my usual joyfulness and I would have to pray and have God's powerfully sufficient and efficient Holy Spirit, bring a washing, a purification, a cleansing that would make me feel holy, pure, and cleansed. And he did.

In times like those the guilt feeling it can leave you with, even though unwarrented, will cause you to take inventory of all the other things you *are* guilty of and make the corrections. I guess that's what happened in this instance. I think the Lord allowed the incident to bring me to become a more repentant, more humble, and thankful believer...and wiser.

Now for the first time I had felt the guiltiness for ever having been a part of any illegal alligator business, as brief and as little as it was, and it was time to not just to have **prayed** for that cleansing. I was pretty sure I needed a complete *overall* /*overhaul,* and thorough repentance and sanctification in *every single area of my life*.

So the Lord changed me some more because I felt guilty to have raised my precious family with some tainted views on some of the hunting laws. I had a new desire to be squeaky clean and let my children know that it is God's way, and all His ways were going to be *my ways,* from then on! But from then on, I just never felt the same about my alligators, and today looking back, find it hard to believe they'd even held my interest at all. Hallelujah, there's a new me!

"Tifton Luckey with his 'Biggest Buck taken in Palm Beach County, 2006' (and then, beats his own record the following year!)"

CHAPTER EIGHT

AFTER AWHILE, CROCODILE!

*"Create in me a **clean heart**, O God; and **renew a right spirit** within me, cast me not away thy presence and take not thy Holy Spirit from me. **Restore unto me the joy** of thy salvation; and **uphold me** with Thy free Spirit"*
Psalm 51:10, 11, 12 KJV

Back in the day, you just didn't hear stories much about alligators attacking people except under rare circumstances and we had no fear of them. Now as far as they were concerned, they did seem afraid of us and would scadoodle at the sight of us and if we carried a shotgun in our hand they would seem to duck under the water and disappear downstream or into their gator holes like they knew what could happen.

We took baths and swam in creeks with them and we always had a gun with us in case it was needed. Several times out at our Two Creeks Ranch I bathed with the kids with soap, shampoo, cream rinse and Gary stood on the shore holding a shotgun when one or two gators of any length were just seemingly hanging out there watching us.

Why, before we were married we swam in the Loxahatchee River at the legendary Trapper Nelson's camp on the riverbank and never ever thought of an alligator coming after us, and there were many there, at times, but usually no great big ones like you'll see in the water now. Gator hides were bringing higher prices and the big ones seemed to get thinned out on a regular basis.

Tifton had cut his hand really bad once when he was skinning one out in the woods. His wet, slippery, bloody clenched fist slid down his very sharp knife as he made a jab into the tough skin. He wrapped up the wound in his shirt driving himself to the hospital. Our fear was that the injury would cause permanant damage with the use of that hand. What prayers went up on his behalf and were answered when he learned of an internationally famous hand surgeon specialist who just happened to be living in the Palm Beaches. She immediately was fond of him and nursed the hand back to normal and kept him in rehab appointments till it was completely restored. Thank You Lord! It would not be his only close call, there were many and some I am sure they never told me about.

Tifton had always been an outstanding hunter who kept fried backstrap (Venison) on our dinner table as well as turkeys, wild hog, gatortail and fish. He was fishing one night when I had a home fellowship Bible study group assembled around my campfire in front of the house. A few times we had as many as 65 men and women seated in a circle on picnic table benches and hay bales. This one particular night I was a little concerned that Tifton hadn't come back before dark. As we told testimonies, sang choruses and prayed together, I also asked God to help Tifton and return him home soon safely. Just then I was relieved to see his headlights coming up the road.

As he pulled up close to the fire the men folk gathered around the bed of his truck, as they frequently do to check out what's in back, a deer, hog, or turkey, for instance and sure enough there was a live gator and a story to go with it. I had not quite understood in all the excitement if it had caught Tifton's fishing line or a gator line, but he got surprised on the canal bank when he dragged it up on the shore tangled in net, rope and line, and Tifton unable to cut it all free, as it began to attempt wrapping itself around him!

He managed by pure strength and determination to drag it in circles all the way to his truck as it tried to bite him with his vicious teeth, but he managed to throw it in the back of the truck so he could deal with it at home under better lighting.

Another time they were all camping at Two Creeks Ranch and he killed a gator almost twelve feet long while his dad and his friends were sleeping near the old camphouse. He had taken a row boat way down Fisheating Creek, that ran through our property, to help retreive it. He did all of this by himself, and when he attempted to get the monster into the boat it was still alive and could have taken him right down to the deepest part of the creek and drowned him and nobody woulda known where he got off to.

When Gary awoke and realized Tifton wasn't back yet he walked way down the creek to find him. After all was said and done, Gator, boat, and men secured, Gary had this to tell me the following day: "You can surely be proud of our boy there, Mama, I am now convinced there is not a thing in this world that brave boy can't do!"

Well, I could not be more proud of Tifton for so many reasons, too many to name. He has been an awesome son in every way. He is good at everything he does, including owning and working his own Luckey Pest Control company in Martin, Palm Beach counties, and surrounding area, as well as Brighton Reservation.

One very hot day I had the day off work, the kids were at school and Gary at work, and I'd worn my bathing suit under my clothes. I'd brought a towel into town with me in case I had time to stop at Jonathan Dickinson State Park swimming hole in the Loxahatchee River. Since my goal on this rare day off work was to get some exercise, instead of driving into the designated parking area I parked farther away and came to the swimming beach by hiking up through a woods trail I was familiar with that came out by the water. I was surprised to see so many cars in the parking lot and shocked to discover none of the large crowd of people, not even one person, was out in the water.

People of all ages were there, sitting on blankets, towels or quilts, or folding chairs they'd brought with them. They appeared miserable to me, out there getting sunburnt, sweating, all staring at me. I dropped my towel on the sand and walked into the cool, awesomely refreshing river water.

I swam, floated, waded, staying out far enough for the water to come up to my neck, probably, having the time of my life. I prayed silently and talked to God, enjoying and thanking Him for His mighty creation around me, the clear water, the fish, a turtle, the butterflies, an amazing array of egrets and a gorgeous Blue Heron watching me from a low branch nearby. I would see an occasional alligator not too far off and figured that's what everyone was staring at.

I could not imagine how so many people could stand to stay in the sweldering heat with the heavenly Loxahatchee River just a few feet away from them. I discovered why when I got out of the water and dried off with my towel and glanced at the sign that had been facing all those folks that had its back to me, it read:

"POSITIVELY <u>NO SWIMMING</u>-ALLIGATORS-NO GUARD ON PATROL!"

I was actually kind of embarrassed that I'd disobeyed the rules though, especially, when a man called out to me and said, "I betcha wouldn't have gone in there if you'd seen the big one that was here earlier!" Not to be undone, or put down, I wanted so badly to answer, "Oh, I've been swimming here for years, in there! I just enjoy the gators more when there *is* no patroling!" (or some such prideful, sarcastic remark), but the 'new' me nodded and smiled sweetly and I simply waved to everyone, goodbye.

God was changing my attitudes and still is to this day some fifty years later. I guess we never stop learning, growing in Christ, in preparation for the Heavenly realms He is preparing us for. We continue to mature. He says we are gold tried in the fire, refined for His Kingdom.

Sometimes it took our whole family to help Gary when he had a bigger alligator to skin. Libby made me laugh today remembering how she would help him by sitting on the gators to help keep them still enough for him to do the skinning. It reminded me of one particular day when Gary was leaving the yard to go to work.

As Gary started pulling away from the carport, a truck drove up with a young man Gary had hunted with before. He asked Gary is he wasn't busy, could he please help him skin the eleven footer in the bed of his truck. He said there was no one available anywhere he could ask. Gary explained that he was almost late for work and could'nt even talk much less do a gator, but that he was welcome to knock on the door, that I was home, and he could see if I was up to it.

I sat on the gator for the next hour and a half and he did a fine job skinning it and I did a fine job giving him a condensed version of the

Bible, Genesis through Revelation! I included all my favorite illustrations, Scriptures, and even sang my favorite Gospel choruses. Poor guy, I don't know if he had ever been in a church before, but he sort of had a "catching up" that day, especially, when just before he left, I closed with prayer. As I prayed I included asking that the Lord please continue to bless the young man in his life and help him grow closer to Him and welcome Him into his heart in a new and closer way than he'd ever known before.

Two weeks later he was killed in a head on collision between Palm Beach Gardens and Jupiter, and then I knew why God had me sometimes doing things like, sittin' on gators. It seemed like the mission opportunities were and are everywhere, every day, and I realized that had been a Divine appointment for sure.

Before we built the ranch house at Lucky Buck, we were living in a mobile home and I had decorated the walls with deer racks, an animal skin of every kind, and some alligator hides that were special. One was one I had removed from Trapper Nelson's cabin a few days after he was found dead at his remote, isolated cabin up where Tequesta is now on the river. I kept it as evidence I had been there because I had my own theory he was murdered contrary to what the police had announced, and maybe I would have a witness report that might be needed in a court of law in the future. I had never seen a hide like that one. It was not black leather but soft and almost light brown in color, which was another reason I'd picked that object as my "souvenier,"even though it was only a remnant of what had been a larger piece at one time. It was probably of no value to anyone else because it was pretty ragged looking. It had been on the floor with other hides with his front door standing wide open. That hide finally deteriorated and was in crumbles so it was eventually burned in our campfire.

One day, one of Libby's girl friends rode out from town with her dad to visit us. She was learning to drive. As we sat in the living room we heard a car pull up outside and it was a local game warden. Now what ever posessed me to allow him inside for coffee is beyond me, but we did, but not until we all had jumped to our feet ripping gator hides off the living room walls frantically! "Where do we put these?", her dad had asked as he held one running down the hall, and I told him we were stacking them in the bathtub with the shower curtain hiding them.

Minutes later, The game warden sat in the living room drinking coffee with Gary, and I was sure he must have noticed the holes in the paneling that were in the shape of alligators, but thankfully, he said nothing.

He was explaining that he had come to discuss having a key to our gate for use when they patrolled at night and there might be poachers in the area. Our property ran along three miles of one canal and then one more mile along another popularly hunted canal that ran between Jupiter and Palm Beach Gardens. Gary declined to do it and the officer said it was ok and that he understood. Yes, I bet he did.

Well, after that event, I did away with my gator hide collection. I mean, my house has always resembled a pioneer or Indian museum, but I have since eliminated all the real animal stuff except for the deer racks, I think. At last count, we have kept only about thirty of those after giving so many away as gifts, decorations, and for crafts friends were making.

My favorite such item was when my grandsons, (Justin and Sean Savacool's), daddy, Jeff, made a specially designed pulpit stand for his close friend, Dan Bowers, to use at his church at Brighton. Jeff was a superb cabinet and wood craftsman who had owned his own shops in Martin County, FL. He resided at Brighton where he lived on the Bower's property and assisted Brother Dan until his passing. I will never forget how happy it made Dan to see it. It was made with richly finished rustic wood and deer horns, mostly from deer Justin had provided. It was awesome.

The most heartbreaking piece Jeff would create was the rugged looking cross with Justin's handcarved initials he made on it that he placed on the Reservation Road curve at the scene where Justin had wrecked. It marks the spot where my first grandson Justin, the first child to make me a "Grandma", left earth for Heaven, and into the arms of Jesus.

A distant relative of Gary's with a legitimate alligator business said we were welcome to ride through his gator "graveyard" in the swampy portion of his ranch land and help myself to all the gator teeth I wanted. It was with excitement and anticipation at the thought of finally having a free supply of all the teeth I would ever require, if I did indeed, want a small business or project making the lucrative Indian beaded necklaces.

It was a happy day riding along through the pasture with Gary looking at the enormity of the skeletons, skulls and gator teeth.....but as sunny and bright as the day was, a growing feeling of darkness overshadowed me, and Gary, who had said he would stop the truck and help me if I wanted to start collecting them, but I could only slowly shake my head and I said, "No Gary, lets just go back home".

What happened? A new Spiritual awareness. A new sense of discernment of what was Godly and filled with His brightness, peace, light, and Glory, and what was dark, gloomy, sad, or unclean with memories coming back of how in my lifetime I had been off track so many times when I hadn't actually thought I was, yes, and at times, *I'd been truly deceived.*

I had been fooled by an unseen enemy, (read Ephesians 6:12), and I knew when there was a demonic presence, I got that bad feeling in the pit of my stomach, the same one that I would get at even the memory of certain past events. It was as if the Lord was speaking to me that He was showing me and allowing me to discover that this was not what He ever had in mind for my life. He was telling me, like the day He had shown me an eagle high up above my head, flying with dignity, head held high, with purpose, with integrity, and had told me to rise above where I was, and what I knew, and to start soaring in **high places with Him** and His eagles.

A conviction began to hit me right between the eyes that all those many years, I had allowed my children to watch their parents, me and Gary, good people, believing people, breaking the law, whether selling a hide, killing a deer out of season, or breaking the speed laws on the highway, we had four sets of eyes watching us, and we were teaching them dishonesty. It was the breaking of the laws of His Holy Word, and those laws instruct us to get right with him and to stay right with Him.

We had become so good at rationalizing excuses for doing some things that somehow we had talked ourselves into believing it had been okay, but, I could now see it had clearly defied God's way. No, we can never be perfect or righteous that's why Jesus became Righeousness for us at the cross. I would be asking my children to forgive us. I was asking God now, and His loving arms were wrapping tenderly around me with the cleansing power and Blood of Calvary and total peace was settling upon me, my marriage, and our wonderful little family. Yes, my back slidden lifestyle was mingled with my strong committments to Jesus, and that had made it even worse! We cannot serve two masters. (God and money, or Satan)

I had felt so guilty, but Hallelujah, now He had changed me! He cleanses and forgives us when we repent and gives us a brand new start. I loved the song in Jesus Christ Superstar when Mary Magdeline, I think it is, sings, "Could We Start Again, Please?" The answer is a resounding, and jubilant victory shout, **"YES!"**

One of my favorite songs, (By James E. Orr, 1936, Public Domain), comes right out of Scripture in Psalm 139:23-24, it goes, **"Search me, O God, and know my heart today, try me O Savior, know my thoughts I pray. See if there be, some wicked way in me, and cleanse me from every sin....and set me free!"** He does, He did, and He will! (Psalm 139:23-24 KJV says: "Search me O God, and know my heart; try me, and know my thoughts; And see if there be any wicked way in me, and lead me in the way everlasting.")

We packed up several moving vans to move to the mountains on March the 15th in 2019. We were energized with excitement for the life ahead in the Smoky's and for the new home ahead God planned for us. I was pulling my Uhaul-type trailer we own and it was so packed with belongings we could hardly get the door closed. We pulled out of LaBelle tired from moving furniture, but happy beyond words. By the time I left Fort Myers city limits, Gary who was exhausted, was already drifting off to sleep on the front seat next to me.

Just before leaving the old Luckey Island Ranch I had put several of my necklaces in my purse I had beside me and reaching for my silver cross with the turquois stones, I pulled it on, over my head. Then as I was driving out of the county, I reached for the old Indian necklace there, the one I had made long ago with the gator tooth on it and held it in my hand.

Rolling down my window to enjoy the warm wind on my happy face, feeling it blowing and tangling my long hair, and thanking God, I smiled. As my Florida memories, happy and sad, were fading away in my rearview mirror, the glorious visions of the Smoky Mountain prophecies ahead, were dancing along with the Blue Grass Gospel on my truck radio......and somewhere between the Caloosahatchee River and the Peace River bridge, I threw my Mohawk-beaded, *gator-tooth necklace* out the window and said, *"See ya later, alligator!"* and somehow, in my memory, and through the corridors of time, I could just hear my seventh grade classmates joyfully echoing in reply, "After awhile, crocodile!"

"Author with Lena Gopher, left, Honored War Vet Dan Bowers, on right"

CHAPTER NINE

THE BATTLE CRY!

---◆-◆-◆---

"For we wrestle not against flesh and blood, but against
principalities, against powers, against the rulers of the darkness
of this world, against spiritual wickedness in high places."
Ephesians 6:12 KJV

I had a Sunday school class for a year at the Brighton Reservation's Seminole Bible Baptist Church. It was the church the tribal members referred to as our, (dear late friend), "Dan Bower's" church, just down the street from my own First Indian Baptist church where my membership was. I was there temporarily to help with piano music and children's ministry. I knew everyone there very well and loved each person. My grandson Justin attended there with his wife, Danette, and her awesome family who had founded the church.

Dan Bowers had been a special friend to me and Gary ever since we'd arrived at Brighton Reservation managing Alices Restaurant and the Windmill Cafe. He often sat talking with us there, or visiting in our home when he'd stop by with his close friend Pastor Wonder Johns. He always made us feel welcome at his home as well, where he and his wife, daughter, and family frequently hosted wonderful barbeques, holiday dinners, and a Christmas gathering when he liked to have our whole family come and help lead in some of the music. I would play the piano in his living room while everyone sang carols.

Dan built an amazing pavillion on his property, a close walking distance next to their lovely home. It was called his barn, but had a stage, a sound system, lighting, fans, and was filled with enough long tables and chairs to hold huge crowds very comfortably. His family and friends would gather for a bounty of awesome foods displayed on a very, very long buffet table. But the best part, besides their friendliness and gift for hospitality, was sitting with Dan at his fire, beside the barn. There under the chickee we listened to him share stories, as he'd add more logs to his welcoming fire, and I can still see the glowing firelight on his gently smiling face, and Gary in his white cowboy hat laughing with him.

I loved holding the children's class outside under the little pavillion, over by the church, a Seminole chickee outside the sanctuary, in the sunshine. The church had met there in the early years since its founding, and before the buildings were built they now used to meet in. On one particular morning I had a larger than usual group sitting and standing around the long picnic table.

There were a few distractions in the large church yard that morning, with singing birds, scampering squirrels, a bumble bee, and cars and trucks arriving for the morning worship service. I think I managed to hold their attention pretty good, though, with an animated Bible story, a picture to color, and a CD player with kid's choruses.

The lesson was from Matthew 14:27 (WEB) which is Jesus assuring us He is with us to give us His peace regardless of the fear or turmoil in our lives. I loved how it had it worded for kids in one of the children's editions of the Bible, and I used it in a previous chapter: **"It's Me, Jesus! I'm here with you! Fear not! Cheer up!"** (WEB) In the regular WEB version Matthew 14:27 reads: "But immediately Jesus spoke to them, saying, "Cheer up! I AM! Don't be afraid!"

I remember using an illustration for this at the neighboring FIBC (First Indian Baptist Church, Vacation Bible School) once, and how inspired and encouraged all the children seemed to be at its message and when I began to tell it, every student was still and quiet to receive every word. So it was on this day, as well, just *as soon as I asked this question:*

"Did you ever see something, like on television that made you sad or scared, I have. Do you know that anytime in your entire life ahead of you, what to do when that happens?" Now every eye was at once concentrated on what I had just said, and away from the paper they were coloring and all the distractions. "Well, yes, I have too", I continued, ".. and this is what Jesus is showing us to do when anything makes us afraid... first, pray to Him to help you, and remember what He is saying to us in this Scripture!" Following a brief discussion, they all had smiles now and I asked, "So, what is it we will do when we get frightened at something or feel bad about something we don't understand, or need forgiveness for?" Almost in unison they all excitedly answered loudly together, everyone at once saying that they would pray, they would remember *God was with them*, He loves us, He forgives us, He heals us, and to *not be afraid*, and that Jesus said, *"Cheer up!"* To that, we all cheered, laughed and clapped.

I remember telling them about the time I spent the night in the dark church we were visiting, with Onnie Osceola and her mother, Lena Gopher. I told how we prayed over our little crackers before eating them and how happy it felt to be sleeping in a church building, even on the floor, without even lights to see. I sort of acted it out and they loved it, laughing and giggling, just like Onnie, her mom and I had that night. It made a great kid's story of having the Lord with you all the time and in unusual times, and how fun it always is to be in God's house.

We formed a circle holding hands and prayed, and off they skipped, papers in hand, joyfully, across the grass to join their families. Pastor Cal Jones, who is one of the finest Bible teachers I have ever listened to, and his wife Clara, smiled, nodded, and waved to us as we were leaving.

Little children on every reservation, children in every state, in every country on the whole earth, are living in a generation like we have never seen before. I know they are experiencing the most ungodly exposure to fearful and painful realities we never had to deal with at that age.

They crave the love and comfort we can share with them that can only come from God, and He says, "Bring all the little children to me and do not neglect them!" The King James Version says of the children, "and forbid them not!" Matthew 19:14 KJV says, "But Jesus said, Suffer the little childen, and **forbid them not,** to come unto me; for such is the kingdom of Heaven."

I thank all the pastors who are ministering to kids all over the country.

I will forever appreciate the anointed ministries I have seen as Brother Walter Taylor, (and wife Melinda), for instance, at FIBC has provided, almost a continuous revival with multiple baptisms consistantly since arriving there many years ago from Oklahoma.

Brother Salaw Hummingbird, (and wife, Brenda,) pastor at the First Baptist Church at the Big Cypress Reservation, conducts a Vacation Bible School also, like none other! He even continues to bless me every day online with his outstanding daily devotions on Facebook. He more than once, directed VBS at Brighton and at one of those morning sessions I experienced a truly miraculous moment in my office as secretary at the church.

I was so preoccupied making the bulletin for the week and completing the daily VBS records for the day, I was sitting at the computer unable to go into the sanctuary where Hummingbird was finishing his sermon to a packed auditorium. As he began the invitation, I could hear what he was saying in the sanctuary because my door was open and so was the sanctuary door.

Suddenly I was overcome with goose bumps and tears! The power of the Holy Spirit came into my office and I slipped onto my knees beside my swival chair. I recognized what it was, *it was overflow of the Glory of God which was happening among the children and pouring in from there*, so great, that it was now flowing into even my tiny room nearby!

I prayed for the kids coming to Christ and could not hold back the many tears, as I sensed a move of God occurring on the other side of the wall beside me. When I joined them in the sanctuary, what a victorious celebration we shared at the huge response at the alter!

Not too long after that awesome revival among the Seminole children, things started happening to me when I was attempting to fall asleep at night. It was almost as if the devil was spitfire mad at evangelism among the people and their children. Now, whenever anything disturbing, distracting, or challenging had ever presented itself, ever since I was young, I would immediately go into warfare mode and pray that the powerful Blood of Jesus would remove any sense of evil near me, protect me, and cleanse me from any of its affects. I would command out loud to whatever it might be, "Go, in Jesus' Name!" and it did. On one particular night the manisfestations seemed accelerated.

Whether or not I opened my eyes or closed them, I could see just in front of me, hideous looking creatures and people with grotesque faces staring at me coming closer and closer. I remembered to say the phrase, "I Plead the Blood of Jesus"! It worked instantly and the images disappeared three nights in a row.

It reminded me that I had once had a vivid dream I was standing on an old wooden front porch backed up against the wall as three witches, all quite beautiful, a redheaded, a blond and a brunette woman with horrifically blazing and evil looking eyes staring into me. They were there to kill me. I had only seconds to do something quick! I screamed, *"JESUS!"* The very moment I did, they halted, melted into the floor boards, and disappeared between the cracks.

Once when my cousin Cathy was preparing creme of mushroom soup on the stove, a group of young people stopped by and said to her they had just the thing to add to her soup. They put real psilocybin hallucinogenic mushrooms in it and they all, including Cathy, sat around the living room holding their bowls and eating it with their spoons.

She said all of a sudden she began to descend below the carpet and into the dirt below the house she was renting. She had no control over the terrifying realization she had just made a dreadful mistake and was being taken against her will to the dark, cold depths of earth, stone, rock, and water below. The group in her livingroom was now a tiny white light high above her head and she screamed in her panic what my mother had said to do and told her to do, whenever there was nothing else you knew to do, call on the name of *"JESUS"!*

When she did this, she instantly felt two angels in white take each of her elbows and gently bring her upward, ascending passed the stone and dirt beneath the earth, to the light above, and she was once again seated on her sofa, the bowl still in her hands. She repented to the Lord and to the group and vowed to never again be tempted to do such a foolish thing again.

Now I should probably explain to you I never watched spooky movies or horror theater, or even violence. In fact, probably to Gary's disappointment I insisted on walking out of at least two theaters that were showing realistic war movies from the Viet Nam era, unable and unwilling to see such awful images. I had always protected my mind as much as possible from exposure to anything I perceived to be inappropriate for a Christian. I didn't want thoughts put into my mind that could produce bad dreams and unhappy thoughts. The war images were too realistic to me and I just knew not to expose my mind to them unnecessarily. The Bible says this in Philipians 4:8 KJV.....

"Finally, brethren, whatsoever things are true, whatsoever things are honest, whatsoever things are just, whatsoever things are pure, whatsoever things are lovely, whatsoever things are of good report; if there be any virtue, and if there be any praise, *think on these things."*

I would sometimes copy that verse on a piece of wood for a plaque, to be displayed on the wall above a television set as a reminder. Not that I needed to be reminded, I had it inscribed in my heart. I knew many Christian people that enjoyed horror movies and it didn't seem to bother them at all. Not me, I was not one of them. I was at war with Satan the instigator of all the darkness. The Bible says he is come to steal, kill, and destroy us. Sometimes he just needs to get his foot in our door, and when we let him in he begins his deadly plan to completely overtake us.

The day I tried to take a nap and manifistations began in my bedroom, I had a lesson ahead and thankfully, it became the Holy Spirit who was my instructor coming to my rescue. I suppose if I could imagine the most detestable image in my head it would be what I saw in front of me that afternoon. I knew the enemy was behind it, because he had attempted to use it to disgust or frighten me, or perhaps taunt me that I was hopeless to avoid it.

There in front of me so close I could have reached out and touched it, suspended in midair, lay a real looking infant baby. Whenever I closed my eyes it was there, when I opened them it was still there. It was not alive, but was bloody, discolored, and hideously obnoxious and revolting to see, almost impossible to look at. I was being forced to see it, however, and at the time I never considered it represented abortions, but today, I think, maybe that it did.

I understood full well there were demonic beings present and evil beyond description. I knew in my knower that it was used to terrify, repulse and intimidate me. I knew that the very fact the demonic forces were causing this to occur, was also their point, their reason for doing it.

It was a strong evil spell used to manipulate me into feeling helpless and hopeless to do anything about it. Regardless of where I turned my head it was right directly in front of my eyes.

It was also for their entertainment, amusement, and hideous enjoyment. The demons wanted to terrorize me and show me I was unable to stop the manifestation and being forced to keep looking at it. Satan knew what the worst thing, the most disturbing thing, would be I could have ever imagined in my mind, and that's why he chose it. (He knew oh how I love and protect precious little babies!)

I began my commands and threats to the powers around me. I exclaimed "Leave me in the name of Jesus!" When nothing changed then I advanced my verbal arsenal to using the "Blood of Calvary" and finally, wordage such as, "By the authority given to me by my Almighty Heavenly Father, and the Holy Ghost, and by the Blood of Jesus Christ of Nazereth on the cross and upon His Resurrected Power, I command you to go this instant!" Nothing happened.

The manifistation seemed to only grow more detailed and ugly. Finally I prayed.....''What's wrong Lord, what am I doing wrong, are you wanting me to learn to start praying *and fasting*, like you were teaching the disciples? Well, I haven't fasted, so please tell me *now* what I have to do *right now!"*

The miracle of what happened next taught me something I would need to know the rest of my life, putting it into practice from that day forward, a little detail I seemed to overlook unintentionally and unknowingly. And, it wasn't going to be any "little detail" but of mighty and powerful importance.

I cannot recall word for word what I heard next. I will tell you how it came across to me or how I can now interpret how it went, in my own words, as I recall God's message. With a kind and sweet demeanor yet firm and intentional, the voice of my Savior instructed me with this: "Betty, when you repeatedly state the words, "In the Name of Jesus" in your mind it is more of an automatic, repeticious motto, which you *mean* in your heart, but *as you say* the words, the evil present in the room with you, doesn't sense the deliberate imminent authority in your spirit and I will show you what you need to do!" He then said He would show me what I should always remember to know, put into practice, and never forget. You can bet on that, His instructions are quite unforgetable to say the least!

He said, "I want you to picture in your mind that you are at the actual scene of the crucifixion." Tears began to roll down my cheeks as I looked at Him, picturing in my mind, the sinless, innocent, God come in flesh my Savior my Creator, nailed to that awful tree. I pictured it so real-it *was* real and I wailed, "*Ohhhh, Jesus...*" and moaned a grown I'd never heard come out of me before. Then He said, "Don't be afraid, go up to the base of the cross and put your hand on the blood". I literally, in my spirit mind, *crawled* up to His feet hanging from the cross and warm blood covered my fingers and palms. "Oh, nooo....", I sobbed, for the agony He was suffering was too much to see, the agony He'd endured for me!" (and you, and all of us).

Then He instructed, "Now, Betty, I want you to look at the manifestation in front of you. It was still there in all its goriness, the blood in living red color, more vivid than before. Then the Lord said, "*now* command the enemy to leave!"

I looked at the vile image before me and with authority from the Great "I Am" who made us into existance and as wariors before Him are commissioned, I spoke I'm sure with blazing eyes of fire as I gazed at it with power and might, not of my own, and not of this world, I said, "Leave this place, and leave my sight, this instant, *IN THE NAME OF JESUS!*" ......and it **did.**

"Author's stairway to the loft, Smoky Mountains, NC log home"

CHAPTER TEN

THE MEDICINE MAN'S INVITATION

---◆◆◆---

Be sober, be vigilant; because your adversary (enemy), the devil, as a roaring
lion, walketh (stalks, prowls) about seeking whom he may devour!"
1 Peter 5:8 KJV

I was known in the Palm Beaches as a Christian activist. Because I would react boldly to important political, educational, or spiritual issues of the day, it often caused my name to appear frequently in the newspapers. I'm sure that the Palm Beach Post and Miami Herald still have files and photos of me that some made me look pretty good, like a community protector or watchman at the gate, and sometimes, I probably did *not look so good*, maybe. The media could put their own slant, their spin on things, and sometimes it wasn't seemingly intentional, they would just get a lot of facts reported wrong. The old saying, "don't believe everything you read" is a true one; however, does not apply to the contents of my book, just to be clear.

I had picketed a fortune telling phsycic fair at a Lake Worth shopping center and closed it down using posters with scriptures printed on them. I had gone to the Riviera Beach town council and spoken against the Riviera Theater when it had become X rated, and they closed it. I had made a plea to the North Palm Beach Town Hall about the lingerie shop with its disgusting 'adults only' obscene backroom on Northlake and they were made to close. I had stopped the wet teeshirt contests an Okeechobee nightclub had started to promote and convinced the Chamber of Commerce that it was not the image we wanted for a Christian community and they developed a new restriction to that affect.

I had embarrassed the Palm Beach County Sheriff when he hosted a law enforcement seminar for narcotics officers from across the country and published their itinerary to include daily and evening cocktail hours. I had argued with him that alcohol was the number one drug and when new stipulations were developed to prohibit county events with county paid alcohol, because of my appeal to them, he was outraged and even his secretary had warned me that if I didn't stop the campaign, that I might be found in a canal somewhere.

Well, I had been working with troubled youth who were complaining that marijuana laws were making a mockery of alcohol allowances and that adults who drank but prohibited the use of weed, were hypocritical. One argument they had was, how come no one stood up to the lawmakers about the alcoholism in families that made the kids need to smoke!? I made a decision not to allow a threat to stop me from standing up for issues.

During the height of the anti-war demonstrations in the early 1970's, anti-war groups as well as Jesus people organizations and simply Christians trying to evangelize to all of them, were actively invading events such as the Republican National Convention in Miami in 1972. It was widely publicized one day that the stratedgy to force the legal demonstrators out of the convention area park was to cut off food supplies. When demonstrating groups would leave the park to get meals, they were not allowed to return. It was effectively preventing their troups from growing in size and those who were there were getting hungry.

That was the same day I bought a nice loaf of baked bread from a nice grocery store and discovered a "not so nice" ingredient inside and I contacted the large local bakery facility it originated from, a well known brand, located a few miles away. The manager asked me to bring it to the bakery and meet him there. When I did, he inspected it carefully and asked me to please not publicize it, but that he could compensate me for it if I would keep it quiet. He had said, "You're Betty Luckey, *on the news*, right?" I answered, "Well, I am Betty Luckey, with *half* a mouse in my *whole* wheat".

With that, he had me drive around back to his loading ramp and he filled my station wagon so packed full of every kind of freshly baked yummy smelling bread of all flavors, colors, seasoning, and variety. There was hardly any room for my children, who sat holding huge plastic bags of many loaves of bread. After driving around and leaving bread with relatives and friends, we headed for the house when one of the children asked me what were we going to do with all the bread. It was then I knew.

I stopped at two Winn Dixie stores and one Publix. I told them that one of them had donated a huge jar of peanut butter and jelly for the non profit Christian groups congregated to witness in Miami, and they all responded by doubling that, so as not to be undone by their rival stores.

We ended up with exactly what was needed to make hundreds or thousands of PB & J sandwiches for the park, and I was able to drive my car right into the park past all the security, down the 12 foot wide sidewalk, park it in the center square, as people of all walks of life and races, and interests, moved away to the side to make room for us. I had brought all my butter knives with me, my children, my brother, Lars Swan, and my cousin Eraca Cleary (Cathy), and using the hood as a deli counter, fed every single hungry soul around....for free!

There had been a commotion at the intersection that required police to move the traffic, but none was there and a skirmish resulted between drivers. Who jumped out of his limo to direct traffic and calm the confusion, but the famous singer musician, Carlos Santana himself! Leaving his limo driver with his lights flashing, Carlos jogs up to my car in the park and asked, "Have your kids had any breakfast this morning?"

I was leaning on the car with a slice of bread in one hand and a knife dripping with strawberry jam in the other, and shook my head "No". He said "Don't go anywhere I'll be right back!" The next thing I knew, someone returned with a huge white bakery box tied with white string along with a gallon of white milk and a stack of paper cups! "Where did this come from?" I asked. The man said the pastries inside had been destined for the Presidential party at the Fountainbleau Hotel, but were somehow intercepted, and Santana had said they were then "borrowed" and were to be delivered here. They were the most incredible gourmet delight in red, white, and blue patriotic designs and frosting, the world has ever known!

When it was announced that the annual Armed Forces Day parade was being cancelled in West Palm Beach, for lack of interest, it struck me funny for some reason, and I thought a great Christian outreach theme would be the Onward Christian Soldiers who would parade in its place and call it the 'UN-ARMED FORCES DAY PARADE". Without consulting anyone else, I called the city manager's office asking if I would need a permit for one such parade using the same dates, hours, and locations, of the previous one. The manager said, no, that he would put it under my name, and it would be registered as previously scheduled.

I was so excited I called my dad and told him my vision of marching with a Bible in front, the Sword of the Lord as the focus, as our weapon of war, and he said he would join me, drive his car with the American flag from one window extended on it's long pole, and the Christian flag out the opposite window, the Bible on the dashboard. He would have his trumpet, shofar, and rams horn there, as well, as needed. (See where I get it? I'm Sherm Swan's daughter!)

I called every newspaper, television and radio station with my press release. It would congregate on Flagler Park by the Catholic Church and end up at Curry Park just as the original parade had been planned. When the day arrived I had no idea what I would find when I arrived thinking maybe it would only be my dad and myself. Was I in for one huge surprise!

There was my anti-war brother Lars, many of the rabbis and priests in Palm Beach County, several churches and scout groups, the International Women's group for Peace and Freedom, musicians from a salvation army band, a bicycle brigade from Century Village, one of the local Jewish communities, fifty bikes all decorated with balloons, crepe paper, and honking horns! Oh, that's not all!

From Riviera Beach, a striking patrol of black cowboys on horseback, whose decorated steeds were behaving better than any mounted parade unit I had ever seen, much to the thrill of the black groups along the parade route who yelled, whistled, cheered and stood as the horse riders carrying American flags marched proudly by, waving to the appreciative crowds.

Veterans from past wars marched in uniform, veterans against the Vietnam War were also marching, choir groups from a variety of churches, a rock band in a pickup truck, a huge assortment of civilian marchers of every race, color, creed, size, and age filled the street and filed along waving to the crowds and marching to the band music and decorated pets on leashes. It was the nicest, most friendly, happy, group of American citizens who showed their support that day and related their interest to a wide assortment of reasons. All the various groups and individuals were compatible and expressioning openly the strong sense of love for God, country, and their fellow neighbor. What an expression of community unity!

At the park there had been set up a sound system and a band playing with an emcee who introduced a lineup of poets, speakers, and musicians, who expressed a wide variety of views, opinions, greetings, well wishes, and inspiration. The vendors who had preciously committed to be there filled the park, along with news media, TV cameramen, reporters and photographers. It was a huge success.

Then the news folks all requested to have Betty Luckey, the instigator of the event come to the microphone. I was pleased to be able to give them a very brief testimony about Jesus, His modern day "Soldiers" of the Cross, His "forces" armed with their weapon of choice, the Holy Word of God, and I closed thanking everyone for making it the best surprise and parade ever! Then I had my proud daddy, standing there with his Bible in one hand and his trumpet in the other, close the day with prayer.

When I got home, Gary had returned from work and said, "Hey Honey, what did y'all do today?" "Oh, we had a parade" I answered. Then I laughed when he said, "Oh yeah, I forgot!"

But, the fame in the 1960's and '70's, was not because I was so active, but because noboby else *was*! When that occurs, you naturally stand out, whether you want to or not. There were campaigns, demonstrations, rallies, and picketing I organized and/or involved myself with, to the point, one day, the Lord convicted me that there would be too many issues yet ahead in my future. He wanted me to quit spinning off in every direction to confront them, and just focus where He most needed me: **evangelism.**

It can be so easy to get caught up, involving ourselves in projects, activities, and programs that are great ideas and I did always give Him all the glory, but, it didn't glorify Him in that I only *thought,* He'd ordained it. There's a thin line and prayer and Bible referencing, is urgent to finding out the difference. It was during those years I learned something very important, only follow where and what His Holy Spirit leads you do.

And from then on I did. Besides, I worried people might be thinking I was nothing but a publicity seeker wanting attention, even though I'm glad I never heard anyone say that to my face. I wasn't, I just felt as Christians we had better stand up for the faith when our communities, country, and generation is confronted with satanic attack that we are able, and commissioned, to challenge.

When Playboy, Penthouse and Qui magazines started showing naked women on the front covers of magazines on all the newstands, I contacted every corporate office and convenience store that had them, and laid out my plan to have women all over and at every church to picket the stores until they provided paper "covers" to protect our men and boys, as well as, our children, and of course, all of us, from seeing it every time they bought a loaf of bread or a candy bar.

I had also said I would bring a lawsuit against them if they didn't comply. Within days, literally within ten days, all obscene literature began putting covers and binders over all the front cover photos. I have always known how to make friends; but, I also sure knew how to stir up some enemies as well. But it worked to get the job done. When television commercials were becoming too risque I'd make calls and let them know we would not buy their products or support those programs. When TV stations had movies or shows that used profanity, I made phone calls and wrote letters in protest.

The notoriety of being the county activist prompted so many news stories to start out with, "Betty Luckey, Palm Beach Gardens mother of four...."! It caused my daddy to always tease me and when I called him or stopped by to see my parents, he would always say, "Hey! Its 'Betty Luckey, Palm Beach Garden's mother of four!" and we'd laugh.

One day the phone rang and it was a local photographer I had never met who did freelance pictures for local, national and international publications. I recognized him when he arrived at my home for what was supposed to be a possible photo shoot. I already was familiar with his name having seen it on news bylines. I knew he was a valid photographer known widely for his great pictures and contributing news stories.

He expressed an interest in collecting a portfolio of photos of me so that he might sell them to magazines or newspapers in the future for stories they were printing. Well, that was something I'd have to think and pray about, there. All he had requested was a few head shots of me in my kitchen, at the dining room table, or by my front door. I had only brushed my hair and simply worn a jean skirt and a plaid western shirt for his visit.

Having learned never to be alone with fellas I didn't know, (and even some I did know), I made sure my dad, my husband, and my family knew he was coming and I was happy that they might join us at any time. I sort of looked forward to having a man of his fame and talent coming to pay a visit.

However, he was not as he seemed and I sensed it as soon as I saw him carrying his equiptment in his hands before he walked in, but being a Southern Belle (lol, that's a joke), with hospitality manners, I welcomed him into my humble home on Empress Drive where we were living between ranch sales. I silently thanked God for being there with me.

He was a handsome looking man, by most peoples' standards, tall with black hair and brown eyes. He had the kind of good looks that I never cared for in the natural, (I love everyone in Christ), but he was the sort of, "too-handsome" a man that knew he was. (Well, many women will know what I mean). He did look sort of Native American and he commented favorably at all my Indian decor kind of indicating he had such ancestry, but I didn't comment, I knew he didn't.

I started our conversation asking him if he knew Jesus. Ha! *He didn't expect that or like it.* I don't know exactly what he had in mind that day, and I may never know. **You'd thought we'd just drawn swords!** He sat on the couch and I was opposite in a rocking chair. His black eyes were deep and penetrating and I knew he was "reading my mail", like they say, as he gazed at mine. Yeah, creepy. Real creepy.

He didn't want any water, and I proceeded to share the "Living Water" from God with him when he confessed to being a lifelong atheist. He knew every argument to attempt to disarm a believer from one's faith. I know because for the next forty-five minutes or so, I got to hear them. But with God's help, as I kept my Spiritual eyes concentrated on Jesus and His powerful and precious Blood, it would repeatedly leave the man with no come-back. I avoided eye contact from that point on because a spirit of hypnotism and evil mind control was heavy in the room. I could feel it.

We never got around to photos and the camera never left his zippered gear. His clipboard and pen were set beside him which he also left untouched and he proposed every argument he could conjure up and I countered them instantly one by one, with memorized Scripture. It was a heated battle. It included everything from the Diety of Jesus, the resurrection, the Holy Trinity, the Virgin birth and Creation. I remained super calm, but he continuosly had to keep lowering his voice. Now he really looked mad and I knew to wind things up and see him to the door before he went off like a pressure cooker.

In fact, I sometimes fingered the little detective special (revolver) I had in my skirt pocket and prayed I wouldn't need it. (I mean there are times you can't be sure what someone might be capable of doing, and I was a "be prepared" Girl Scout from the old school), so I told him it was time for my husband to return and I needed to get my chicken in the oven.

He closed the conversation and the door, by admitting this: "Betty Luckey, I actually came by here, not for the photos, (I knew that in my knower), but to find out what makes you tick. I can't seem to get around your Jesus. There is a strong barrier I can't break thru and I'm going to leave you now with your Cross and it's Blood!" (That's *my* caps on 'Cross' and 'Blood', *he* was being sarcastic)!

The moment I heard his car leaving I turned on the stove, then I seasoned a nice big, fresh, whole chicken in one to two minutes, I placed on a baking sheet and popped it in the already preheated oven at 350 degrees, just in time to answer my ringing telephone.

It was the photographer! I recognized the angry voice even though he didn't say hello or introduce himself. "Betty, look at your chicken now and tell me where the power is!" He abruptly hung up the phone.

I opened the door of my oven that, of course, still read "350" degrees, what I mean is, the chicken was not in the oven until the preheat light had just gone off, but *just as it had gone off,* and it had not been in the oven over **three to four minutes**, or at the most, probably 5 minutes. Not only that, it was a big heavy chicken, not a small one, and I had been planning to need to serve it more than an hour later and it would have needed every minute of that to cook thoroughly.

I pulled out the oven rack with my pot holder, and black smoke billowed from the open door and there in my pan was a little black, shriveled up, burnt up, smoking chicken. When Gary got there he took it outside and tossed it over the fence into a canal behind the house. We were amazed but not impressed. Had the man still been there, I think I would have said simply, "Mister, is that all ya got?" I believe it was two words that crossed my mind at the time, "parlor tricks". I was and I am a follower of the God who made the chickens in the first place! Now that does impress me! Hallelujah!

One day I did not have one visitor, but two. We were living in Okeechobee. I was home alone. It had been a normal day with laundry, cooking and housework, being it was my day off from dispatching at the Okeechobee Sheriff's Department. I had been in a lot of great prayer time earlier in the day, when all of a sudden I felt like I was not alone. I wasn't.

There in the room with me was an Indian man, a medicine man, older maybe, than my dad was, probably. When I closed my eyes he was still there. When I opened them, there he was looking at me. He was dark complected with kind eyes. I think he spoke to me in his native language but I knew the words in English in my spirit, but I'm not sure. He wore something like loose denim britches and an open suade, worn-looking shirt. He wore beaded jewelry and a medicine man's pouch hanging from a leather strand around his neck. He had what he was calling, an "invitation" for me.

He said he wanted to nurture me, to teach me, in his ways. He would be my mentor in things spiritual and of the miraculous. He would show me ancient thoughts and practices that would give me stronger power than I could ever have any other way. He said I would heal the sick, control the things around me and foretell the future.

I knew I was about to decline his invitation but at the same time I thought perhaps some sort of respect might be in order, and that maybe I should probably say no gracefully and graciously. What I mean is that I felt I'd better not make him mad, as I refused his services...**wrong!**

Then I remember being ashamed of even entertaining such a foolish and potentially dangerous thought. I was to treat him no differently than I did the manifestations of the grotesque, hideous, fear-instilling, terrifying and horrific entities, or Satan, himself. The Lord has given to us the authority *through Him,* with power over all of the demonic and we are to dismiss them *fearlessly!* It is vital not to "entertain" them or patronize them for a moment more. We are to proclaim they leave that instant in the Name of Jesus, and mean it, and they will, by *His* authority! They're not afraid of you and me, but they are afraid of Him.

I decided instead on an outright, shoot-from-the-hip, almost indignant, "Betty Luckey" resistance. After all, I knew I was dealing with a demon who was attempting to appeal to my Indian-ness, to impress me, to make me feel some sort of pride that he had "chosen" me. No, I had his number and knew he was evil and I wanted no part of him.

I also want the world to know that the only reason I was wise to him was because the Holy Spirit had me on alert, discerning who he was, and so many Scriptures I knew were lending themselves to my uderstanding of what was happening here. My point is, look at all the people who may have already become entrapped into deceptions like his, or other similar evil beings, manifestations and visitations.....or invitations.

The Bible strictly warns us, revealing how demons connive and deceive to get their foot in the door of our lives, and for some it may seem quite tempting and appealing, but this is what everyone has got to know: they will do everything in their evil power to kill, steal and destroy you. That's why the Bible says we must stay sober because the devil stalks about seeking those to destroy.

It is also important to realize how some, like the medicine man, came across as harmless. That is how sin operates, too, starts off like a simple little matter that won't "hurt anything" so that it can slowly progress with you to the point in your life you feel hopeless and helpless to be released from its grips, chains, and bondages. Praise God He has provided through Jesus that all those chains be broken and we are set free! Thank, You, Lord!

I told the Indian spirit guide my only teacher and guidance came from the Holy Spirit of the Most High God Almighty, the God of Abraham, Isaac and Jacob, and through the Blood of Jesus Christ of Nazereth, my personal Lord and Savior and that additional assistance was inferior, unnecessary and unwelcomed.

At that moment he stepped aside when an aged, dark brown, almost boney hand with long, unkempt fingernails appeared on his shoulder and from behind him emerged the oldest human being, or spirit manifestation I could have ever imagined, only this was not an imagination, it was for real! The elder Indian man said "Then if you will not hear my son, you will hear *me*." (Not unlike a script from an old western movie.)

The elder medicine man spoke with more authority, and he also spoke in an Indian sounding dialect with words my spirit uderstood. I looked up into his eyes and they were yellowed with age and bloodshot, framed by very wrinkled skin and stringy disheveled gray hair. He wore an old leather skin or hide from a wild animal with holes cut out for his head and arms. I felt his invitation included reference that what he would teach me, I could use his training and supernatural gifts to honor my God with. I immediately had a check in my spirit to not become coerced or bamboozled by his deception, either, I looked above their heads and spoke to the Lord. I said, "Thank You Jesus, You are all I ever need or ever will!

Surprisingly, the elder man smiled at me as he nodded his head and spoke softly, saying, "Daughter, You decided well!" Then the two very real spirit guides, apparently two ancient-looking entities perhaps, or appearing as such, disappeared before my very eyes, and I was sure glad not to be his daughter, but a child of God.

In the days following I frequently thought about how many people would have given anything to have such a personal invitation, and I recalled in all the movies and books the tales about the young Indian and his vision quest. Well I never sought one, I hadn't roamed a wilderness or gone off fasting or seeking, what I had was a visitation with an invitation, but it came to me right in my own living room in a chair in front of my television set.

I wondered why the medicine man seemed to approve of my decision. He had told me that I had decided well. I mean, that was weird. Ah, the answer was this: I knew I didn't need an Indian spirit guide and he knew it also. Plus, he knew that there is no higher guidance than the Word of God....and nothing could ever compare to **His** Glory, whether *he* followed it or not, I may never know. I felt confident though, if it had been a test, I'd passed it.

Through the years I would sometimes wonder how many folks are confronted with occult spirit guides and overwhelmed with the excitement of the offer, thinking they're being honored, to have those abilities, and actually are now operating in them. I should re-word that rather, I should say the guides are desiring to operate inside the humans.

I understand there may be a rash of it everywhere, just as Satanism, the reports about the worshipping of Satan, has spread in every country in the last decade. The Bible says as much concerning the last days. One strong impression the two medicine men exhibited was their mild manner and innocent demeanor that could really fool folks, especially children. Think of the generation of children mesmerized with magical thoughts, readings about learning curse and spells and then have one of the demonic spirits appear to you to help teach you? The Bible strictly forbids any witchcraft, sorcery, and divination. Everyone needs to know that in reality, they are anything but kind, honorable, respectful, and wise. Resist the devil and he will flee from you. Those Indian guides I met? They were there to lure and entice me to fall for their deception, that their real purpose was to kill, steal, and destroy, and they fled.

CHAPTER ELEVEN

THERE'S A WITCH ON HER WAY!

"Beloved, believe not every spirit but try the spirits whether they are of God: because many false prophets are gone out into the world!"
1 John 4:1 KJV

I enjoyed about five years of employment as a toll collector on Florida's Turnpike and prided myself on friendliness and cheerful greetings to every single patron who ever passed through. My transactions with them required eye contact as I would punch out the appropriate ticket according to the size of the car or rig they were driving, as they rolled down their windows when approaching my toll booth to enter. Then of course, when they were exiting, they were paying money and I was making change and receipts for them. I always said, "God Bless you," or "Jesus loves you," as they drove away. I don't know if employees are still allowed to do that, but for about five years I surely did.

If the traffic was sparse or was spaced far enough apart and there was time, I

"Author with her cousin Eraca (Cathy) Cleary on the left, in Midway, KY"

was always prepared and excited to share the Gospel at every opportunity and there were always so many. It was great having daily opportunities to share my testimony with tourists, residents, people stranded, hitchhikers, and sometimes folks needing counseling, and those with prayer requests, including emergency and law enforcement personnel.

One evening it had just gotten dark and the weekend traffic was heavy and had been continuous. It was bumper to bumper but moving along well. In spite of conversations around me and between me answering frequent questions from drivers, I heard a familiar voice, as the Lord told me three times, "Betty, a witch is on her way". As I continued to hand out tickets I kinda just let that sink in.

I had another worker in the booth with me so I began speaking to God through inaudible prayer, as much as was possible, with all the activity around me. I asked the Lord what He wanted me to do and he had some "intel" for me so I listened carefully.

Someone, He said, was a witch, who would come through my lane in a few short minutes and she would attempt to shock me. Her purpose was to alarm me, intimidate, and make me fearful. He said I should only glance in her direction but not look into her eyes. He said not to touch her but that as soon as she would take hold of my ticket release my hold on it quickly and I was to look immediately at the following car behind her and punch out the appropriate card for the next driver. He said not to look back at the witch as she left. I asked how I would know when it was she and He said, "Oh, you will know!"

That was an understatement.

I began a silent continuous dialogue with God, praying and praising and focusing on Him and the power of His Blood. I sensed and knew when the witch was turning the corner at Indiantown Road and it was now about five cars away. Of course I said nothing to the collector beside me who was receiving money on the other side of the booth from the cars exiting.

As the non-descript car was 4, then 3, then 2 cars away, my heart raced and I breathed slowly, silently repeating the name, saying, *"Jesus"*. I punched out her ticket and with a friendly smile and a bold, "Good evenin'!" I glanced to see two eyes with lightning blazing like a fourth of July sparkler that was penetrating from each eyeball surrounding a blinding spotlight from her retina, a hideous wrinkled red face, not a mask, it was just the eyes, that when I saw them in a split second, sent an electric shock down my spine, through my feet, with a jolt like an earthquake and I grit my teeth punching out the next ticket, as I said in the most casual, happy, nonchalant voice I could muster up, "Thank you, have a nice night," as if there had been no affect on me at all.

As she scratched off and the hot rubber burning smell of her tires hit the night air, she let out a blood curdling scream of laughter that echoed beneath the station overhead ceiling, and I didn't even look back. "What was *that?*" shouted my co-worker as she grabbed me by the arm!

"Just a witch," I said calmly and then answered the next driver, as he asked, "How many miles to Orlando?" I said with a big sigh and a happy smile, "One hundred forty four miles, Sir"!

The Lord had all ready shown me previously, that as we become more and more familiar with supernatural things that evil forces may attempt to act out and to be prepared for such shananigans but NEVER was I to fear. Now when He tells us not to fear, we can trust Him. He gives us that instruction so many times in the Bible that you come to realize, this is not an option, this is always a direct command and He is the Commander and as His soldiers, we are to obey His commands. If God be for us and *He is,* who can be against us, so then, who's there to fear? No one and no thing, Hallelujah, Praise be to God!

He had also taught me that there may be times, that the appropriate response is to ignore what was just seen or heard, just as if it hadn't happened. Sometimes, He did not want to allow the enemy or maybe others around us, to think he may have impressed us with his "party tricks." We can rejoice that God sometimes (or maybe most of the time), spares us demonic manifestations that Satan orchastrates in an attempt to bring glory to himself, or his evil works of darkness, and their effects on us.

One night I was on a lonely stretch of highway on my way home on Indiantown Road and had to bring my truck to a halt at a lonely four way stop at Pratt Whitney Road. I thought I detected movement on the corner and then I discovered slight movement on all four corners simultaneously. I realized there were four men standing one at each corner on the grass. They were dressed exactly alike and looked alike. I would have assumed they were hitchikers but none held out the traditional thumb and all four just stood staring right at me with blazing colored eyes, having a hypnotic looking, glow-in-the-dark kind of stare.

As I drove off I said, "Lord, what was *that?*" He said, "Ignore it, nothing that concerns us, all is well, Betty." My family was following a mile behind me, and when I asked them at the house if they'd seen the four men they said no, there had been no one there and they had passed no cars.

Back in the '60's and '70's there was a rash of new age religions, cults, and the occult, causing a buzz among the youth, music, Hollywood celebrities, television, movie entertainment, and newly formed groups, as well. There was much talk about Zen, Eastern religion, mind control, Scientology, Transendental Meditation, new age publications, including books like Urantia.

My cousin Cathy, who is now called Eraca, from California who was living near West Palm Beach at the time, asked me if I would come visit her ladies group she had joined, as they were studying a book that had a lot of Bible material in it. I had declined her invitation previously, but when she mentioned the Bible, I thought I'd better be more protective and see what she might be getting into. She had even ordered me a copy of the book. I thought of myself as her "big sister" cousin, at times, and at other times, *she was more the "big sister"* and I needed **her** advice.

I followed her directions and pulled up to an average looking home in Riviera Beach where many cars had crowded to park in the driveway and on both sides of the street. I was late, but found a spot to park my truck a short distance away. All the house windows appeared to be open and a voice from inside said, "Come on in!" before I could knock. "Oh good", I heard a familiar voice say, "Its my cousin Betty, come sit here next to me on the couch!" A multitude of women's voices greeted me at once and the leader who was seated in a chair facing all the others, welcomed me, and then continued teaching from her book.

The ladies appeared mostly middle aged or much older than we were anyway, and they filled the living room, smiling sweetly and listening intently to the teacher and fanning themselves with fans or booklets. (hot day, no AC). I had just gotten settled on the couch when something caught the corner of my eye, something, as if it was a balloon floating a couple of feet from the floor, aimlessly roaming through the room, and then another one. There may have been three. It's hard to keep count of balloons that not only won't stay in one place, but seem to fade in and out of existance altogether.

Now, I wasn't employed in law enfocement yet, at that time, but I had already been known for my detective tendencies my whole life. I didn't care at that moment what the woman was saying, I was looking at something I had never seen before and because it was pastel, and lit up, I looked around the room to see if there was perhaps a hidden projector or a mechanical or technical explanation for a transparent ball to float around a room containing not only iridescent reflections but perhaps I perceived it to have also,...*personality!?*

Somehow, it seemed *the thing was alive and could think!* I poked Cathy's arm and found she was already looking at me, smiling and nodding. "It's ok, Betty", she whispered. Well maybe it was ok with her but it wasn't ok with me. (I also thought if those balloons could think, they were telling each other, "Oh NO!! Betty Luckey's here!")

Cathy interrupted the session as she told the leader, "My cousin can see our visitors today". "Oh, yes!" fondly exclaimed the lady, "We are so honored and delighted that these little visitors have chosen to join us today and grace us with their presence! There are some here who cannot yet see our dear little friends! It is highly unusual that a nonmember is able to see them so soon and we are most delighted to have you with us, Betty," she said with raised eyebrows, peering over her glasses at me, almost squinting suspiciously, as she continued reading from her book.

"Those are orbs," Cathy whispered.

"I'm out of here," I whispered back.

I got up, walked out the door, and drove home in my truck to familiar territory where cows are cows, tractors are tractors, people are people, and God is God.

Incidently I was given the book, Urantia, and when I glanced inside at what appeared to me to be sacreligious, anti-God, deceptive material in it, I took it to the campfire to burn. The book would not burn. I used liter pine wood and even poured lamp oil on it and still it wouldn't burn. Finally, I placed my hands above the book and prayed, "And now by the power of Jesus Christ and His precious Blood spilled out at Calvary's

Cross, I command this book to burn to ashes in His Holy Name, the precious Name of Jesus, Amen, Amen, and Amen!" As God is my judge, it was only then, that the book disintegrated into blackened ash that blew away in a gust of wind from the evening breeze, Hallelujah!

To me, Cathy was so much more like a sister to me than a cousin. When her beautiful mother had passed away from an illness in San Francisco, my Uncle Roy was left with Cathy and her younger sister to raise, so my parents drove to California and we picked up my two cousins and brought them to live in our home temporarily until their dad could get moved and settled into a new home before coming to bring them back, I was thrilled. I had a new baby "sister" and finally a sister cousin, close to my own age that made my life suddenly more fun and adventurous.

One night after we had been reading "Tom Sawyer and Huckleberry Finn", we did what they did in the book. They snuck off in the night to the cemetery. Looking back I shake my head in wonderment of how in the world we thought that was ever a good idea. Maybe it was to prove to ourselves there was nothing to fear. What it proved was that walking through a cow pasture on a full moon to the back of the town cemetery and through the fence, makes you hungry, cold and sleepy, so we quickly returned back through the bedroom window and into our beds.

The next morning I remember telling our parents what we had done and they looked at us in disbelief. I don't think they could decide if we needed to be punished for doing it or for lying and saying we had done it. They seemed to only sit there in shock and we had a conversation about dangers and house rules, and of course there were warnings and such, but something tells me they could never bring themselves to believe we actually went to the cemetery at midnight in the moonlight. But we did, and no, we weren't in the least fearful. Having Cathy with me at home, at church and at school, made every day fun, interesting, and I was never bored again. We have lived on opposite coasts for most all our lives since, but I still miss her. Whenever she would come to Florida, it would bring a renewed close friendship and we would inevitably make new memories.

It was during this period in my life I was becoming spiritually awakened to all the various false teachings and religions and had many opportunities and invites to join some of the groups. I was usually introduced to the local head honchos of a variety of these faiths, but was quickly dismissed by the leaders as someone not suited to their false teachings. I testified of Jesus as Lord and Savior to every one of them, and was never approached again to participate. There were a few additional stories I could probably go into detail about to better describe this, but after awhile you want to just say, "Yucky", and think on only very Godly, clean and Holy subjects.

There was a time a group of people I was witnessing to were so excited about a guru from India who was so "wise" they were all trying to quote him and trying to get me to ride down to Ft. Lauderdale to hear him speak in a park. The big draw was that they thought he was so enlightened because he had a supernatural glow everyone loved to go see. He always met folks in the park at noon on Saturday, I think it was.

When we arrived at the park it was in the middle of the day with the noonday sun brightly illuminating everybody there, but especially the "wise" guru who used white clothing to his advantage for sure. He was not only glowing, but his stark white robes, sandals, and turban were so white that the blistering sun had him lit up like a 5000 watt flood lamp.

"Aren't you coming with us, Mrs. Luckey, we're taking flowers over to him?" I heard them call out to me as they approached the speaker at the microphone with the white, long flowing beard. Putting on my sun glasses in order to see them, due to the blinding reflections of their "teacher", I shook my head and headed north on Highway US1.

I just remembered one more story, when Cathy and I were volunteering to run a hurricane shelter because it was near impossible to get folks to help to do that. The county had set up a day to have emergency officials teach prospective shelter managers first aid, shelter management, weather vocabulary, everything connected with storms and making people safe. Well we sat there for over two hours listening to experts in their field speaking. The authorities were represented by the Sheriff, the fire chief, the EMS commander, emergency management, etc.

As the men sat lined up on the stage with spot lights focused on them, a black velvet curtain or drape across the stage behind them, I had stared at them so long I began to see perfect colorful auras radiating from each man. The colors varied between each one though. I whispered to Cathy, "You seein' that?" She laughed at me and said, yes, and that she had just happened to bring something for me that today! She handed me a small booklet that said, "How To Read Auras." Now I was really ready to go.

In the car as we were leaving, I gave the pamphlet back to her saying I didn't want to read auras and that if Jesus had wanted me to, He probably would have included it in the Gospels. She then proceded to state how diagnostically beneficial, etc., it could be to see the electrical magnetic forces around someone and be able to know by the colors, if the person was physically sick or even spiritually healthy or not, or something like that.

Then I said something I probably should not have. I proposed that as we left that street, we should look at the next car to pass us and I bet there would be no aura, that the auras were so visible back at the Red Cross auditorium because of the lighting and eye strain. Cathy smiled.

There was no traffic at all on the four lane road we pulled onto. I went slowly so that whatever car would come by next would have to pass us. The plan was to stare at him, or her, to look for an aura that I was certain we would not see.

Here it came, a brilliantly painted Volkswagon bug with no windows. The guy driving not only came up slowly next to us, but he rode at our side, looked directly at us, leaning almost out the window to show us he had huge wild eyes with a blazing brilliance to them, and obviously a set of fake vampire teeth and he growled loudly at me and Cathy. It jolted us both!

Then he speeded up with his ear-deafening engine and disappeared over the hill ahead. I pulled over into a parking lot. I prayed out loud for Jesus to forgive me for "dabbling" with subjects I knew in my spirit to be forbidden to believers. I thanked the Lord for warning us against any forms of witchcraft or the occult. I asked Him to fill me so full of His Holy Spirit I would never be tempted or deceived into thinking those things were harmless or could even be tampered with by Christians, like even the horoscopes.

I mean it had not been that he scared us, no, and we certainly forgot to look for the aura (lol), but what were the odds in the natural that right when we are "testing" an occult art, that a demonic looking person or practical joker, whatever he was, would come by at that very moment? I felt God was teaching us a real lesson that day. I knew what it felt like when the Holy Spirit is convicting and correcting me. But its a really good thing. The Bible says "For whom the Lord loveth, He chasteneth" (disciplines), from Hebrews 12:6a KJV.

When I was thirteen I had mentioned to my daddy some reference to horoscopes and he made me promise that regardless of how tempted I would ever be to read one, like seeing it in the paper, that I would train my eyes to refuse to look in its direction, I agreed, and to this day I will not look at them in any publication, and I turn the page as soon as possible. The Bible means business when it says, in Leviticus 19:31 (NIV), "**Do not turn to mediums or seek out spiritists, for you will be defiled by them, I am the Lord your God**"!

I have a great praise report of one victorious event that took place when I was serving as a chaperone in Haiti with sixteen teenagers from Maranatha Church of God in Palm Beach Gardens once.

The church had several pastors on staff and they had enlisted me to go with the mission group along with church mission director, A.T. Lowery, also an EMS ambulance driver, Mark Howell, who I knew from church and law enforcement, and the youth director, Pastor Doug Mitchell. One busy Saturday morning in a Port-au-Prince, outdoors market square, it may have been, we held church!

The local Haitian pastor who was hosting our group, had arranged for a flatbed truck with a sound system to be parked right in the center of all the activities. We began with recorded music that drew a huge crowd. Pastor Mitchell stood at one microphone, his Haitian interpreter at another mic next to him. I could not have been more pleased how things were going.

Doug would declare a Biblical statement in English, followed by the interpretation by the Haitian man and the responsive crowd would nod, smile and clap appropriately, when all at once a disturbing strange voice joined in on the mix, disrupted them with a witchy sounding shrill voice that was louder than our microphones! The woman would mimic their voices with her own "interpretation" of the message, taunting, ridiculing, and distracting from everything being preached from the flatbed.

The crowd would look at the stage, then at the woman, back to the stage, then to the woman, like a tennis match. The three voices went round and round and the crowd would stare at the stage (the flatbed) and then at the woman in the back of the audience. They all got louder and louder, Pastor Mitchell's face got redder and redder, and even though we were all standing in the hot sun getting sunburned, I knew he was probably getting frustrated at the devil for the major interruption!

I took off through the crowd heading directly toward the sound of her cackling voice! When Mark saw what I was doing, I later heard him tell folks, he took off to try to get to the woman before I did because he didn't want to see me get hurt. He says "I got there just in time to see Mrs. Luckey lift her hand up high above the woman's head and declare, "I speak to you devil and declare you come out from this woman this instant, by the authority and in the Name of Jesus!" and she fell to the ground! Hallelujah!

Well the Haitian pastor took it from there and I went back to check on Pastor Mitchell, who continued on with his sermon and never missed a beat!

The woman who was delivered was the town sorcerer, a known witch woman who did voodoo. From that day forward, they said, she praised the Lord and would invite everyone to their revival. In fact the pastor there said she positioned herself by the front door of the church and every evening welcomed people at the front door as they arrived! He said she became a faithful christian and member of the church and from that day forward spoke only with a kind and loving voice.

Had I ever done anything like that before? No. I had not even practiced deliverance of that sort....I was used to praying deliverance in more like the "quiet, inside-a-prayer-group" type ministering, why, I had no thought what I was going to say when I got up to her. But the Lord knew what He needed to do and He used me to do it, and with no preplanning on my part, that's for sure. I learned that day, when the Holy Ghost wells up inside you with a Word....you better just let it out! And that's all I did.

This chapter is entitled, "There's a Witch on Her Way" so I guess this story is the one about "The Witch Who Was on her Way... *to be Delivered!*"

"Cherry tree by Author's front door at her home in Cherokee County, NC"

CHAPTER TWELVE

SURPRISE!

———◆◆◆———

"Eye hath not seen, nor ear heard, nor has it entered into the heart of man, the things which God hath prepared for them who love Him"
1 Corinthians 2:9 KJV

Well, if you didn't already start to think I might be a bit off my rocker, no tellin' what you'll go away thinkin' after you read the next six stories. These are true tales I don't tell just everybody about.

Speakin' of rockers, I'm sure enjoying my rocking chairs these days though, and nothing beats sitting out here on the porch looking out over these Smoky Mountain woods and creeks and taking in the sunsets and the moon sets and smelling the fresh mountain breezes and remembering the excitement I had when the Lord let me see some mighty unbelievable things, for sure.

One afternoon I had been driving alone up the Beeline Highway, State Road 710, back in Palm Beach County toward our home at Lucky Buck Ranch. I had the truck windows rolled down, wind blowing my hair, singing Jesus music at the top of my lungs. I was praying and praising and driving along miles of nothing but pastures and woods when all of a sudden something caught my eye way off to the side of the road.

There to my right was a huge stand of tall pine trees blowing in the wind, and just as I was going to pass them by, it seemed just like they, too, were singing and praising the Lord, just like I was. As God is my judge, may He strike me dead if I'm lyin', every one of those hundreds of trees, bowed before Him in Honor, in praise, in thanks to the Creator Who made you and me and every tree!

All the trees leaned forward, way over, as if on bended knee, as if bowing before their Lord and King! Now seeing this caused tears to flood my eyes and I had to pull over to the side because I couldn't see to drive. Happiness filled my heart and I remembered all the Bible references telling about trees singing and *clapping! The forest of pines then strtched back up straight,* right before my eyes. It was not as if I had envisioned them doing this, no, I saw them do it! They bowed in praise and honor to their Creator!

I had been rejoicing and continued to rejoice and even the trees, as well! Some time Google all the Scripture about trees praising God. It was the first time I had ever seen it happen though, and it was almost as exciting as what happened to my daughter Sheri not that long ago, late in 2021.

Sheri was out helping her husband Simon get our Bloodhound, "Hank," (Williams), back by a gate he got out of, to chase a deer at the house. While he was running up the mountain after Hank, Sheri waited at the gate in fervent prayer, first, for the dog not to get away, and also for Simon not to get hurt running up some steep terrain. Both of them, Sheri and Simon were both still recuperating from the coronavirus that had left them, at least temporarily, with much less energy than they had been used to.

Now standing right next to Sheri was a tree with a low lying branch near her head. She could hear Heavenly sweet, happy music! She said it resembled maybe, like a cheerful Irish melody never heard before! She descibes it with such emotion she almost does a happy dance as she imitates its wonderful sound.

Where was the music coming from? There was no phone, no radio, no music playing closeby or at a distance when she realized.... it was the branch with the green leaves singing! For real! The tree was praising the Lord, and in its way, as only the tree could, I imagine, was assuring her that God answered her prayer and that Simon was safely returning with Hank and all was well.

That wasn't the end of it, folks, listen to what happened next. Sheri runs back in the house to get her phone. She wanted to bring it outside and photograph the branch. A strong tree branch from way high above that gate, had spearheaded to the ground and set firmly into the rocky soil below *precisely where Sheri had been standing when she heard the tree singing, just moments before! In fact, it was now preventing the easy opening and closing of the swinging gate!*

Well, now she was able to film the branch in the ground as well as the branch that did the singing. Simon was able to adjust the gate, and repair the place Hank had escaped, but the limb that penetrated from up above I guess, will always have to stay there, too deeply embedded in the ground to remove easily, and as a reminder of the supernatural activities of the day. We would begin to contemplate all the possible meaning behind the strange event and I guess we still do. Hmmm....if she hadn't heard the tree sing, she would not have left the spot where the limb shot into the ground where she'd been standing. Do you think God used the singing tree to warn her?

One day I was praying for all the Native American Pastors, their wives, their churches and ministries, the musicians and what Indian ministry the Lord might have in mind for me, when the strangest manifestation appeared before my eyes causing me to slow way down on the highway, that thankfully was devoid of all traffic at the moment.

There, surrounding me, in front of me and behind me, in the grass and on the shoulders of the road and to the sides of me, were animals looking right into my eyes! At first I thought I was seeing animals from the Indian medicine wheels from Cherokee, Iroquois, Seminole and Creek Tribes I was familiar with. Actually it was more like the Seminole clan circle, maybe more like a clan circle, than medicine wheel. They were almost spaced out semetrically and in a perfect circle and evenly apart, just as they are on the wheel. I was at their center, inside the circle.

I had to look carefully, removing and replacing my red-lensed prescription eye glasses I have always worn. I blinked my eyes repeatedly and pinched my arm just checking to see if I was really there. I asked God to speak to me but realized I needed nothing more said, He had already spoken with the vision: *"It was his Holy will that He would always anoint me to be inside the very center of His will for ministry to tribal people everywhere!"* and I thanked Him with tears of joy! It was another confirmation that He was preparing me for ministry to people with the message they needed to put all their trust in Him, not animals and wheels, just Jesus.

It seems as though so many events in my life were confirmed when I asked God to lead and direct for guidance about something and He would use a bright, red, colorful, healthy, Cardinal as a confirmation that yes, I was on target pertaining to something as I prayed. At times I was in the woods, or on my porch, or looking out a window, in the pasture, or at my desk window up in my loft.

However, the most profound moment was on a day a dear friend died and I didn't have enough gas money to attend the funeral. We were living up on the Lake Wales Ridge in Lake Placid, Florida, and I was praying at my desk. I believed the Lord had probably allowed me to discover my truck had an empty gas tank and I had used it as a sign I shouldn't try to make the three hour drive to Jupiter to the police officer's funeral.

Bruce St. Laurent wasn't just any cop. He was about to become my son-in-law many years before and was engaged to Sheri when she called off the engagement, way back when they were very young. He had been her drummer in her band for a long time. Now she had been wearing his engagement ring that she returned to him.

When he had become despondant over the breakup I had spent a couple of hours praying and counseling with him. I had helped lead him to the Lord long before this and my dad had baptized him. When he said he had nothing to live for any longer, I asked him what his dream had been for his life and he said he'd always wanted to be a policeman.

I was elated! I told him to go for it and he said it wasn't possible because he was now leading a lifestyle away from the Lord, which included even helping a friend who was in the drug trade. I told him to repent of those things, ask the Lord's blessing to become a cop, and find favor at the local Jupiter Police department. He did, and boy, did he have favor!

Bruce not only talked to the chief confessing everything illegal he had ever done, he was hired, graduated from the academy, and one day I opened the newspaper and read he had been named Policeman of the

Year, or something similar. He was their motorcycle cop and a good one! He married a beautiful woman with children and together their family became even larger. He was a very happy husband, father, employee, and successful police officer.

Bruce was assigned the Presidential motorcade when the President came to Florida for a campaign, and he was killed in an accident on the highway as he rode patrol in the procession to the event. Of course that brought news media world wide and his funeral would be one of the largest ever in south Florida. I really wanted to go and I was working at my desk in our home computer room feeling a little sorry for myself when the phone rang.

My Seminole friend Mable Haught asked me what I was doing and said she thought I was going to that funeral on the east coast. I explained money was too tight and now it was probably too late even to think about. All of a sudden, at once, and in unison, red Cardinals and other birds too, of all colors, *filled my bush beside my open window and began to squawk and holler!* The biggest Cardinal of them all stood on the branch closest to my screen and yelled at me the loudest! I never saw a bird so mad and indignant! He was scolding me for not having the faith to have planned to go. I laughed and told her what all the racket was about. Maybe I can't talk Cardinal, but I sure can interpret Cardinal real good when I hear it! Mable said it was not too late, that she would meet me at the Brighton blinker light on Highway 70, that I was supposed to go! She was right.

I grabbed my empty purse and drove to the blinker light where her husband, Terry, was parked and came to my window handing me a hundred dollar bill and I made it to the funeral in time to have a wonderful seat. God provides. The birds knew it, too. The Bible says the Lord takes such good care of the birds they don't have to work or sew and he feeds and clothes them and how we are much more valuable to Him than the birds.

I am about to tell you something that happened to me one day when I was alone in the pasture, fasting and praying, rejoicing in songs, with my Bible, at our Two Creeks Ranch along Fisheating Creek at Venus. Well, it occurred in the creek itself as I walked along wading in my barefeet, feeling how soothing that tea colored, tasty, cool water felt on my feet.

We had been searching for a week for a bull that had got out and now I could see how easy it could have been for him to have gone over or under the remaining tight strand of barbed wire. It was stretched across the width of the whole creek, and I was now looking at it, just ahead of me, about ten feet away.

That strand represented the boundary fenceline to the neighboring property that I would not be able to walk into without illegally tresspassing and it was not possible out there to get permission from the ranch foreman's office many miles away with no phone reception. I looked at the barbed wire and wished it wasn't there.

Now this is the truth, y'all, I prayed that somehow I would feel it was God's will that I could go to the other side so I could look for any cow tracks beyond the curve just past the fenceline. It was strict business to me not to go onto posted property that wasn't yours and you could never be sure the other ranch didn't have hidden cameras, hunters or game wardens hiding there on tree stands that would catch you if you did. I remember praying what was probably a sort of pitiful prayer by an old cattleman's wife trying so desparately to help her husband. I prayed please Lord, if that animal came through here, please help us find it, and if its ok for me to cross this line, please let me know.

Just then, the piece of wire that stretched tightly between two heavy, naturally-cured posts, one on either side of the creek, popped in half, each half of the strand floating on the top of the water to the side as if welcoming my entry like an opened swinging gate! I could imagine an angel with wirecutters sayin' "Come on in!"

Shor' nuf, I found tracks ahead and knew Gary would be able to retrieve the old bull later that day, and I thanked the Lord for His huge miraculous manifestation and surprise in the middle of Fisheating Creek!

One of the most startling things I ever saw was a real live vision when I was traveling along a high mountain back country road somewhere between Franklin, Cashiers, Highlands, and Glenville, NC. I was praising God, singing along with the radio a Bluegrass hymn and started to pass a very small cemetery up on a little knoll overlooking the most breathtaking view. I also had to slow way down as I rounded the curve, and it gave me a moment to see the very old, weathered historical cemetery markers from generations long past.

All at once everyone who had been buried there was standing beside their tombstone waving at me and smiling! (Hey, I can't make this stuff up, folks, trust me!) There were middle age, young and old men and boys in overalls, an old lady in a bonnet and apron, little children in homemade clothes, a couple of soldiers in uniforms, ladies all in long pioneer dresses, some with shawls, and a few men in suits with vests. All ages, types, sizes, and races. All so happy they were besides themselves....literally!

I slammed on my brakes and waved at them, smiling back. I mean, my daddy taught me to always be friendly and not to ever be stuck up, and I discovered that day, it included every smiling, waving folk, dead or alive. They disappeared when I heard an old truck behind me and I had to move on down the one lane road. But I wiped my joyful tears at the knowledge that when we go to be with the Lord we are not even in those graves, and like Jesus we have risen to everlasting life! I just traveled on down the mountain and continued singing that song, "Yes, we'll understand it better by and by"......"*By and by, when the morning comes, when the saints of God are gathered home, we will tell the story, how we've overcome, and we'll understand it better by and by!*" ("We'll Understand it Better By and By" by Charles Albert Tindley, 1905).

I could just hear all those people back up on the knoll singing with me like the country choir we have at Notla Baptist Church in Cherokee County, NC.

Seein' all those graveyard pioneer people reminded me of another song I'd always asked for my funeral one day, if Jesus doesn't come take me in the rapture first. This is one I can still hear late Ms. Betty Jean Robinson singing for us, "Ain't No Grave Gonna Hold Me Down!" Now *that's* a good one to Google up and listen to! That and "O Happy Day" by Edwin Hawkins Singers.

So, these are my stories how I've overcome. This wonderful life has been an amazing trip with Jesus up His mountain. There were twists and turns in the road, there are valleys and shadows, washouts and landslides... but there was and there is, sunshine, bright happy paths, and His summits of Glory, *His Glory,* bringing us safe and secure in His love, for eternity.

And, let me add, may all my true and real adventures climbing His mountain, just Glorify *Him*, and not me. You know, when you try to write a book something like this one, where you're also trying to leave your family generations coming up, a way to understand who you were and what you were all about, I don't want my great grandkids to read it and think I was just bragging. *If I brag, it's only on Jesus!* He was and is my hero! I just can't figure out how else you can write an autobiography without it being all about yourself, lol.

I have a cemetery plot on a mountain plateau up at Peachtree right next to Gary at Green Lawn Memorial Gardens. It's surrounded by picturesque mountain ranges, I think of as kind of a special place like an eagle's nest, nestled high in the sunshine where I sit as a resting place to collect my thoughts and replay happy memories. The park bench is located between Gary, his brother Glyn and his wife Pam's grave sites. She was a best friend of mine and we had moved there in the mountains to be close to them in the first place.

Sometimes I spend time in prayer there thankful that Little Brasstown Baptist Church, (Glyn's dear church where he taught an adult Sunday school class and sang in the choir), was thoughtful to have placed it there.

The tombstone I share with Gary has my name on it already. Its not really a sad thing to go and see it there, because of Jesus. He has my husband and family members in Heaven where, because of Him, we know the real Gary's not in the ground, he's talking Glyn's ear off in another far up location, and we can celebrate Life.

Gary's grave is described, just like this sad song tells it, as Vince Gill sings it in the song he wrote, "Go Rest High on the Mountain". It was too much of a tear jerker for me to want to use it the day of his funeral, but the words sure reflected how we were all feeling. What was so difficult for us to accept was that in the days prior to his passing, he was sedated on a ventilator in ICU unable to have visitors and calls and I knew that for Gary, that had to be an utterly unbearable, undescribable torture for him. But he was always so brave and so many of the words Vince wrote were so fitting:

Oh, how we cried the day you left us, we gathered 'round your grave to grieve, Wish I could see the angels faces, When they hear your sweet voice sing.

Go rest high on that mountain, Son your work on earth is done, Go to Heaven a-shoutin', Love for the Father and the Son.

Twenty-five years later Vince added this last verse and debuted it at the Ryman Theater in Nashville with his wife Amy Grant:

"You're safely Home in the arms of Jesus, Eternal Life, my brother's found! The day will come I know I'll see him, In that sacred place, on that Holy Ground."

By Vince Grant Gill, 1994

Vince sang this with Patty Lovelass at the memorial service in 2013, of George Jones, one of Gary's favorite country singers.

Up at the top of Jesus' Mountain we can see forever and one day I'll be waiting for each of you there with open arms, if the Lord doesn't come and get us all first! .....but always remember......I sure love Y'all, more than you will ever know! And don't forget, clinging to your faith in Jesus is the most important word I leave with you because of Him, "There ain't no grave, gonna hold us down, Hallelujah!"

"'Gran'maw Rambo' (Author), police academy gun range in cammo vest"

CHAPTER THIRTEEN

...BUT SHE'S HADESWITH A SHOTGUN!

━━━━◆━◆━◆━━━━

"Last of all, I must remind you, that we are all fighting in
a Spiritual battle. We are weak human beings, so let your
strength come from our Great Warrior Chief"
Ephesians 6:10, First NationsVersion (FNV)

When we leased over 2,000 acres for cattle in Palm Beach County west of Palm Beach Gardens, Florida, we named it "Lucky Buck Ranch." The day that a realtor opened up ten acre tracts for sale along its western border, we jumped at the chance and were able to purchase a tract. We made plans to live temporarily in a mobile home we moved there, until I could start working to help pay for a new house to be built.

Our 10 acres we bought was adjacent to the 2,000 acre lease that was "land-locked," having no legal or convenient access road until we made one entering through our new property. At the time we had no idea just how long we would have the lease, which was specified as year to year, but we were blessed to have it for over twenty five years.

My only interest for employment was in law enforcement and the only position available in those days was as dispatchers, few and far between were female officers ever hired. There were no women in the police academies locally and when a female officer was hired in an agency, she had usually received her certification from another state and had moved to Florida.

I had my application in at every agency but it was the one at the Florida Turnpike that was accepted first. I liked it because the toll collectors listened to the Florida Highway Patrol Troop K on their radios constantly and soon became familiar with all the codes and procedures. They had a reputation for having the best dispatchers in the whole state. It was training to be a dispatcher every day that I spent in my toll booth glued to the police scanner that broadcast every night across my speakers above my head.

The previous Jupiter midnight toll collector had been attacked one lonely night at her toll booth and had quit her job and no one wanted to replace her at the remote station on Indiantown Road. I was a willing volunteer and so happy that we would be able to start building the ranch house Gary and I had designed on a napkin one night at Pizza Hut.

That it was a dangerous position, actually, never occurred to me at all, because I knew God would protect me everywhere at all times, and boy, did He ever! This job was good because I would work the midnight shift and Gary would work the afternoon shift at Pratt Whitney, that way we shared the same truck, and we were always with our children, who were never left alone. The old Ford F-150 and F-250 pickups we owned at different times did double duty big time during those years.

I especially loved my summer schedule when the kids and I would have a daily routine that included the Jupiter and Hobe Sound beaches. At seven AM I dropped Gary off at Pratt Whitney Aircraft, a fews miles from the ranch, then hurried home and cleaned the house putting a roast in the oven.

My favorite was a venison, or wild hog roast, potatoes, carrots, onions, green beans or peas, (something green), seasonings, a little water, occasionally, whole tomatoes or corn, (whatever I happened to have), sealed with aluminum foil, or a tight fitting lid, to bake in the oven all day on 300 degrees.

The kids would help do laundry, make their beds, and run the vacuum, their reward ahead was a day at the beach. So, as soon as our work was done we could leave and get in the truck, so the kids were always motivated to help. Off we'd head for Dubois Park on the ocean in

Jupiter, or Hobe Sound public Beach, with a tuna sandwich and potato chip lunch all packed in a cooler with sodas and cookies.

We all stayed brown from the sun and slender from all the excercise. In the afternoon on our way home, we picked up Gary from work and when we got to the house, and yum, did it smell good, our whole supper all ready for us to serve in the dining room, and the house all clean. Then everyone took a late afternoon nap.

I loved having the house already cleaned up to come home to each day. Frequently, I slept until time to put the kids to bed, when I would then take the truck and leave for work. Gary often took the kids with him to the pasture to check the cows or hunt and fish while I slept. It would be a successful schedule routine that worked really well making it possible to manuver jobs on a tight budget with four children and one truck.

Many friends and relatives would comment on how dangerous it seemed to them it must be for me to be the lone toll collector on the turnpike at the Jupiter exit on Indiantown Road all through the night. Back in those days it was so dark, isolated, no homes, businesses, just surrounding pastures, groves and farm fields. The Lord made me fearless and I was able to study the Bible there and pray. There were many possible close calls where a hitchhiker, an escapee, or a man would attempt to rob me, but God protected me through all of it, Hallelujah!

One such incident was about three o'clock in the morning and there was no traffic. Even the Highway Patrol radio in my booth had been perfectly silent since the last hourly security check, and it was quiet until a stranger who had emerged apparently from nearby shrubbery, appeared suddenly in front of me! He had the wildest look in his eyes and spoke with a snarly, taunting voice, but with authority.

Raising his arm he held his hand inches above my head. He said, "Don't be afraid, this will not hurt. You can ask the 'men in my unit'. (He was alone). I will crack your skull with one blow but I promise you will not feel a thing." He raised his hand and took a big breath!

Now the last vehicle that had passed through my toll booth earlier was a semi truck driver who had handed me a shiney, bright red apple as he reached down to get my ticket. We smiled and I had thanked him and set the apple on my cash register. Without taking my eyes off the intruder, I reached over and grabbed the apple. I shoved it in his face and commanded, *"Eat this!"*

The unkempt, wild-eyed pedestrian snatched the apple and sat down on the grass at the curb a few feet from the booth and began devouring it. I keyed my mic without him seeing me and spoke clearly on my sound system, which was also monitored in every toll station on the entire Interstate, was also heard in every patrol car from Miami to Wildwood, and scanners of many law enforcement agencies in the both Martin and Palm Beach Counties.

"10-24, 10-18, (and of course, including the original Jupiter Exit #), 10-24, 10-18"! Which was to say, "Trouble, Send Help! Hurry, Come Quickly!"

Just as my suspect tried to stand up a State Trooper car sped into the station and up onto the grass next to me, his blown patrol engine smoking and hissing violently, and leaped from his car with a drawn revolver he pointed at the man's head, shouting obcenities at him! Police radios all overstepping one another at once on my radio and scanner, indicated almost every cop on duty regardless of his agency was enroute or arriving all at once! My Trooper soon had a barage of backup that had assembled and surrounded us in record time.

The man laid in the grass on his face as they cuffed him and when his rap sheet was read over the radio the officers all assured me I had been in serious trouble. The man was not only wanted with multiple warrants for his arrest, but was a fugitive with a murder charge from a state penitentiary mental hospital in another state. I thanked God for helping me, for keeping me safe, and for the truck driver and his awesome, life-saving apple!

From that day forward my officer friends wanted to see me hired as a dispatcher at their own command centers and I began seriously studying police radio procedures, memorizing all the signals and codes. One day one of the state Florida Marine Patrol officers was driving thru my booth in his car pulling his patrol boat. There was no traffic in sight, and so he said, just out of the blue, "Ok, Luckey, give me signals and the 100 codes!" (not just the common codes, but all the extra ones everyone always had to look up to see what they meant, because almost nobody had ever learned them.

When I rattled them off by heart he was shocked, and immediately called his supervisor and arranged for an interview for me that very day. I was hired on the spot and dispatched for all the patrol boats, cars, helicopters and planes for six counties for five years, for Florida Maine Patrol District Six. The office for the district was conveniently, for me, located on Hwy US1 at the Palm Beach and Martin County line, in Jupiter, beside the tall radio tower.

That location, incidently was almost across the street from where Gary and I had first honeymooned and lived back in the first year we were married in 1960. Our romantic little trailer was parked by the Intracoastal Waterway with its turquois sparkling water, waving palm trees, and idyllic procession of yachts and sailboats. Little did I know that some twenty years later I would spend five years looking at that special tropical scene from my communications console beneath the tall radio tower on the corner of Countyline Road.

Before I left the turnpike various officers had supplied me with several knives, mace, a pistol, a detective special revolver, and a machete. But, it was my ol' standby I kept there from then on, my 12 gauge double barrell Remington shotgun I hid in the booth concealed by my raincoat. The revolver, I kept in my empty turnpike moneybag so that if a robber had said "Hand me your money!" I would have slipped my hand inside the open zipper, aimed, and confidently said, "Sure!" and shot right thru the bag. Well, that was my secret plan, anyhow. I never had to implement the plan, and actually, guns were off limits to turnpike personnel, according to the handbook. BUT, like the cops always say...."Well, would you rather be *carried* by six? Or would you rather be *tried* by six?" Food for thought.

Well, now I'll confess to a major mishap I pulled off right from the foyer of our house because a loaded rifle was leaning in the corner by the front door. Just as I was passing through the foyer I heard a hog or a deer running through the water in the yard down by the front gate following a bad rain that temporarily flooded the area down along the front fence, a pretty good distance from the house. But it was an umistakable sound, "ka-chow, ka-chow, ka-chow!" I reached over, grabbed the gun, opened the front door wide enough to see the fatest hog crossing our property! I fired once and it fell.

Gary was at work, Tifton at school, and so I managed to handle the very heavy, healthy bar hog (one who'd been castrated, enabling him to gain weight and be more flavorable), dragged him with a chain on my truck to the backyard. We had a children's old swing set I decided to hang him on. Before I did I took the post hole diggers and dug a hole under where the swing had been. Then I punctured a hole in each hind ankle, inserted the chain from the swing, hoisting it up above the hole in the ground.

When I gutted his belly, everything that needed to, fell into the hole and I used a shovel to fill it back up with. I skinned it and sectioned it placing the meat in heavy plastic bags, and into a large cooler in the back of my truck. I drove to a meat market at a grocery store in Indiantown, and for only fifteen dollars, the butcher had it all in neat little white packages he had labeled and dated! When I got it home I made several trips from the truck to the freezer, when Gary pulled up from work.

"Hey, Honey, where's that old hog you shot today? If its a boar I'm just going to haul it way out in the pasture in the palmettos. Otherwise, I better get busy cleaning it right now before it gets dark. I told him to go look in the freezer. "That's impossible!" he said. I just smiled sorta proudly like, at least until I learned what I'd done.

It was Tifton who broke the news to me. It was the neighbor man's prized pig he was raising and it got loose from the pen. He told him what I had done and that he would bring all the meat to him right away. He was a fine fella, and very neighborly, he understood how that could happen, he refused any meat or money, and said he was so tired of having to feed it every day, that it was for the best. He said he wanted our family to have it and enjoy it. He said anyone who could shoot a hog at that distance deserved it, and I sent him half the meat anyway. I had learned how to cut up wild meat just from having to help Gary my whole life, but that was my first time doing a hog alone, and from scratch.

I was a toll collector for the Florida Turnpike for five years before I began dispatching and working as a 911 operator. I dispatched for FMP (Florida Marine Patrol) for five years, Lake Park Police Department five years, Martin County Sheriff's Office, Indiantown Substation, five years, Okeechobee Sheriff's Office one year, and for two years I was a security guard in Nashville, TN. I worked for Seminole Indian Police Department twice for a total of five years, at Brighton Seminole Indian Reservation where I retired in 2004.

While I was with Lake Park Police I graduated from the Palm Beach Police Academy, without much help from their department. The supervisors in charge had fought to the finishline to keep female officers out, probably for similar reasons women were not allowed in combat or as regular members of various armed forces for so long, way back when.

I solved my own problem (after at least getting their approval to allow and sponsor my application), by paying my own way. Yes, budgeting had also been a factor with City Hall. My Lieutenant had an ongoing argument we teased about, that I better not graduate because then he would be required to hire me, and he wanted me to stay in dispatch. But my dear dad and husband wrote the checks and I was an official recruit in their six month school in Lake Worth, Florida, making high grades. I was nicknamed, at the academy gun range, *"Gran'maw Rambo" not* because my scores were that good, but mainly because I was the oldest woman to graduate.

I gotta tell you about one funny story when I appeared for my first day as a police rooky. I was met with one of the Sargeants who would be riding in my patrol car with me for a probationary period. This would be the norm for the next few weeks and would depend on how long they felt I would need to prove myself, and get acclimated to my new position.

Of course everything I did he watched with eagle eyes and waiting for any moment of opportunity to supervise. I guess I gave him none. My first call was a man slumped over in his car at Dunkin' Donuts. I saw my supervisor rolling his eyes at the traffic fearfully as I sped through town with my lights flashing and siren blaring, at the same time giving information on the radio. I knew he wanted in the worst way to ask me to slow down, but he didn't. I loved it! I was thinking, "Thank you, Lord, I'm really cut out for this, huh!"

I pulled up to the reported car and my Sargeant watched me go up to it first. Reaching down through the opened window I took the man's pulse as I held his cold wrist and at the same time radioed dispatch for an ambulance for a possible signal seven, (deceased person). My Sargeant looked white as a sheet and seemed to stammer a little the rest of the morning.

Day two: The same Sargeant assigned to me said, "Luckey, yesterday, if I appeared a little shaken I will share with you that in all my years here in this agency, that was the first call I have been on (given to him on the radio or his officer he was riding with, who was in training), that the person was deceased, as hard as that might be to believe. I just want you to know we are proud you did everything correctly and professionally." Whew, I signed with relief. Then, at that very moment, the first call of the day came in, so I answered.

The dispatcher said, "Possible signal four (car accident) inside Kmart parking lot. " I responded that we were "10-51, 10-97" Enroute *and* had arrived. (I was almost there already). I spotted the car that had driven into a parked car, opened the driver's door, and radioed in, that I had a possible heart attack victim who needed an ambulance 10-18! I opened the door, leaned into the vehicle well prepared to begin any necessary emergency CPR but discovered an older deceased gentleman who had already expired with unmistakable evidence to that affect. I updated my code on the radio to possible signal seven. I looked around for my Sargeant who was on the radio in my patrol car.

Day three: I waited in the patrol car for my acting supervisor to come out of the station and join me for another day of "training". Instead of getting into my car, my Lieutenant came to my open window. "Luckey, you'll be riding solo today. You're doing fine. Sarg says he might be supersticious, but he can't take a chance riding again with someone named "Luckey" and have another person die on us three days in a row!" If you have any problems, call me". Yippee! My probation was over.

I'll never forget the day one of the local police chiefs (another one of the good ole boys who wanted the force kept male), was visiting with one of our detectives at our station and saw me for the first time in my police uniform with gun belt, etc. He stopped what he had been saying to the man and shouted, "Luckey! Is that you? Who in their right mind let the fox into the henhouse!?!" He was kidding, of course, but that's the sort of stuff we gals had to put up with back in the day.

After I had been on the road a few months I got a call of two angry, intoxicated black males in a bad fist fight in their front yard inside my zone. The caller had said they were fixin' to kill each other.

I was the first to arrive. My Sargeant and Lieutenant were on their way, as well, but they were coming from some distance, so I got out of my patrol car and yelled at the two of them. I pointed to one and said, "Break it up, go stand by that tree! And you (I pointed to his "buddy", I said), "You, go stand over by *that* tree!" as I pointed to a different tree close by. They sheepishly hung their heads when my superiors confronted them minutes later. The two were local men with long rap sheets and my backup said they never drove through town so fast before. My Lieutenant asked them why they were obedient as to do what I said so quickly.

The older man said, "Any lady wild enough to break up me and him?....is wild enough to use that gun she got on her hip!"

Back at the academy I had attempted to help a new recruit, a young, pretty African-American girl who was smart as a whip, and a great shot with her revolver, but who, for some reason, she could not explain, was just terrified of shotguns. One of the instructors at the range had suggested once that I might try to help out and maybe encourage her.

We became good friends while she was there and when she expressed her fear of shotguns I told her that she had so much going for her that I could see her rising up in the ranks in police work and not to allow *any* ole gun to hold her back. She knew the technicalities of the gun but when she stood in front of a target with ear covers, goggles, and an instructor beside her, her knees would shake, and her hands would sweat. She truly was horrified at the prospects of shooting a shotgun!

I think it was my attempt to show her how to attack the gun boldly, fearlessly, and with more aggression, even if she needed to pretend, or fake it, that caused me to, more than do my best when it was my time to qualify, and with the girl and everyone there watching, I tried to set an example for her. Anyhow, I was so sad to hear she was no longer in the class and that she had withdrawn from the academy. I felt very disappointed for her and knew that it was law enforcement's loss.

We had started the class with twelve female recruits and maybe twentyfive men, and now were finishing with a fraction that amount. Test scores, skills and so many factors that made up our grades proved the various ways they eliminated the women, *and* men, police departments were actually needing all over the country. I would frequently hear the fellas, though, almost boasting about how many gals were dropping like flies, so to speak. I tried not to be resentful but thankful that I was still succeeding and I knew it was because of my strong faith in my God.

After all, He caused all the miracles recorded in the Bible, times when He allowed little David's small stone to kill the giant, or when out numbered armies became the victors, or when He caused the Red Sea to part and the enemy became swallowed up in it after God's followers were safely through! I felt the presence of God with me all through the academy and whenever I would excell on the range, for instance, I knew He was answering my prayers and it was He who was giving me a good eye and a steady hand. It also helped that I had never smoked and didn't drink, unlike most of the recruits.

One of the excercises required at the academy, was similar to the one I would later become certified in at a Clearwater Beach Specialized Training Conference for Female Officers. The last test responsible for a final score, was held in a very large gymnasium and was sponsored and manned by the Florida Department of Law Enforcement and the FBI. The obstacle course contained a maze of situations an officer might encounter in a building, in an alley, in a house, in the woods, etc., and several administrators of the challenge were stationed discreetly out of sight and would suddenly attack with various weapons. None of the recruits had a weapon, aside from the examination excercizes we were given with our night sticks, or side handled batons. We had to learn to out-fight, outwit, or overcome our apponant at any given phase of the manuever including taking away his or her weapon.

The maze began as one person at a time, entered one end of the gym and working your way through all the various scenarios, you were to make it across to the exit door at the opposite end of the gym. I prayed so hard as I managed each encounter, that I no longer felt any blows or hits from my opponants and I seemed to simply automatically, without thinking about it, propell myself to the next challenge. I remember trying to run as fast as I could between conflicts and do each combat as swiftly as possible, well, we were also being timed.

I recall once that I was almost through, but thinking I might not hold out and began to feel weaker than before. That's when I said, *"Jesus, You take it now and bring me through by Your power, not my own!"* In another moment I remember saying, *"**Jesus, help me!** Remind me at this moment* how I am **Your** *Warrior,* and then I went and added with an *audible* shout, *"I'm Your redneck, wild woman, Mohawk Warrior"* and I absolutely plowed into some officer who looked at me with eyes wide open and seemingly unsure which tactic was going to be needed next! I remember grunting, growling, and then finally shouting a victorious *"Hallelujah!!!"* as an FBI man held open the gym door for me to run out! I remember him saying, "You made it!" I could hear other recruits cussing throughout the routine from various parts of the gym, but one of the recruits said, "Yeah I could, too, but I also could hear Luckey praising God at the top of her lungs all through it!" Lol, Thank You, Jesus!

I was 43 years old when I graduated the first time (Palm Beach Academy), and 52 when I graduated (Indian River Police academy) the second time. Martin County Sheriff Bob Crowder had told me it wasn't required since I was already certified, but that if I wanted to join the other posse members I was welcomed to and the county would pay for it, we'd be bonded, and it would also update all the different categories of my training certification with the latest information, so I did.

The instructors at my first graduation had asked me to share a brief devotion and to pray at the start of the ceremony. I "preached" on Romans 13, that's the Scripture instructing us to obey those in authority because, as the First Nations Version (FNV) Bible words it, "The Great Spirit is over all the powers and authorities that rule the lands. Since He is the One who created them to serve His purposes by providing protection and order for all..."and it goes on to instruct police in authority that they are "the Creator's servants against evil doers." Romans 13 KJV: "Let every soul be subject unto the higher powers. For there is no power but of God; the powers that be are ordained of God."

It was a pretty intense pep rally in Spiritual Warfare, but, maybe over the heads of many there, so to speak. My preacher-daddy who was in attendance to see me graduate, said he had never been so proud and said many of the graduates looked surprised to hear me read the Bible speaking of law enforcers as "God's forces"!

Well, it pleased me to make my dear daddy proud but I have to admit what was even more profound to me, was when I heard it said by many officers for years to come, what they heard said about me at a mass meeting of all the heads of the Sheriff departments, the Sheriffs, police agencies, and their Chiefs, who were all attending a huge meeting jointly. Well, included on the stage at the podium was the head Director of the whole academy.

They say there was a question and answer period in which my name came up. Remember south Florida was smaller then and all the agencies were a fraction the size they have since grown to be. It was known that I was graduated from the first academy that included women for the first time and that I was also the oldest female to finish the difficult school successfully. It has since been said they *made* our class more difficult purposefully, to ensure female applicants could pass the tests and qualify to be officers, (or could not, maybe?).

The Police Chief from Palm Beach Gardens asked in front of the crowd, "Tell us how Betty Luckey did in the academy, just how well did she score at the range?" They say everyone listened up with interest.

I was so shocked at his reply, and admittedly, it was also with tremendous relief, (I mean you have to know how hard I'd worked at it with God's help just to get *into* the academy, much less graduate) :

The Director announced, "Luckey was average...**but *she's hades with a shotgun!*"** *(I had to chuckle to myself remembering how desparately, and yet, unbeknown to the others, I was trying to encourage and inspire my young friend there that day!)*

When I think of all the many meetings I atttended in law enforcement and classes in which there were officers enrolled who represented all the various agencies, I recall the funniest thing I ever heard one of the instructors say. He announced that it was twelve o'clock and time to break for lunch. He added, "For all you Sheriff deputies, it's high noon!" He said, "Now you must be back here in exactly one hour and in your seats!"

He said, " That is one o'clock for all of you police officers! That's 1300 hours for all you Marine Patrolman and State Troopers! For all you game wardens, that's when the big hand is on the 12 and the little hand is on the one!"

It would be so many years later as I was in my early seventies and we drove over to eat at Gary's cousin's restaurant in Lehigh Acres, FL, near LaBelle. We were disappointed that Diane and her husband Bill Harrell were off that night, but pleased the restaurant was packed and every table taken. As soon as we arrived a young couple got up to leave and we didn't have to wait for a seat. The place was filled with all ages, no children, mainly just middle aged and retired couples, all happily enjoying their delicious meals, when there was a ruckas at a table in the corner.

It was a table filled with several males in their late teens to mid-twenties, I'd guess. They were getting louder and louder and the patrons got more quiet by the second as we listened to their gang-like manner, abusive conversations and offensive language. They were chiding one another with descriptive filty phrases in a mean, teasing, and tauntingly ugly argument that seemed to become more agressive by the moment.

I took a quick inventory of the men in the room, all of whom were looking away from the direction of the unruly young fellas. I'm certain, they were embarrassed their wives were exposed to such conduct, and I decided there were no apparent able bodied vets in the room, nor was there law enforcement, and the waitress staff too busy to probably notice. I thought how that would never happen had Billy been there. He and Diane provided the finest restaurant in town, always very Christian and frequently featuring Gospel music. I decided if anyone was going to defuse a potentially explosive situation in their fine establishment, it was probably going to have to be me.

As soon as their language became incredably sacreligious with profanity of the foulist nature, including the name of my precious Jesus, I had enough! Leaving my purse at the table with Gary, which he knew was containing my loaded revolver inside, I walked empty handed over to the boisterous group and instantly everything in the restaurant came to a silent halt. Gary said every eye was on me as I went and stood eye to eye in front of the biggest, the oldest guy in their group. He was tall and heavy and I felt like little David before the mean, bad giant. I spoke softly and directed everything I said only to the big guy. Talk about shocked, now he looked *shocked!*

The other six or seven men looked wide eyed at the woman who had such gall as to come up to their table that way. I knew the men were probably on some drug that had them very hopped up, but I also knew they could be capable of anything. I said to him nicely, maybe gently, but firmly, "There are ladies in this room who have never heard such talk as this before in their whole lives. This is a Godly restaurant and we need to respect the people here tonight who are trying to just enjoy a quiet evening meal with their wives. Do you think you can help me out here a little bit, Sir?"

He nodded very slowly and stared at me like his old grandmaw had just popped into the room out of no where, and he said to me, "Yes ma'am". I whispered, "Thanks," and made my way back to my table where Gary sat with his hand on my now *unzipped* purse.

The gang members spoke softly amongst themselves for a minute then, much to the relief of everyone, they simply piled out the front door leaving cash on their table. As each couple left the restaurant, some thanked me, some patted me on the shoulder, but I think all of the patrons at least nodded, waved or smiled at us. I thanked the Lord that He is faithful when we boldly and bravely with **His** power, authority and guidance, trust and *obey **Him**, as **His warriors.***

One day at Lucky Buck Ranch we thought we heard several pickup trucks pull up into our yard at the same time. Each truck had several young men inside wearing western shirts or tee shirts, and baseball type caps on their heads. I recognized only a couple of them, the rest seemed like they were from out of town. The men in the first truck were getting out and stood waiting beside their truck, as I watched Gary, carrying his loaded 12 gauge, walk out the front door to join them. I supposed he'd taken his gun with him when he hadn't recognized them.

After they spoke for only a few short minutes the men drove off and Gary waited till he saw the last truck drive out our gate, to come back in the house. The girls were curious and all asked him at once, "What was that, Daddy!?" "That was the local KKK, kids," he explained. They were looking for a big pasture to hold a big rally in soon and willing to pay real good money to use it. However, by the time Gary gave them his personal opinion of racial equality, probably, and announced he had a membership application in at Temple Israel in West Palm Beach, they got the message that he never wished to be asked such a thing again. We were proud of him.

There would be an incident once I would report to the Sheriff's Department when a man we'd known most all his life, had called the house to speak with Gary about a hunting trip. The man was not the least bit sober and when he attempted to leave a message with my daughter, he was very crude and innappropriate when he spoke to her. Minutes later he was driving up to our house, and already knowing my husband wasn't at home, probably thinking I wasn't either. I went out my front door with a loaded double barrell shotgun and commanded him to get off my property and never ever return or I would shoot him. He circled around and left through the gate.

I didn't learn until later that Tifton had gone to his room for his gun and was hiding on Niki's front bedroom floor by her low open window watching intently the exchange out in front, gun barrell propped on the marble tiled window sill, with the man in his sights. I unknowingly, had young, but quite capable, backup "at the ready" and in place, had there been trouble. Kind of reminds you of what pioneer families experienced in the old wild west stories. When you live way out in isolated remote areas in the country, you have to be your own security, because it takes too long for the law to get there! I thank God that He is always here with us.

On two other occasions I knew of Gary to hold his ground and refuse to become involved in drug drops in his pastures from aircraft. I had said, "Wow, that must have been tempting, wasn't it, to turn down all that money?" Why it was certainly enough to buy a lot of land with and he would have never needed to ever lease grazing land again. In fact, it was common knowledge that there were cattlemen who had made their millions in exactly that manner.

"Tempting?" Gary asked, shaking his head, and then answered me, "Nope! Just say, 'Nope to dope'!" It was Gary who was no "dope" and he would firmly stand his ground on all his political and religious beliefs regardless of the opposing arguments or pressure. He was an example to me to always try to be more like him that way.

Gary was firm in his ways with or without his shotguns, though. I truly believe he would have been a great fighter had he enlisted in the armed forces.(It was a "water-on-the-knee" old broken bottle injury, that had kept him out). His daddy, James Franklin Luckey, who was nicknamed, "Red" for his temperous attitudes at times, if he was threatened, still had a reputation among the LaBelle old timers who were still living, that he was not to be messed with.

His great grandfather was Samuel Anthony Luckey, Sr., (June 16, 1846-May 27, 1925). He had lied about his age to become a (wounded)

Confederate soldier (and as inscribed on his Ft. Myers CSA (Confederate States of America tombstone), he served as a Private in Company C, 51st Georgia Infantry, enlisting when he was only sixteen. "Luckey's had Stamina", that was how a newspaper once headlined their story of the Luckey family bravery and determination.

You know what? God put me and Gary together as a real pair, let me tell you! lol. I came out of the bloodline of John Weakland, a pioneer who married an Indian and was ready to fight off a band of angry men with a fence rail singlehandedly, to save the life of the local Catholic priest, depicted in stained glass windows of a church to prove his heroism to this day!

My Swedish daddy, who was always set firmly in the ways of God, brave enough to stomp on top of a coiled up rattlesnake to protect a hundred kids in Vacation Bible School! Those two ancestors hadn't needed a shotgun either! God calls on us to be warriors. He also equipts us and trains us, and works through us to defeat our enemies. He instructs us to be brave and fearless.

Our weapons are not carnal but spiritual, by the pulling down of strongholds. By the power of the Holy Spirit we bravely march to battle and aim at the enemy as you do with a shotgun, using God's Spiritual arsenal, firing efficiently against evil, the waring targets who come against us, our families and generation, and God's Kingdom, and the weapons include prayer and love! "What shall we then say to these things? If God be for us, *who can be against us? (Romans 8:31 KJV)*

OK, one more shotgun story and I might be through.

One day, it was a special day, the Florida Game Commission labeled it the annual "Doe Day". That meant, because for conservation reasons, it was adventageous to eliminate a substantial amount of deer to offset the over bred deer population statewide. It would be legal to kill does, usually forbidden, in certain areas under certain conditions, for one day only. Well, because Gary wasn't feeling good and seemed a bit weak and shakey for several days and was on medicine, I decided I didn't like the idea he was going out to our Two Creeks Ranch in Venus, on Fisheating Creek, to hunt for does that day by himself. I decided to ride along just to keep him company.

We got out to the creek before light and I sat with him against a tree in the dark while the mosquitoes buzzed around our ears and got stuck in my mascara. I was happy when it got toward dawn and I could see movement on the other side of the creek. First one deer was visible, followed by a second one, and then a third. My heart raced faster and I could tell Gary's "buck fever" was full on, that's when your excitement at a deer causes a rush that can interupt your normal shooting ability and sometimes prevent a steady hand.

I was thrilled to realize that we would indeed be able to leave with venison for our freezer and I could imagine the heavenly smell of my frying backstrap in my cast iron pan already! Just then Gary shot, perhaps prematurely, but he missed, probably because it was difficult in the pre-dawn fog to see that well. I could barely make out the three deer as they scampered off and Gary laid his gun down on the ground. So determined not to miss out on the steak dinner, I grabbed up his shortgun, and leaned against the tree, saying "Please Jesus, help me in Your Precious Name!" just in time to see the deer run past back in the opposite direction and I was able to pick them off one at a time as they went by, the first one, then the second one, and then miraculously, the third one! "Thank You, Jesus"! I said. "Thank you, Betty,"! I heard Gary say, as he took the shotgun from me and more shells, and then went chasing across the shallow creek water following after them.

One at a time he located where they dropped and I heard each shot to their heads as he successfully finished them off! Not long afterwards he had all three in the back of the truck, ready to start skinning them at the camphouse. I heard him on his cell phone telling Tifton, "So, I sure was glad your mama was with me. She hates killing a doe...but *she's hades with a shotgun!*"

"Author with her youngest daughter Niki"

CHAPTER FOURTEEN

THE STRAWBERRY CANDLE

"Even though we are walking in weak human bodies, we are not
fighting with human strength. We do not make war in the ways of
*this world. Our weapons have **Creator's power** to break through and*
tear down strongholds. These strongholds are high-minded and wrong
ideas about the Great Spirit and His ways." IICorinthians 10:3-4
First Nations Version

There was one particular night when everyone had fallen asleep and I went through the house turning out the lights and felt as though I was being watched. Then as I hurried down a hallway *I knew* I was being followed, as well, and even though the intruder was unseen and from another dimension, a different realm than my own, he was directly behind me and at my heels. I knew without seeing him he was male, had red eyes, and a desire to have me dead. This thing wanted me dead and had come to do it and I knew I had only a couple more minutes to figure out how to stop it.

This had all begun at a time late in the evening, as I looked forward to getting to bed, but with a very happy and contented mind, I was at peace and was glad to have just finished last minute touches cleaning up my kitchen for the night. This surprising event was just sort of out of the blue, and certainly, unexpected.

At first, I was prone to yell ahead to my husband to come help me, when the reality began to sink in: there was nothing Gary was going to be able to do to protect me or the family. The "thing" was bigger, stronger, "seemingly" a lot more powerful than we were! In spite of being unable to see him with my natural eyes, he was more real than if I had been able to actually look at him. I began a warfare prayer to God and asked Jesus to come help me quickly!

I could tell he was an evil entity taller than my roof, yet able to accompany me from room to room as if his eyes were close behind, perhaps only inches from the back of my head. Glancing in at my children as I passed their open bedroom doors, I was so relieved they were peacefully sleeping. I scurried even faster into our room where Gary was alseep and slightly snoring. I quickly checked the corner beside him to be sure his loaded shotgun was in its place where he always kept it perched against the wall. I rushed around the side of the bed to grab it when the Holy Spirit stopped me in my tracks. He reminded me that my Bible was directly beside me on the dresser.

The Lord reminded me that no gun, nor any kind of weapon, would be sufficient to stop the evil spirit in my room that wanted me eliminated. Or, if it wasn't to take my life, it wanted to terrorize me. However, He assured me that the weapon He was providing me was all I needed! My Bible.

I was now backed up in another corner of the room by what I perceived as a most chilling, obnoxious, forboding, murderous, and inescapable monster of Satan's demonic kingdom, who was looming powerfully over me and I grabbed my Bible, whirled around to face him head on, and holding my opened Bible toward a hideous face I refused to look at, I did only one thing:

I bravely held the Bible toward his red eyes and tipping it slightly to see the verse I'd randomly flipped open to, I read aloud with a strong and commanding voice (that made Gary suddenly sit up in bed wide awake!), I simply, but loudly, declared the words I had opened to....*"Fear not, for I am with you!"* (Isaiah 41:10a NKJV). Those seven words alone were mightier than a shotgun blast!

Immediately, it disappeared. Gone! I hugged my Bible to my chest. Rubbing his eyes, Gary said softly, smiling, "Well Honey, that's comforting, I'm not afraid of anything and I'm glad you're here."

"Not *me,!*" I said, "The **Lord** is with us! You didn't see that thing in the room right here?" I asked him. Then, I noticed he glanced back to be sure his gun was there, and said, "See what?" I noticed he got up and carrying his double barrel, and then walked through every room before returning to his bed.

It was not the first time and it would not be the last event in our life where there were things we "saw" or wanted to handle, quite differently; but, the most serious of those I am fixing to tell you about. Before Gary died in 2020, he gave me permission to share this with you, "in hopes it helps someone else, or saves a life," he had said. This time it would still be a strong faith, that would be required, and God would be faithful to deliver us from a far more sinister evil attempting to infiltrate in our lives. It also involves a request I put out to God, for a sign from Him, like a fleece (in the Bible), and includes *a little strawberry candle.*

It was New Years Eve 1971 and I wanted so badly to go to church to attend my dad's annual midnight candlelight service. When I tried to talk Gary into going he said he was too sleepy to ride into town, but he smiled at me and teased that if I would come "tuck him in bed" first, then it was ok with him if I went alone. At the prayer service I thanked the Lord for my family and God's many overflowing blessings on our life together. Little did I know at that moment how mightily He was *still* blessing us for real!

It was during this period of time that Gary was probably battling personally in ways, most folks, never realized he was. He was successfully juggling his career at Pratt Whitney Aircraft, where he had already been employed for over ten years, while paying for a house in town, pasture leases, cattle purchases, land to build on, and trying to hunt and fish in between just to keep meat on the table. He was working very hard to get ahead, and I was very proud of him.

Other men in his department loved their weekends off so Gary took advantage of lots of available overtime working six days a week! He loved it even when he worked holidays because it meant the pay was time and a half, sometimes double, but, it also meant that he didn't have days off hardly ever. Yep, he was probably burnt out; but, that old Luckey stamina, made him so motivated and determined, it didn't show. Well, in some ways, it guess it had started to show.

Gary was also battling at that time his personal faith in God, and on some days he expressed atheistic views and some days he was agnostic. Some days you'd hear him singing favorite hymns at the top of his lungs, other days he sounded grumpy and he'd make an extra trip to the gas station for beer. Looking back, with what I know more about now, there was a real battle for his soul going on.

I knew he was struggling in many ways, and besides prayer, the secret to keeping the boat afloat was to make sure every bill was always paid on time and good records were kept, and the checkbook balanced. We had already eliminated charge cards and buying sprees, and lived on a tighter budget than our friends and relatives. It had always been his plan to become a millionaire, but getting there was becoming harder than he thought.

No other man I knew of with three children was even attempting to manage what he was, so when the day came and I so happily announced I was expecting again, to my shock, my loving Gary was not so loving or happy. However, he took it far more seriously than I ever expected he was capable of. I knew he had always had a more liberal view of abortion, unlike myself, who had no tolerance at all for acceptance.

I spent so many days of crying, and trying to convince him I had not missed a birth control pill on purpose, which he was accusing me of doing. I was begging him to let me keep the baby, praying, fasting, and mourning over what he was trying to require me to do. He still returned home from work one afternoon and handed me several thousand dollars he'd just borrowed from the credit union. "Betty," he said putting the money in my hand, "This should cover an abortion in New York City (they were illegal in Florida), where you can stay in Jamestown with your Aunt Betty, your air flight, and expenses, this should cover it. I'll keep the kids. Its either an abortion or a divorce. I can barely manage financially with three children, and four would put a halt to everything I'm working to accomplish." My heart broke, he was believing Satan's lies.

I drove to town to my mother and dad, who held me, wept with me and prayed. It was my mother who took me gently by the shoulders and looked deeply into my bloodshot eyes. "My dearest, Betty Winsom, your first committment has been to a husband with a holy promise to obey for better **or** *for worse*, and I have the faith to believe that when you make the trip to New York, you will *by faith* obey your husband, and *we will completely trust God to take loving care of our precious baby, as He wills.*"

We three agreed in prayer and I wiped my tears and could hardly wait to return home just to hold each one of my children tightly in my arms. It was inconceivable to imagine living life without any one of them. I already felt the same way about the child in my womb. I loved that baby already and I knew in my heart I'd let no one harm him or her.

It was the darkest of days for me even just knowing my own husband, my other half, could consider such a thing, even more, I was shocked he could even conceive of planning it. I was horrified that he would expect me to have to agree to it, was another thing. Would I have actually gone through with it? I'll tell you in a minute.

I know what it feels like to *fly* and to *cry* nonstop from Florida to New York State with very kind airline stewardesses trying everything in their power to help comfort you, all the way there, in every way. I never did turn loose of my candle. At the Palm Beach International Airport, my brother, Lars, ("Chip"), had ridden with me and my parents to drop me off. Some would call him a hippie, maybe, with his anti-war army jacket with its peace signs on it and his hair, which was longer than my own. He had given me a parting gift, a token of his love and concern, to have with me, that somehow said it all, a small, pinkish red candle that smelled so good, like fresh strawberries.

That little candle expressed to me that what my brother was trying to say was this: "I love you, Betty, I know you are broken hearted, and I will be thinking about you and praying for you about *everything.*" Actually, my brother will never know how much it meant to me that day to feel his sincere compassion and thoughtfulness.

In Jamestown, my Aunt Betty and both of my grandmothers hugged me and assured me of their prayer support, and thankfully, in no way showed any signs of condemnation at the unthinkable and unspeakable thing I was there to do. We did not discuss the procedure or even the scheduled trip into the city the next day, although everybody knew. Looking back, *it was obvious we were all expecting God to come through with a true modern day miracle for His Glory!*

At Aunt Betty's beautiful colonial white brick home filled with antiques, she showed me to her guest bedroom upstairs and set my suitcase by the closet and I set the candle and a matchbook on a small vintage saucer on the bedstand. We had just enjoyed a delightful supper with my grandmothers and I declined the dessert Betty had just offered me in her country kitchen. I told her I decided to spend some time in prayer before bed and I'd try to sleep to be fresh in the morning for our early trip into New York City. She hugged me tightly and prayed with me, reminded me of the phone beside the bed, and said good night.

My Florida obstetrician's office had provided the information for a respectable doctor in the state for abortions and through their recommendation, they had made my appointment for me, at ten the following morning. All I knew was that I was taking one day, and one hour at a time and giving the Lord a chance to work or time for Gary to change his mind.

I'm positive I would have canceled the appointment and returned to Florida with my baby still safely secured within me. I would have given Gary his money back and told him if he wanted a divorce, well, now he had the cash to do it. I had learned, though, that sometimes, God likes to *wait till the last minute*, so I was willing to go through all these motions, if in some event, by some chance, or by some awesome miracle, Gary would have a new heart. That, to me, would be our best solution all around, and I knew Gary needed a Spiritual breakthrough in his life. So I acted totally in faith.

I'm sure there were many times before, when I had petitioned my Creator in prayer with requests so heavy that the pain was almost unbearable, but I assure you, none had ever been as deeply agonizing as this one. "Please God Almighty, I am lighting this little strawberry candle **and before the flame burns out**, I beg You, in Jesus' precious name, to show me unmistakenly, a sign, that I am NOT to have an abortion tomorrow! Please forgive me for coming this far, and I would proceed with it only if that is Your will, but I know it is not."

My prayer continued, "Please may Your will be done and You have Your way with me and my new baby. Please even take my life along with this child, if *that* would be Your holy will, for I am willing and desiring in my heart to stay with my baby, no matter what! You know I have no murder in my heart. I have faith to believe that it is Your will I live and that my baby will live, but I must hear from You, O God, and I now put the two of us in Your mighty and powerful hands. I now place my Gary there as well, for your will in his life. I am thanking You ahead of time, in Jesus' name. Amen, Amen, and Amen!"

I wept as I continued to gaze at the yellow fire and its golden light that reflected across the darkened room. I kept praying for my husband and my children at home, I prayed thanksgiving and I prayed praises to Him, the God we can *trust*! The candle was now a pretty little pink puddle in a floral china dish, as I watched the amber glowing flame begin to flicker..... *when the phone rang!*

I heard Aunt Betty call me from downstairs, "Betty, its for you, pick up, its Gary calling!" I could hardly speak and he heard my sobs. All I could say was, "Hey".

He said, "Betty, I have a lot to tell you, but let me start by letting you know our daughter Libby is OK. There has been a terrible accident tonight but I'm here at the hospital with Libby, and she's not hurt, just some scrapes and bruises." And then I heard clearly God speak next:

"You see, Betty, it is I, who GIVE and take life, NOT YOU"! I immediately told Gary what I had just heard the Lord say, and I burst into tears of joy!

Gary continued on with all the details of the accident in West Palm Beach that had happened within the past hour or so. My cousin Cathy had been driving with her little boy, Lloyd, and had our eight year old Libby with her, when she wrecked at a four way stop and rolled her VW bus. They were all ok and were being checked out there in the emergency room.

When they had rolled the van they were unable to open any of the smashed doorways and were trapped inside with the engine on fire. They could hear people yelling to warn everyone to get back away from the flames because the engine could be about to blow. People could see the three of them trapped inside but could do nothing. Everyone in the crowd that had gathered ran back to a safer distance.

Just then an off duty fireman from Riviera Beach, Rufus Blue, a very strong looking black man, they said, leaped from his vehicle and with his bare fist, beat in the windows, and got all three of them safely to a far corner of the intersection. It was then that they heard the blast of the loud explosion they had just been so miraculously rescued from! Thanks be to God for sending Rufus! Hallelujah!

I told Gary I would be canceling my appointment and be flying home, and to have my folks meet me at the airport; but, he said no, he would be there himself to pick me up and our wonderful, newest addition to our growing family! We both cried together on the phone and Gary said he was so sorry and could not believe how he could have made such an awful decision. Talk about a last minute "reality check"! I assured him we were both forgiven and that the experience was going to make us better parents and better human beings than we would have been otherwise, and I knew it was certainly already causing me to be a better person, mother, and a much better follower of Jesus than ever before.

Needless to say, our wonderful Niki, born October 1, 1971, (exactly nine months from my New Year's Eve prayers), was the 'apple of her daddy's eye', as the saying goes. He loved all his children equally the same, with the strongest most genuinely devout fatherly love I'd ever seen in a man for his children, but I will never forget that awesome special sparkle I'd always noticed in his eyes when he looked at his precious, youngest little girl, Niki Lynn! As we watched her fall in love and marry Brad and have two great kids of their own, Ernie and Daphne, I could not thank God enough for all our lives and His blessings on them.

As I watched Niki and Brad working hard, getting their Master's degrees and teaching in colleges as professors, purchasing property and fine homes, raising their children, each one with their own skills and talents and accomplishments, I beam with pride, I just can't help it. But thanks, (and credit where credit is due), my sincere thanks is to God, for it was He alone, who gave life to all of us! I am also thankful he created us as parents to use, to make it all happen.

I could never imagine my life without my Nikole, or Ernie and Daphne! They have made my life complete and the love they have for me, alone, makes my life worth living. I love the song "Because He Lives", which is about Jesus but is also appropriate for my Strawberry Candle baby. Written by Bill and Gloria Gaither in the late 1960's, note the lyrics on the second verse:

"How sweet to hold, a newborn baby, and feel the pride, and the joy (she) he gives, But greater still, that calm assurance:We can face uncertain days, Because He lives

Because He lives, I can face tomorrow. Because He lives, all fear is gone!

Because I know, I know, He holds the future. And life is worth the living, just Because He lives!"

One day when Niki was about twelve, we were going into Sears Roebuck store at the old Twin City Mall in North Palm Beach, and as I was walking behind her I saw what a beautiful young lady she was becoming. I felt pretty much righteously indignant toward a couple of boys who were turning to watch her, and especially at a grown man I saw who, also, was looking at her. Just then she said, "Oh..look mom, a strawberry candle!" as she smelled it then set it back down on the counter, "I just *love* strawberry candles!" she added. I had never told her about the one I'd had, "once upon a time," and I was so glad she hadn't looked up to see the tear I had to wipe from my cheek. But it was a tear of joy.

I believe that old enemy was at work in my life and Gary's, attempting to deceive us by trying to take life, joy, and our faith away from us, but God used a weapon that overcame what plan the devil had, with a far greater weapon, His Holy Word (the Bible), patience, prayer, faith and trust in Him, and....love, God's love. Oh, how I love my Niki, and is she a delight to me!

JESUS SAID:

"It is not the will of your Father which is in Heaven, that one of these little ones should perish! "Matthew 18:14 KJV

"Whoever receives one such little child in My name receiveth Me and whosoever offends one of these little ones which believeth in Me, It were better for him that a millstone were hanged about his neck and that he were drowned in the depth of the sea!" Matthew 18:5,6 KJV

"Florida Alligator photo taken by Seminole Tribal Member Allen Huff"

CHAPTER FIFTEEN

WILD MAN OF THE LOXAHATCHEE RIVER

———◆◆◆———

*"For the Word of the Great Spirit is alive, powerful, and sharper than
any two-edge long knife. His Word cuts deep into the inner being,
separating soul from spirit and joints from marrow. His Word uncovers
the true nature of the human heart, its thoughts and intentions"*
Hebrews 4:12, First Nations Version

I told you in the previous chapter what had happened one night when I was pursued through my house by an evil spirit and cornered in my bedroom desparately needing a weapon to defend myself. It was the Bible I had grabbed and flipped open to what became my battle cry! Without looking for a verse, I had turned to face my terrorist and read the verse I'd miraculously opened to! It proclaimed God was there with me and when I held my Bible up toward the spirit and speaking from it loudly and fearlessly, read the words, **"Fear not, for I am with you!"** (From Isaiah 41:10 NKJV) The demonic entity immediately and instantly disappeared. The exact wording in the Isaiah 41:10 (KJV) King James Version is: "Fear thou not; for I am with thee; be not dismayed; for I am thy God: I will strengthen thee;

yea, I will help thee; yea, I will uphold thee with the right hand of my righteousness."

That would be a prime example I had learned, in how to sometimes deal with an unseen spirit or demon. Remember when the devil tried to tempt Jesus, Jesus said to him, "The Lord rebuke you, Satan!" (From Zechariah 3:2 KJV). The devil was not afraid of Betty Luckey, but he was terrified of God's Word! Mother always had a plaque on her wall, *"Satan trembles when he sees, the weakest saint upon his knees!"*

I knew way back in my teens that the Word of God not only terrifies a demon, it can cause even the strongest, rough and tough, grown man in the flesh, to run! I'm fixin' to tell you about the "wild man of the Loxahatchee," Trapper Nelson.

Trapper had many names. He was also known as the Tarzan of the Loxahatchee. Tarzan, because he lived in his handmade log cabin he made from trees he had personally felled with an axe on more than 800 acres he owned along the Loxahatchee River near Jupiter, Florida. He would be labeled Tarzan in countless magazines who always had him pictured tanned and bare chested.

His property was a pristine tropical paradise on undeveloped or uninhabited property so private and isolated Trapper could bathe nude in the river, hunt, fish, trap, and garden wearing nothing but khaki shorts, barefooted, year 'round. He lived off the land, selling skins and hides from wild animals.

He would one day take advantage of his unique opportunity to allow the public into his world, who had come by boat to reach it, and pay good money to see the animals he trapped, watch him wrestle alligators, and allow them some recreational pavillions, picnic tables, and hammocks to rest in. He named his place, "Trapper's Zoo and Tropical Garden". He not only drew the curious public but Hollywood celebrities including Gary Cooper, and Palm Beach socialites.

It was the later group who were infatuated with his rugged handsomeness and Tarzan appeal, and they say he was frequently asked for dinner by the affluent "Janes" from around the world who wanted to meet him. He was tanned from living in the Florida sunshine and muscular from chopping wood and finding lots of excercize in his "living off the land" lifestyle.

People began to make the treck out to his place just by word of mouth and then the "Jungle Cruise" sightseeing boat began bringing tourists from town and his business began to boom. Everyone wanted to get a closer look at the "wild man," the modern day Tarzan, look at the cages of turtles, panthers, coons, and gators, see his authentic handhewn cabin, and have a first hand look at his rustic, idyllic, and truly unique homestead.

Trapper even provided a big, heavy rope swing which hung from an old majestic, very tall cypress tree at the water's edge. You would hear the fellas sometimes, swinging out over the water on the rope, bellowing out the famous Tarzan call as they'd let go of it above and into the river. It was quite entertaining to many retired folks from town, and winter visitors from out of state, who came to watch.

This was the thrill of a lifetime for the Jupiter kids in those days and others who liked to come in their boats or drive up there to Jupiter or Jonathan Dickinson Park where canoes could be rented. It was a traditional and popular event from West Palm Beach when high school teens would converge at Trappers on senior "skip days". In fact, that's how Gary had first gotten started going there in the first place.

I never quite had the nerve to try the rope swing. I was afraid I'd have to let it go too soon. It looked so easy watching everyone else, doing it, but it was a really different perspective when you were standing on the high bank with the deep black water down below. I once took the rope tightly in my hands, backed way back from the embankment and started to run toward the water, but chickened out. Now Gary and his brother, Glyn, what was a different story, and they had it mastered. Gary could make the rope go farther out than anyone, splashing so hard we all got wet on the shore, and then he'd swim underwater from the deepest part of the river and back, just to go do it all over again!

Problems with legal matters eventually had Trapper dismayed as he dealt with authorities concerning new restrictions and requirements for zoos and tourist attractions, not to mention the costs required to meet them, and then, of course there were the rising taxes. He reached a point after several years that he no longer wanted to deal with it, cut a few trees across the paths of the river so no more boat traffic could reach his place, and only a few locals ever made their way to his camp much after that. Now there would be an additional name he would be labeled, "recluse".

Trapper's real name was Vince Nostokovich from a Polish family originally from Trenton, NJ. But I'll let you Google all the information if you're interested, and I grant you, his story is very interesting, even without reading the many books that were written about him, you can hear many a fascinating story about him just from checking out websites from Mister "Google". People in Jupiter knew his name to be Vince Nelson, but everybody I knew only called him "Trapper".

The only way you could get to his remote location was by boat and you had to already know your way through a maze of swamps and mangroves, passed some pineland with palmettos, but also gorgeous lush oak hammocks with Spanish moss and cypress trees. You could get lost easily by boat and by car you wouldn't even know how to reach his cabin unless you figured it out and Gary did. Every newspaper and magazine article or tourist report would always include that his place was "inaccessable by land", so most folks never looked for a way.

The story I have to share with you about the man, you aren't going to find on Google, or in any of the books. Just this one. My dad, Rev. Sherman Swan, at that time was pastor in Jupiter at the First Southern Baptist Church he had founded on Pennock Lane. Years later he would be the founder of the Tequesta First Baptist Church when he led the church to sell the property to another denomination, so they could relocate to a more ideal location on Tequesta Drive. It was following those years he founded and built the First Baptist Church of Palm Beach Gardens, next to the Gardens Mall.

(Whew!) Well, I'm kinda tellin' you all this because you gotta know my dad was an established, solid Christian, preacher-man, and pastor. He was what the Southern Baptist Convention probably now labels as a church "planter". He would respond to God to start a church when God called him to do it. He would sometimes use a store front building, meet and pray with a few interested people, and before you knew it, had it incorporated, land bought, building built, and stayed there with it, him and mama pastoring, until it grew into a well established church. Then when he felt God showing him another location needing a church, he would do it again.

He was a tall, always smiling, gentle man, a full blooded Swede from precious Christian parents. Daddy had been in the US Army Air Force, and could yes, stomp right on top of a six foot diamond back rattlesnake, but I guess what I am trying to say is that the Wild-Man, Tarzan, the gator wrestlin' Swamp Man, Trapper, had no need to fear my extremely congenial Daddy. But something caused him to spontaneously snap, had spooked him, and here's what happened.

It was time for the church to have an annual picnic and all the youth put in to go to Trappers for it, so we did. I think it was the first time my parents had been there, unless one time before on a boat ride, maybe. Most of the kids were swimming in the river but we also had horseshoes, badminton, and boat rides going on. Mom was busy helping the other ladies fixing food on the tables and thoughtfully, had even brought all of our table cloths with her from our home. Everyone else came by boat and we had loaded up dad's station wagon with supplies, so since Gary knew the secret way to get in from the roads, we had Gary's car also packed full of food and drinks we picked up at the church, and had my parents follow us.

Trapper had always allowed us to sneak in that way. The very first time we did it, Trapper was stacking logs on his very huge, well organized woodpile and looked up just in time to catch us driving through the bushes. When he glanced at us we both just smiled and waved at him. He didn't wave back, or smile, but never confronted us about it, so we usually just kept coming in that way. I would later hear wild but true tales how he had caught tresspassers and they met with his anger and threats, even lost their rifle once when he reportedly broke it in half against a tree. I guess he gave us his approval since we did bring him a snake every time we went there instead of paying his usual "entrance fee". At any rate, in spite of the man's lack of friendliness to us, we had some sort of favor with him.

Everyone was busy doing things when my dad asked me to come with him to meet Trapper and thank him for letting us all come out there for the event. I think Dad's friend, Roy Rood, who knew Trapper, had handled all the arrangements to have the picnic there that day. Dad also had a brand new Bible he purchased just to give to him and had written on the inside front cover, presented to "Trapper Nelson", the date, name of the church, etc. I wish I still had it. It would have been a great souvenier of what happened next.

Trapper, who always seemed to make himself pretty scarce when folks were there, and sometimes you'd not see him at all, was standing alone, not far from us, in a grassy clearing near his cabin. We both walked up to him and he and daddy introduced and shook hands. Dad was thanking him for allowing our church group to come to his place, and I remember they nodded and smiled about some trivial humerous comment. It was maybe about even the chickens who seemed to be out enjoying the beautiful weather and all the activities. It was quite a pleasant moment, though, up until the Bible appeared.

It was then my dad had pulled the nice leather-bound black Bible with the shiney gold lettering on the front that read, "HOLY BIBLE" out of the thin brown paper bag. At first Trapper just looked down at it, and as dad began to reach out to hand it to him, and was saying...."Trapper I would like for you to have this as a gift from the church, for........." Trapper turned, no, he didn't just turn, he spun around, spontaneously away, his back to us, and fled running like a deer, into the woods and out of sight! I never saw the man again, well, except for only his blood stains.

I will never forget that my Dad had the most shocked expression on his face and said, "Betty! Did you just see that?! Why, he ran like a deer!" I have to tell you I don't know why Trapper did that. I don't recall that Dad ever shared the story with the church, but our family wondered why he ran. All I know is that it happened exactly as I'm telling it and I had heard their entire conversation and I saw it it happen with my own two eyes.

I guess I will just have to leave all of you wondering the same thing that I have wondered for over sixty-three years. It tells us something about him that perhaps could never be known about him otherwise, but what was actually revealed in his electrified response, I'm not sure. What that could be, I'm not positive, unless it is like in Hebrews 4:12, when it describes that the Bible is the Word of God and it splits (cuts, pierces,) divides asunder (into pieces), the soul and spirit! You reckon ole Trapper's very being, when confronted with God's Word, was being ripped, somehow, *"asunder"*?

Listen to what the following verse says worded in the First Nations Version:

*"Not one thing in all creation is hidden from His sight. All things
are stripped bare before the eyes of the One to whom we must
give an answer for **how we have walked on the earth!**"*
Hebrews 4:13 FNV

I never returned to Trappers from that day forward, not until 1968, the week of his death reported on July 30th. Why, the news was all about his body being found by John Dubois, a friend of ours, who had the fishing bait shop by his house on the Jupiter Inlet at the ocean. I had been a guest in his home where his wife Bessie, the famous Jupiter historian, had told me some of the adventures she shares in several books she authored. Gary would buy bait from Mr. DuBois and fish at the jetty catching big snook.

Funny story: Roy Rood, Jupiter pioneer and highly respected local business man, (and the man who sponsored and promoted my application for Girl's State for Tallahassee when I was a high school junior), says he will always remember his friend Trapper Nelson standing there at the bait shack. He said Trapper would be eating a whole box of Hershey bars and drinking a quart of cold milk after *rowing* a boat from his camp to the inlet. Yep, I knew those icy cold Hershey bars quite well because Gary always bought them for me from Mr. Dubois, to eat while I waited seated on the jetty watching him fish at night in the moonlight. I had been doing that since I would watch him fish when I was pregnant with Libby.

It was John who had an out of town patron at his place, who had prearranged and waited for Trapper to meet him there, and when he didn't show up, John knew something was wrong. He drove right out to his place and found his body on the ground under his pavillion, a gunshot in his abdomen area (some reports stated in his left chest), his shotgun beside him. The shell had entered his upper chest and exited the back of his head. He had been there several days. The coroner signed off the death certificate as suicide. There had been no autopsy unless you would consider that to be the local officers and the medical examiner's observations, when they examined the deteriorated body on the picnic table at the scene, which I don't. He was then cremated, and his ashes tossed across the Loxahatchee River water.

As soon as I read it in the papers I said "Charlie, his brother, sat in jail so long he had figured out a perfect crime. He had said as much when he was sentenced to life in prison for the death of their former business partner (which was also by shotgun), convicted because of Trapper's testimony. At that trial when Judge Curtis Chillingworth announced his decision, Charlie spoke out for all to hear and record, that when he gets out of prison he would kill his brother Trapper, and the Judge. They never found the Judge's body or his wife's but they had reportedly been taken into the ocean for a late night boat ride and never returned. It would be another party, two men, who would eventually confess, however, it still may have been done for Charlie's benefit and theirs. It was strange the two deaths occurred so closely in time and following Charlie's release.

So when I realized that the land at Trapper's place would proably be off limits, maybe forever, I wished to go there one last time. Of course Gary wasn't so keen on the idea but he agreed to go to satisfy my "detective" tendancies, and my brother, Lars, was with us. All the way out there I kept thinking, "Suicide? Suicide, no way!"

I carried our 21 month old son Tifton on my hip as I walked around the camp at dusk. I followed the guinea hens to where they were gathered beneath the pavillion, scratching in the blood stained dirt. The place we had enjoyed as youngsters, such happy memories, now was gloomy, foreboding, creepy and something else, some additional aspect that perhaps called for fear and warned of danger.

I felt like I was being watched, but there was no sign of a soul. I found the cabin door standing wide open and observed something shining in the doorway partially hidden in the cracks between the threshold boards, but when I stooped to bend over, wanting to pick it up to read what the dogtags said, Gary chided me not to touch anything. I was disturbed as to why the chain and tags were there. Was it something investigators missed?

The cabin did not appear ransacked to me at that time. It had always had a simple and plain, bare decor....like, no decor. Only the tanned gator hides he used to have tacked up on the walls were on the floor. Maybe someone was making sure that a suspected "treasure" people always said Trapper hid, wasn't behind them. There was one piece of a hide on the floor that Trapper had tanned to a pure pale brown, a very old hide, unusually soft and pliable, almost like suade but rough. I was fairly familar with gator hide and had never seen one like that before. Fascinated, I felt of it with my fingers and took it with me out the door.

199

Still holding my son in my arms, I hurried to get him out of there. Not because I just stole an historical hide, but I had already started to get that gut feeling you get when someone wants *your own* hide! It was dark now and the crickets and frogs were sounding off like they do in my ears now at seventy-nine years of age. The mosquitos were beginning to buzz around our heads and it was a welcome sound when I heard Gary cranking up the engine on our old truck.

There was a very sinister cloud looming there heavily in the warm night summer air, not just in the natural, but quite significantly in the spiritual sense and realm. I prayed for our protection and was grateful to get out of there and return safely home. The remnant of the gator hide would remain on my wall until the day when we ripped off all the hides when the game warden unexpectedly came for coffee! I would have to trash it anyway as it had started to deteriorate and I didnt want it collecting any Florida bugs. I had wondered if it was perhaps the first one Trapper had tried to process that way.

Well, of course that night at Trapper's cabin we had our shotguns with us, as well, but don't forget, they're only as efficient as the target is human. I notice online that Trapper's homestead is listed somewhere on a website as one of the" haunted" sites in the world open to the public. I'm not too sure about haunts, but there were several times across the span of my lifetime, the threats have seemingly been from a source the Bible refers to when it says this:

> *"But remember, we are not fighting against human beings.*
> *Our battle is against the **evil rulers**, the **dark powers**, and the*
> ***spiritual forces** of the spirit-world, above and around us".*
> *Ephesians 6:12 FNV*

Right about here we probably need some humerous, comic relief, right? Okay, here's one of my favorites, and it seems appropriate:

Did you hear the one about the elderly lady who got pulled over by the cop? When he asked for her driver's license he noticed she had a carry permit in her wallet. (a permit to carry a concealed gun legally)

"Ma'am, are you carrying a concealed weapon at this moment?"

"Oh, yes, Siree, I have my loaded 38 detective special right here in my purse!" she responded.

He continued writing her speeding ticket, and added, "Anything else?"

"Oh my, yes!! I have my loaded 9mm Glock right here in the glove box!"

He then felt prompted to ask her, "Is that *all?*"

"Oh no, sir, my Smith & Wesson 357 Mag is right here under my seat!"

The officer put down his ticketbook, saying, "Ma'am just what are you so afraid of?!"

With a smile of confidence she replied, "Sir, not a cotton pickin' thing!"

That's exactly how I feel about my Bible!

"Book cover of Author's first book, 'Operation: Devil's Garden'"

CHAPTER SIXTEEN

OPERATION: DEVIL'S GARDEN

———◆———

"Oh give thanks to the Lord; call upon His name; make
known His deeds among the peoples! Sing to Him, sing
praises to Him; tell of all His wondrous works!"
Psalm 105:1-2 KJV

When I wrote "Operation: Devil's Gardens" in 2005, it was in response to God's Word, where in the Bible, such as in the verse above, He instructs us to share with everyone everywhere what marvelous things the Lord has done in our lives. One translation says to tell every day what He has done.

The concept I was explaining in that book was that having grown up in south Florida, a land so filled with tropical beauty and abundant blessings, there was, just as the Bible teaches us, an undercurrent of evil perpetrated by an unseen enemy, Satan. It was the old devil in the garden story at work once again, not in Adam and Eve's lives, but mine and yours as well.

What appeared to be paradise and garden-like on the outside, was actually a sinister battleground of fear, terror, deception, and attack with stealing, killing, and destruction the demonic forces colaborated on, attempting to keep the inhabitants from personally knowing their Creator.

There would be repeated Satanic attacks, espionage, and ambush. What that has always called for, is for the soldiers in the field to obey the close instructions of our Commander-in-Chief, God the Almighty, through Jesus Christ, His Son.

Because God sent His only begotton Son, Jesus Christ, to destroy the works of that enemy, we, as his warriors, are deployed to the same mission and have been provided weapons, warfare, battle plans, and some awesome victories! The book I had written describes many of those, recording them in hopes of encouraging my brothers and sister fighters in combat to rise as eagles, sit with the Chiefs, stay alert as His watchmen, and maintain the "mountaintops" as His fortress.

In the first chapter I relate the miracle of God releasing eleven Haitian pastors from the West Palm Beach jail who had been incarcerated when their boat they were in drifted into the Palm Beach Inlet with no immigration identification or authorization to even come there from Haiti. The men had been charged by an evil dictator for speaking out against the Communistic government and given a choice of execution or a boat with no equiptment. They picked the boat.

The Lord had spoken to me that morning when I was in prayer and sent me on a mission. He told me to go to the West Palm Beach jail and say,"My name is Betty Luckey, I've come for the Haitians". For the next two to three hours that would be all I dared say because I had no idea about the prisoners and their dire dilemma, and God had not instructed me to say another word, so I didn't.

The book goes on to tell the time I heard the Lord again speak audibly to me, in my spirit, anyway. He had said to get 100 Spanish Bibles for someone, but I had no idea who, and Bibles were back ordered all over the country at that time. He not only led me to a man who provided the Bibles, but had me running down a migrant bus along the Florida Turnpike and give them to the driver. Lo and behold, (like my daddy always said), the sobbing man had prayed the night before asking God for 100 Spanish Bible. He had said prayed for this to be a sign from God that he was indeed, being called to be a missionary to Mexico. And then....he miraculously finds my house way out on our ranch in the woods so he and his pastor, who then interpreted, so I would know the "rest of the story!"

There is a story as well, of another "100 Bibles" for a Christian rock concert my daughter, Sheri was having in the Lake Worth bandshell and had requested them to throw out to the crowd at the close of her last song. It sure was a miracle how the Lord supplied those Bibles and the exciting event even included Channel 12's Wheel of Fortune.

One time when I was asked by the church youth to help them have a float in the North Palm Beach annual "Christmas in Dixie" Parade in Lake Park, God surprised us by providing a free, old broken down bus to use. Miraculously, it was the biggest tow truck company owner who answered their phone that day. I had called to inquire how much it would be for us to have it towed to the church so we could clean it up of all its broken glass and trash. Mr. Kauff had said his dispatchers were so busy that he picked up the ringing phone himself, something he had never had to do before.

When he asked why I wanted a bus in such bad, unusable condition, I told him about the kids and the parade. He said he had a deal for me. If I would allow him to arrive at the church and tow it in the parade, the kids could all ride inside and wave from the windows. Then he would return us all afterwards and drop off the bus in the church parking lot. What a miracle!

You never saw so many Cabana Colony (the closest community developement to the church), kids so excitedly work on a bus, cleaning, painting in big letters, the following, "Lay not up for yourselves treasures on earth, where dust and rust corrupts, and thieves break in and steal, (the 'corrupted' bus illustrated that quite well), but lay up for yourselves treasures in Heaven!" And then a big red heart on the back door of the bus stated, "For where your treasure is, there your heart will be also!" (Matt. 6:21 KJV). You have to remember this was in the sixties and the hippie looking bus with the phsycodelic, fluorescent painted letters and symbols, were quite the rage.

Mr. Kauff had arrived that day of the parade, hooking us up with his shiniest, most spotless and elaborate, granddaddy wrecker of all time, so shiney it was looking like it was made of mirrors! As he pulled us down US Highway One passed thousands of people and news media, his siren blaring, animated horns blowing, and his fabulous array of flashing spotlights sending radiating colors across the community. The kids shouted Christmas greetings, threw out candy, and the crowds clapped and cheered!

It was no surprise to anyone we won the first place award for the best float in the parade. The Palm Beach Post said, that, in a parade that was filled with blaring rock bands from several local nightclubs and bars, and countless manger scenes in the backs of pickup trucks, marching bands all competing together at once, and businesses represented promoting the shopping season, only one stood out.

It said there was one "float" alone, that expressed a true meaning of Christmas concerning Heaven, that won first place, from the First Baptist Church of Palm Beach Gardens. It was a bus packed with happy smiling children and teens who waved and greeted all, as did the tow truck driver himself. Now the picture of it was published everywhere and our message spread to who knows how many people. The youth had wanted an outreach project and had picked a good one! They knew, also, that it had been an answer to their prayers.

The award was a check from the sponsoring city for fifty dollars. A local business woman who purchased junk cars for a living, stopped at the church after the parade, picked up the bus, giving my dad an additional fifty dollar check for the church. The youth were so happy to be able to present the two checks to the church the next day. It would provide for an unexpected insurance premium that had just come up, and was not in the church budget, and due that very week, for 100 dollars.

What was also amazing was that our group of kids had consisted only of a handful, however, 50 showed up to transform the bus, and to ride in the parade, and every seat was taken. Why, these were all the neighborhood kids we'd been trying to reach! We would hear of testimonies throughout the years of how much it meant to them to have that experience, like the time I took 50 boys fishing!

I loved working with children back in the days in my younger years when I had the energy to do it. My mother had also enjoyed children's ministry and would often use her artist skills by doing chalk drawings, flannel board Bible stories, and skits and plays. In her latest years she would come sit in a chair in front of the platform and tell a children's story while all the little kids in the sanctuary had all come to sit on the carpeted floor in front of her. (Mohawks are story tellers and basket weavers).

One year at Christmas she gave four little kids each a part in a skit and all they had to do was each hold a letter in their hand and spell the word "STAR". They each had a part in a short poem to recite that began with that letter. (For instance the first child would say, "S" is for the *Savior*, born on Christmas day" and so on down the row stationed on the stage). They never made it through their parts because the audience broke into uncontrollable laughter when the four kids walked on stage backwards and in big bold letters, they spelled, "RATS"!

One of the chapters was "Fishers of Men"or "The Fishermen". The Vacation Bible School teacher for the Junior Boys, aged about 9-12, had an emergency and had to leave town the night before it was to begin the following morning. She forgot and accidently took all the VBS materials for her class with her in the trunk of her car. Dad called me late that night to ask me to take the class and he would try to find literature for me.

I felt the Lord instruct me how to answer him. "That's ok, Dad, God assures me I can just teach the fishing story right out of the Bible. I'll use that idea we had once making registration slips of fish we cut out of bright yellow paper with each boys name, age and registration information. We'll learn, "I Will Make You Fisher's of Men" song, and make fishing poles all week and Friday I'll take them all fishing in the woods."

"Thank you so much, Betty, you just saved the day, you better plan for 10 though, and I'm not sure if that's probably too many to try to take fishing," he'd said. Its a fun story how the next day I had 8 boys who were excited to see the fishing regalia I'd brought to decorate the room with. They all filled out their yellow fish we strung across the class room with fishingline. They all took home the rest of the yellow fish, all the extra copies to pass out to friends.

I drove to the "Outdoor Store" in West Palm Beach to see just how much a few cane pole were going to cost me and I was shocked how expensive they were going to be. Then the fella working the counter said he'd get his dad, Mr. Elkins, the owner, to see if he'd give us a special discount. "What can I do for you, Mrs. Luckey ?" he had asked.

I told him what I was trying to do. When he asked me how many boys I might have I started to say 10-12 but instead I knew God was telling me something else and I heard myself blurt out...50! He said, Mrs. Luckey, pull your truck around back and I'll fix you up. It will be a gift from the

Lord!" I hugged his neck! He sent me on my way with fifty top of the line bamboo poles and all the tackle needed for each one!

When I arrived at the church the next morning 49 boys between 9-12 filled one whole side of the sanctuary so that became our new classroom. Everyday each boy worked on his cane pole, rigging it up with line, bobber, hook, and sinker with his name proudly displayed on the side. By Friday there was one more and I took all 50 of them to C-18 canal off Beeline Highway, down the youth camp road, each with a sack lunch, and Jesus and I taught them how to fish.

The Bible records several miraculous fish stories but we had one of our own to add to it. There would be many testimonies come out of that fishing trip I would hear of in later years. Ladies in the church asked, how on earth could one person, a woman, at that, take 50 boys to a dangerous canal near the Everglades, with sharp fish hooks, and no one get hurt?

I had their answer. When God puts something together, He orchastrates the whole thing, and it wasn't the fish we were after, it was the fishermen. The lyrics to the song were "I will make you fishers of men, fishers of men, fishers of men, I will make you fishers of men, *if you follow Me!" (Jesus).*

Another story in my book was about how I had taken my four children to an isolated farm field sandwiched in the middle of no where between Indiantown road and the Beeline Highway. The farmer had already picked his black-eyed peas and said anyone was welcome to whatever they could find left. Oh, how we loved canning black-eyed peas and snaps and we excitedly piled out of the car with our empty bushel baskets and paper sacks in the hot sun.

The reason it was so hot was because it was going to storm and I knew we had to hurry. That it would storm, was an understatement! We no longer got positioned, all spread out in separate rows and started picking, when the most ferocious tornado-like winds rolled in suddenly, sending every pine tree surrounding the field, bent over in unison, like gigantic bows, like weapons of warfare! The wind was also sending a pine-needle invasion of pin sharp artillary aimed for our heads like miniature Indian arrows in a tribal war!

We ran for the car dropping our sacks along the way. The torential rain beat on the car like hundreds of little pounding hammers. In the car I prayed the engine would start because sometimes it waited till the second or third try before it did. Balls of ice were pelting the car and between that and the crashing thunder, we couldn't even hear one another speaking.

When the engine cranked I put it into reverse quickly and may have accelerated too fast, my wheels were spinning! It got worse as even rocking the car by switching from forward and reverse and back, only lowered the car in the mucky dirt and sand until I had the axle sitting on the ground!

Now we weren't going anywhere. The rain had caused all the soil under and around the car to instantly flood into huge puddles and there was no way the kids could get out and help push because the lightning was continuous and we were too close to pine trees that frequently would drew dangerous lightning strikes. We were too far from the highway to try to walk out.

Finally I heard Libby's voice say, "Mama, let's all pray!" We formed a circle as we sat in our seats and held hands tightly. Sheri, Tifton, Niki and I prayed along as Libby led, "Please, dear God, please send your Holy angels here to push us out of this hole, in Jesus' Name, Amen. Even little two year old Niki said, "Amen!"

Now Tifton, who was probably no older than seven, was already very wise to the ways of the woods. Why, he had been stuck in jeeps, trucks, hunting buggies, and cars, having grown up hunting along side his dad ever since he was as young as Niki was then. He knew every kind of way to get out of a bog hole and knew we didn't have the tools or manpower on hand, not in a violent storm like this one. I was moved as I had watched him join in the prayer with his eyes tightly closed and say "In Jesus' Name, Amen!"

Sheri said, "Try the engine now, Mom!" I looked at all the kids, at how expectant they were and hoped they'd not lose faith when the car didn't move. Oh *me* of little faith!

Because what happened next was a true miracle! Why that old station wagon just simply rolled right backwards all the way to the highway just as if we were in the parking lot at the old Twin City Mall! There were immediately cheers and thanks to God! All the way home we sang "No, Never Alone!"

The lyrics are, "I've seen the lightning flashing, and heard the thunder roll. I've felt sin's breakers dashing, trying to conquer my soul. *But I've heard the voice of Jesus*, telling me still to fight on. He promised never to leave me, never to leave me alone!"("No, Never Alone" Anonomous writer, Public Domain according to Google).

Everybody piled out of the car at the house, running inside, all talking at once to tell their daddy all about the miracle. That night when they were ready for bed and saying their prayers, I heard them discussing what the angel may have looked like who pushed them out so easily. One of them said, "I bet there was a bunch of them!" Someone else said, "No, I think it was one big angel, all by himself, who was taller than the pine trees!"

Once when it was time to go see the accountant to do our annual income taxes, we had a major crisis for which I was seemingly to blame, but again, God came through with a miracle.

For weeks we had looked for a cattle receipt from the Okeechobee Livestock Market, necessary to figure income taxes with and it was no where to be found. Gary was so particular and efficient with our monthly record keeping that everything was organized for the trip into West Palm Beach. With all the paperwork together in a big leather pouch, except for the missing recept, it would mean that our only alternative was to estimate the cattle amounts and Gary was upset about having to do that.

We had all searched for it, turning the house upside down, and I was the one who must have mistakenly thrown it out with the trash. Gary was now waiting in the truck in front of the house and, holding my purse in my hands, about to go out the front door, I begged God one last time, that if the receipt was still in the house, would He please tell me where it was.

Gary now blew the horn. But I heard the Lord's voice: "Betty, go down the hall and open the door to the garage." I can't tell you how I wanted to jump for joy! "Go across the floor to the black plastic bags of newspapers over there against the far wall. Put your hand down into the middle inside of the one in the center and close your fingers!" It was the receipt!!!!!

I could not stand. I fell limp on the cement floor, tears pouring out of me from thankfulness...and relief! I was impressed that the Lord had three things to teach me from this, and He said yes. #1 He is always right here with us, #2 He cares about everything we go through, big and small, He said, #3, He sometimes waits until the last minute.

"Yes, Lord, about that, how come You wait till the last minute?" I laughed. He said, "Sometimes, Betty, I have to let you know I'm here and that its Me! After you have done everything you know to do, then I show you what I can do to help you."

He certainly showed me He was with me and had assignments for me concerning my piano playing on two occasions. I heard His familiar voice when He instructed me to leave what I was doing immediately, and drive to a church. I arrived at both churches just in time to hear the pastor's wives, I'd never met, ask the "visitor" (me), who'd just popped in the front door, in front of a packed sanctuary or auditorium of people, if I happened to play the piano!

It was at the Jupiter Farms First Church of God, meeting at a very large home until their sanctuary could be constructed, down unmarked streets in a rural neighborhood, where God led me through a maze of dirt roads to the home surrounded by cars and trucks. Walking up to the door, an usher opened it, smiling, and gave me his seat in the back. It was an amazingly large garage with a platform, a pulpit, and a brand new piano. Mrs. Wheatley, the Pastor's wife was at the microphone ready to lead the crowd in a hymn when she saw me come in.

"Welcome! You don't play piano do you?" she asked over the mic. I left my seat and headed for the front. I introduced myself and she had me sit on the brand new piano bench. She continued to explain to the congregation that she was so delighted the brand new piano had been delivered that very day, but how she had called every pianist she could think of, and no one was able to play for the evening service. She was wiping the tears from her eyes and I noticed other folks had also reacted in the same way. She said when she was praying that morning, the Lord had assured her He would send someone that evening. I played for them for about a year, when their new building was ready. But it was the piano at the Seminole Indian Reservation at Brighton, that was the most amazing miracle and I played there for closer to 28-30 years.

The prophetic signs leading up to that even included the gift to me of a valuable silver and turquois Squash Blossom necklace, from the parents of a lovely young woman. She had been killed in a head-on collision by a drunk driver as she was on her way to our Maranatha Church in Palm Beach County to hear Benny Hinn. Her mother was waiting in the crowded sanctuary holding a seat for her daughter when we all overheard sirens zipping passed outside and then only a few miles away. The parents made a trip out west in her honor purchasing some silver and turquois pieces the girl loved. Her grieving mother kept them close to her in a box, until one day she heard the Lord tell her what He wanted her to do with it.

Now this particular day I was sitting in my church office when this dear mama came in and with tears handed me the box. She told me the Lord said to take it to Betty Luckey at the church and give her the contents. We had never officially met one another before. God told her He was healing her from all her mourning and didn't want her to keep hanging onto her treasure box and weeping for her daughter, that she was with Him in Heaven, and all was well. I accompanied her to the door and hugged her as we cried together.

The night before I had asked the Lord for a sign that would clearly speak to me that it was indeed, Native American ministry, He wanted me focused on. Not twelve hours later He had me holding the most precious of necklaces, a valuable Turquois and sterling authentic Indian Squash Blossom from a western tribe, a tribute to and in memory of a mother's child who had loved Indian people. I would wonder what the Lord was about to do because I had my "sign" He was about to do it.

One Sunday morning, not long afterward, the Lord prompted me to hurry, and to drive an hour and a half from our Lucky Buck Ranch to Brighton at the last moment, making the trip at high speeds and in record timing. I only sort of remembered how to get there after having visited the church when I was 14 and the pastor at that time, was the Seminole Chief, Billy Osceola.

I pulled into the parking lot, which had lots of trucks and cars, but no one outside stirring. A little Seminole boy, Anthony Fish, came out toward my truck so I opened my window. He was the son of the pastor, Brother JB Fish, and he said, "Aren't you coming in?" For some reason I felt intimidated at the last minute thinking I wasn't sure I'd even be welcomed. "Think its ok?" I said. He smiled nodding. I slipped inside and sat on the last pew.

His dear mama, Carolyn Fish, had me introduce myself. She then added, "You don't happen to play the piano, do you?" When I said yes, there was a gasp from the crowd and tears from Carolyn's eyes. She proceeded to explain that they had not had a regular pianist there in 22 years and that a few nights before, at Wednesday night prayer meeting, someone had suggested that for the first time, they pray for one. So they did, and here I was!

She pulled out the piano bench for me to sit on, and that would become my seat there for most of the next twenty eight some years as they voted me the piano player at the First Indian Baptist Church. It was a miracle. I would also one day be the Pastor Wonder John's secretary for several years until he passed away, and they would have me teach the adult Sunday school class.

Yes, I was seated with the Chiefs, I was flying high up with God's eagles in realms of Glory, (He had given me peace, joy and purpose!), able to minister and evangelize to my tribal brothers and sisters, and even though the terrain was considered to be Florida flatland and wetland, to me, it was one of God's mountain tops where I walked and talked with Him. It was a part of my life experience so filled with the miraculous, and I would always feel was a very beautiful piece of "Jesus' Mountain".

"Grandson, Sean Savacool, Grand Ole Opry, front left center stage, 2022"

CHAPTER SEVENTEEN

LORD, PLANT MY FEET ON HIGHER GROUND

*"Then shalt thou delight thyself on the Lord; and I will cause thee to ride upon the **high places of the earth**, and feed thee with the heritage of Jacob, thy father; for the mouth of the Lord hath spoken it!"*
Isaiah 58:14 KJV

The hymn, "Higher Ground" had to have been one of my Dad's favorites because we sure sang it more than others, it seemed. It was written by Johnson Oatman, Jr. in 1898. I liked it too, maybe more now than I did then because the lyrics have a lotta meaning I have more understanding about now than I did back then. I mean it's actually a really good "mountain climbing song" when you check out the words:

"I'm pressing on the **upward** way, *new heights,* I'm gaining every day; Still praying as I **onward bound**, "Lord, pant my feet on **higher ground!**" Lord, lift me up, and let me stand, By faith on Canaan's tableland; a higher plane than I have found, Lord, plant my feet on higher ground.

My heart has no desire to stay where doubts arise and fears dismay, though some may dwell where those abound, *My **prayer**, My **aim**, is **higher ground!***

The words of that hymn express everything I'm trying to say about our lives with Jesus on His mountain top! I always loved the high places. My parents would tell you that is where they'd always find me. When I was little I'd sit down at the top of the slide and want to stay there up high where I could see everything. The ferris wheel would probably be the only ride I'd want to take at the fair, well, besides the merry-go-round. Sometimes, I chaperoned church youth at Disney World in Orlando, like for our annual trip to the Christian festival weekend there for "Night of Joy" for instance. I made it clear to the kids my "headquarters" was at the top of the Swiss Famiy Robinson Treehouse where they could find me if I was needed. (No cell phones in those days).

At Jonathan Dickinson Park in Martin County, I loved to go up to the wooden tower with all the benches where you could see as far away as Indiantown to the west and at low tide, the Bahama Islands way out in the Atlantic Ocean to the east. I once held a surprise birthday party for the well known talk show host, Mitch Sandler, up there, and it was full of all his wonderful friends he talked to every day on the broadcast phone calls, but had never before had an opportunity to meet in person. I served cupcakes and icy cold fruit punch in paper cups for everyone. He was on his daily radio program with a slew of faithful listeners who actually showed up and made their way up the historic wooden tower to join us.

Mitch hosted a cable television network talk show also, interviewing special guests and local celebrities. Hey, I was one and he featured me more than once, as He would put it, I was his favorite Christian, because he, being Jewish, had found me to be a loving friend who loved him unconditionally, and made him come, as he put it, "awfully close to becoming a Christian, like I was." I gave him a beautiful Bible that day and he wept openly in front of his fans.

Mom and dad bought an acre on a high mountain near Glenville, NC and would go there to camp in a small camper trailer they parked on the sight, we named "Eaglesong". My parents left it to me and I sold it because Gary and the rest of the family were not at all comfortable with the steep dirt roads you had to take to reach the property. I loved it, though, but when I sold it, the proceeds helped us buy the large home in Lake Placid, Florida, we purchased to bring them to, in their final years. I knew one day I would reinvest that money in a new place in the North

Carolina mountains and I did. How Mom and Dad would love the home I have here now, and I can just imagine my Daddy and how he would have been out here on the porch rocking chairs with his autoharp, playing and writing new songs.

There is nothing so inspiring for prayer, meditation, artwork or writing, than the views and the perspective they provide that lower valleys and flatland, just don't, for me, anyway. I liked it when we made a trip out west about some twenty two years ago and walked along the crest of the Grand Canyon walls and up to Devil's Tower in South Dakota and went to see the Native American horse monument carved into the Black Hills and walked some of the hiking trails in Yellowstone.

We had our young, (at that time, he was young), grandson, JT Luckey, with us on that trip and I can still see him racing on up ahead smiling back at us, along trails that teetered on the steep inclines and edges of crevices having no guard rails, that would scare the wits out of me to ever attempt. Not JT, he was a natural outdoors man and brave adventurer, even early on. His grandfather on his mother's side was Native American. Sometimes I could barely watch, like, when he showed me trick skateboard moves off a high loading ramp, once, in downtown Okeechobee, Florida.

I was telling some of my elderly Seminole friends about how brave he was surfing, unafraid of the circling sharks, and could ride the highest waves. I had also watched him ride a bull at the Brighton Seminole rodeo arena for one of the trainers. He was so impressed, said he was a natural, and that he wanted to take him on as an apprentice but the family knew it meant a lifetime of future aching bones and muscles or worse, and decided against giving consent. One lady asked, "How come he does dangerous things, like that?" I answered simply, "Well, for starters, he's like his dad, Tifton, and just because *he can!*" (most folks can't!)

JT has his own company in Martin County, Florida, "Luckey Environmental Services". He provides a wide range of expert and experienced complete lawn care, (grass, shrubs, palms, spraying, fertilizing, and weed control). His specialized services include inspections, pest control, fungus, insect and nutritional treatment and more. He drives the biggest pest management truck I 've ever seen on the road, and yes, he's still riding the high places and we're really proud of him.

Speaking of heights, I recall Mother telling me the Mohawks were discovered to be so good at fearlessly handling altitudes, that when New York City needed workers to help in the construction of the tall skyscrapers, it was the Mohawk tribal men they hired for the scaffolding. That's a well known fact.

My closest Cherokee friend knows the Appalachian Trail like I know my way around Walmart. She is known for her brave experiences hiking on the highest and most difficult pathways and her phenomenal photography there. They call her "Mission Dee" because she leaves Bible verses hidden along the trail for other hikers to find. It's a ministry she does for Jesus, to share His love and salvation. I just recently spoke with an old friend, Dan Westerman, who said he hiked the trail and had found some of those verses Dee left and it had meant a lot to him and helped in his walk with the Lord.

What a sight when you approach Albequerque from high above and suddenly there across the valley below are millions of twinkling city lights of every color, sorta like when you come up on Chattanooga unexpectedly, and you get that same surprise how the lights at night sparkle like the stars do.

Just as a mountain, a watch tower, or the highest summit in a territory creates the best strategic military advantage, I find it to be so in the Spiritual warfare we are in, as Christian soldiers. Look at how often Jesus took his disciples, followers, and crowds to mountains to teach them and pray. He is still doing that today, I know because I'm staying as close by His side as possible! What's cool is that we can climb those heights and hang out with Him whether it's outside our vehicle in a parking lot, or inside the privacy of our bathroom. To be with God in His presence is to know no physical boundaries because He carries us to His mountaintops no matter where we're standing, sitting, walking, sleeping, or travelin', Hallelujah!

I can't wait till I go to Eagle Mountain, (Monteagle) TN soon, tour the University of the South and attend a church service at All Saints Chapel in Sewannee, where there are outstanding views down below of North Carolina, Tennessee and Alabama. I am actually planning to be there this Sunday in their morning service.

When I was once a busy young wife and mother, slightly discouraged needing some encouragement and hope for the future, I was in a lonely isolated mobile home in our pasture when I heard the Lord's voice urgently prompt me to almost run to the back door and open it and look up. When I did, He showed me a huge Eagle soaring passed, up in the blue sky, it's white feathers aglow with golden sunlit reflections that were indeed awe-inspiring! This would be what I would refer to as His calling me to "fly with the Eagles" call. This is what He said to me:

"Betty, I want you to stop looking down, and start looking up. No longer concern yourself with all the struggles and cares of this world and seek only Me and My Kingdom and all those matters will be taken care of. If you will just trust and obey Me you will have no reason to not be happy, safe, and joyful. I want you to *climb higher*, no more distractions, difficult paths, and dark valleys, but keeping your sights, your eyes, on the sure, pure, and peacefully secure "skyway" my Eagles fly, *with My Holy Spirit*, gaining heighth, strength, and nobility". It reminded me of my Papa's Indian Chiefs, and I wiped my eyes and promised that I would. Hallelujah! What a life changer!

I love the old Jupiter Lighthouse and I'm glad I climbed those historical steps while I was young enough to do so. When I was fifteen I entered the Lighthouse Centenial Celebration beauty pageant and came in number five, Now that's bad; but, it's pretty good when you consider we didn't wear makeup back then. They still have a photo of me in a scrapbook in their museum in my one piece red swimsuit with a Hawaiian print of big white hibiscus on it and I wore a real white hibiscus blossom on one side of my long black hair.

Maybe every young girl, well, at least *some* young girls, may dream of some day getting to be in a beauty contest, and I had, so at least I had the opportunity and I have to admit I was very happy the day I visited the Jupiter Lighthouse Museum and found my picture there when I was fifteen, and I came in number five.

My son asked me on the phone today about my "bucket list", that list of things you'd like to do while you're still alive, and I hadn't given it much thought till then. Tifton was specifically asking if I had ever been able to make a trip to Dollywood, since we live up here in the same mountain range, and yes, I remembered it is a place I would love to visit. There, as well as the cathedral, "All Saints Chapel" at Sewanee, TN. Maybe at least one more trip to my favorite white sand beach near Sarasota, "Siesta Key"

Beach where Gary and I loved to take the family to. I was happy knowing Gary had achieved his "bucket list" before he had passed away.

Gary loved Donald Trump and never once missed watching him speaking at his rallys on television, but wanted to see him in person at least once before, as he put it, he would "kick" the bucket. So I surprised him with tickets to see him at the ballfield in Fort Myers not long before we moved to the mountains. I never saw Gary laugh so hard, jump to his feet clapping, and shouting with thousands of others, all the patriotic chanting. He really had fun that night.

My friend, Seminole Alice Snow, a tribal medicine woman I had done mission trips with, asked me to solve a mystery for her once. She said her favorite thing to do was to visit museums, and she had been to many famous Native American museums in the country, but there was supposed to be one right there in Okeechobee, Florida, not far from the reservation, she was asking me about. She said Mr. Buxton, our local funeral director had invited her to go see his museum for some time and she'd always wanted to, but never got around to it. She said she wanted to see it before she died, so she called Mr. Buxton and he was so delighted to have her, she said.

He had invited her to come meet him at the funeral home so she shook hands with him inside, and then he just simply took her on a tour of his very large facility, a very attractive complex, a compound of buildings and services. She said it took well over an hour to see it all......but there was never a *museum*!? She said it even mentioned it in the phone book. So I looked it up and she pointed to the word, "mausoleum" and when I read the word out loud and defined it as a burial choice and what they can look like........she began to chuckle and shake with laughter and with somewhat, relief! Now she understood. Alice was fluent in the Indian languages, Muskogee, Creek, Miccosukee, and English, and maybe more, but occasionally words can trip us up, as she discovered. She had fun laughing at herself about it. It reminded me of a speech I had to give.

When I was a regular student at Palm Beach Junior College, (not when I was in the police academy there), I was in an Ancient History class that required every student to give a speech at the end of the semester. It was the final grade that was comprised of the paper we had to turn in just prior to the talk, and the brief talk. Normally, I was never nervous at speaking publically, but on that particular day, they had combined several history classes to allow everyone to hear all the speeches.

There were those other teachers sitting in there to listen to us, as well. Our talks were timed and were only to be about five minute summaries without notes, but I noticed my hands were sweating. I was *really* alarmed when *everyone howled* at something I'd just said...and mine was a very serious, not a humorous speech!? When I finished and took my seat, they were still laughing at me. I whispered to a classmate, "What was so funny?"....she replied smiling, "Twice, in your cute, Southern accent, in stead of saying 'homo sapien' you said 'homosexual' without batting an eye!"

Back when I was in elementary school a terrible thing happened one night at a revival service at our church in Midway, Kentucky. Everybody in town knew and loved our local barber, Mr. Rupert Breeden, but there was one thing he would want to do with his life before he ever passed away, and that was to be a song leader. That night my dad asked him if he would bring his hymn book up to the pulpit and microphone and lead in the singing. He looked so delighted and with a huge smile, he announced the page number. I was watching a large beige-colored moth, flying around the room, circling above the heads of people on the platform, and maybe trying to make it's way to the light up on the ceiling directly above the pulpit stand.

The pianist played the introduction and Mr. Breeden, holding his hymnbook in one hand and raising high his other hand to direct the music, took a big breath and letting it out loudly, with the first word of the song, the large *moth-looking* **bug** *flew right into his wide open mouth* and down into his throat, clogging up his breathing passageways as the crowd gasped watching him changing skin color, unable to get a breath!

Rupert dropped the hymnbook on the floor, clutching his throat with his left hand, he waved goodbye to the congregation with his right hand! As he moved his head from left to right, he gazed at his longtime friends and relatives, scanning across the audience, nodding at them and waving "good-bye!" some waving back!

The next thing I knew, my dad was in front of him with his back to us so I wasn't for sure just what all daddy did, or in what sequence, but he lifted Mr. Breeden's arms, gave him a pound on his back, I think, gave him a glass of water he held up to Mr. Breeden's mouth, that had already been prepared for the evangelist that night on a shelf in the podium. You could hear people praying out loud, the song leader-barber giving out with a roar of a "snorty-chokeral-growlerous "roar in the key of lower "C" and he was able to swallow the culprit and finish the glass of water to the celebratory shouting and clapping of the startled congregation!

From that day forward, whenever someone even looked like they might choke or be short of breath, or unable to quit coughing, our family would start waving goodbye to them and we would all go into fits of laughter, but I assure you it was not funny the night it happened.

I liked to go up in the Bazaar International lookout tower on US1 that was there in the fifties and sixties, and where I once worked in a gift shop. It was there I got to wait on Jackie Kennedy, the Nation's First Lady at the time, and would have rung up the little package of tiny paper decorative umbrellas she bought for her daughter, Caroline, but the owner let her have them.

When I had a surprise 16th birthday party for my brother Lars (Chip), I had invited all his friends, picked them up in a large van, gathered at his front door and rang the bell. I called it the "Magical Mystery Tour" Party and was he shocked to see everyone at his door singing the popular song at the top of our lungs. We "took" him away, alright, just as the lyrics say, to a whirlwind itinerary of secret destinations and it was an unforgetable time for him and all of us, as well.

We went up in the tower at the Bazaar, down the Juno Beach pier with the crashing waves spraying their ocean mist on us, the Lake Worth pier with fishermen showing their amazing catches for the night, we visited the local rock and roll radio station where their familiar disc jockey unlocked the door and let us all inside, showing us what it looked like and giving everyone free music to take home, and then he talked about it over the air wishing Chip a happy birthday and playing Magical Mystery tour in his honor.

Then we drove back to Chip's where we prayed to bless the food and my brother's life, where Mom and Dad had the tables ready with cake and ice cream, sandwiches, potato chips, and cokes. The prettiest girl there kissed him goodbye, right on the mouth, and off I went to take everyone back home. The only bad part was that the "prettiest girl" also had Mononucleosis and had not known it at that time, and both she and Chip missed the rest of the school year at their homes recuperating in quarantine.

I thanked God for helping me put together a delightful birthday for my brother, and He indeed continued to bless and *protect* him, when in 2001 he would survive the attack at the World Trade Center. He was at work that day in management at the Border's Bookstore on September 11, 2001. He would get everyone safely out of the store and was walking across the bridge, when he looked back just in time to see the building collapse. I cannot tell you how relieved I was, with my parents in Florida, as we huddled together in prayer, when he was finally able to make a call to let us know he was ok. God had assured me He was spared before we ever got his call, and I was able to announce that to my distraught parents. That, too was a miracle. He still lives in New York City where he is an artist and writer, and provided the design for my front cover for this book he had just completed and had entitled "Mountain Top".

Speaking of bucket lists and mountain top experiences, we are still celebrating the fact that my grandson, Sean Savacool, Libby's son, achieved a real dream come true, that most musicians *only* dream about. This past (April 9, 2022), when he played on that great stage at the Grand Ole Opry, in Nashville, Tennessee, at a concert he did with popular country singer Waylon Payne.

Sean has been living in Nashville for many years, purchased a home there, and he plays with several country bands, sometimes touring in Europe and across the country. Some of the music he has played in, has been featured on television programs, and in movies. Ever since I took him to see Lulu Roman do a concert there, when he was eleven, he had wanted to play his guitar on that stage, he said.

I loved showing his picture on Facebook with my comment, that our Luckey family is so proud of him playing at the Opry. I said that I just knew his daddy, Jeff Savacool, his brother, Justin Savacool, and his grandpa, Gary Luckey, were all watching from the balconies of Heaven, and were still giving him a standing ovation, they are so proud of him and what he has accomplished!

Sean's mother Libby, and her husband, Phil Fraund, live and work in Nashville, as well, and also volunteer feeding the homeless under the ministry of Pastor Bob Beeman, the Sanctuary International heavy metal pastor to musicians around the world. This is something Libby had always wanted to do and had mentioned it since she was a teenager. In fact, Libby has performed many years on stage with Sheri singing backup, playing bass, and dancing so beautifully, gifted for worshipful and praise music. Phil, also very talented on keyboard, had played on stage with them in Nashville and in concerts;out of state.

Now I have grandchildren, not active solely in sports, but musically involved, too. Daphne wins championship ballgames; but, plays in the school bands and orchastras, as does Ernie, who now has his own band playing concerts and he's only seventeen. You know what? I can't think of a single member of our family and extended family, I'm not so proud of. I thank You Jesus, for answered prayers and for all these Blessings! Thank You God, for.......*Higher Ground!*

"Our 'Two Creeks Ranch' at Venus, FL on Fisheating Creek"

CHAPTER EIGHTEEN

TELL ME 'BOUT THE GOOD OLE DAYS

*"And thou shalt teach them,(God's ways), diligently **unto thy children**,
and shall talk of them when thou sittest in thine house, and when thou
walkest by the way, and when thou liest down and when thou riseth up."*
Deuteronomy 6:7 KJV

The verse above has always blessed me and Gary and we did obey the teaching to speak of these things God tells us to share with our children, and we have passed them down "unto the children's children and their children's children". There was an elderly Swedish ancestor of my Dad's Swan family, I believe his name was Jonas Johnson, who prayed the same prayer every day, that God would bless his children's children and their children's children and their children's children. I have always felt God's answer to all those prayers. It made an impact on my Dad to pray the same, and I have since carried on our "Family Tradition".

I can still hear my mother and dad laying in bed before falling asleep and praying aloud together. I would hear them name each member of the family by name, never leaving out anyone! I do that now, and it makes me feel so relaxed and happy to know I have placed each one in the Lord's care for His protection, healing, guidance, wisdom, salvation, and happiness....and then I sleep like a baby. I believe that as a child, when I would overhear my parent's precious prayers, it helped me sleep soundly then, too.

Some of my fondest memories are all the countless evenings when Gary would get a blazing campfire going and we'd sit around it in a circle, family members, sometimes their friends, visiting relatives, and new folks, too. It was common for one of the kids to say, or sing, "Whoa-oa Grandpa...tell us 'bout the good ole days!"

If you don't know what I'm talk' about, just Google the Judd's (Wynonna and her mama Naomi Judd), hit song, "Grandpa, Tell Me 'bout the Good Ol' Days!" And oh, how he would have 'em to tell! In fact, to this day I run into many of the fellas who grew up coming out to our camps and loved hearing Gary telling all his old hunting and fishing stories. We always said we'd record them for posterity's sake, but we never did get around to it. Today you'll have to ask Tifton. He had a front row seat when each story happened, and again, when it got told over and over thereafter, not to mention he was in most of them!

I'll have to leave all those hunting, woods, cow tales and adventures to him, but I can give you some of mine, and there were many nights the kids would say, "Grandma, tell us about the time..." and I would share the unbelievable, exciting, and miraculous events that shaped our lives. God was with us.

This is a pretty good place to admit something that you have probably just discovered. I am not a writer. I 'm really bad at doing an autobiography, and in English class I butchered my compositions as I attempted an orderly, chronological and proper essay structure. Why? because I just don't think and talk that way. I also delight in run-on sentences and sometimes making up my own words or how to spell them.

My mind is usually zipping by so fast and from one thing that leads to another, that you can see how I hop around from one decade to others, without putting them like most every book is supposed to be. Well, my "mountain" has been exactly like that, so thanks for bearing with me this far. *Just imagine we're sitting around that campfire and one story just leads right into another one and this is just how I'd be a'tellin' it!* Maybe someone would say, "tell us another one, Grandma!" So here goes:

THE BALL OF ICE:

One bright, hot, and sunny day in South Florida, the sky was blue, no planes, birds, or clouds. I stepped out the front door and walking halfway to my truck I could hear a shrill but soft, starting high and becoming more audible, lower-toned, moaning and whiring sound as if something was spinning from outer space coming in closer and closer! The sound came descending like a plane from the sky, becoming louder as it came down faster. And then suddenly, the loud "THUGH!" sound on the ground, directly in front of me!

I started to cover the top of my head but before I could, it landed on the grass right where I was going to step, in the direct pathway I was making toward the truck. What landed at my feet? *A PERFECTLY ROUND BALL OF ICE, about the size of a tether ball!* Remember those really big balls at school, a lot larger and heavier than a basketball.

I dialed 911 asking if they had any other calls about a ball of ice falling from the sky, landing in the county, and the amused dispatcher replied, "No Ma'am, you're the first one today!" She told me not to touch it, and that she was sending a deputy to look at it and hopefully it wouldn't melt first before he got there because it would take him awhile to reach our ranch.

I yelled for Gary to come outside and we bent over it, circled it, and decided it was clear to whitish-cream colored, and didn't apparently smell of gasses or chemicals. It began to sweat in the sunshine and although we didn't dare to touch it, it simply seemed to be a ball of ice that was just beginning to melt. It had a crack down the center but had not yet broken in halves, although it looked as though it might do so before the law arrived, anyway.

The deputy inspected it and concluded that, yep, it was a ball of ice inspite of no known aircraft having been above our home to my knowledge. If there had been, it would have been at such a tremendously high altitude that it made no sound below. The officer put half of it into a clear plastic evidence bag and wrote on the label, to take for testing; however, we never followed through to find out what the testing may have concluded.

He said when an airplane releases liquids from their sewage compartment, which is usually above the ocean, he thought, it forms a round ball because it spins as it falls through the sky spiraling downward. When he left, Gary placed the other half in a large plastic garbage bag without touching it, and stuck it in our freezer just in case it turned out to be something.......oh, *"sensational"*.

Gary teased me that had I been alone at the ranch and the ball had hit me on the head taking my life, and had the ice then melted, no one would have known what killed me, it would be a real murder mystery, he chuckled. Not only that, he made a joke that it would have made me irate that an airline had so carelessly caused it to happen, because they emptied the urinals, and yes, it became a funny joke whenever Gary told folks about the ball of ice and how it'd done me in. But the real joke would be on Gary and it was yet to come.

Almost a year passed and Gary had become quite the homemade ice cream maker. For many years he had only used the old fashioned hand cranking style where you have to repeatedly pour layers of ice cubes with salt until finally it hardens. Since he had a new electric one, he got in almost a daily habit of providing all of us with the delicious homemade ice cream the Luckey family was known for, usually vanilla flavored, made with their Eaglebrand canned milk recipe, rich and yummy!

One day we had unexpected company and they put in for some of Gary's famous ice cream, which tickled him big time. It was never any trouble to him, and he could never stop eating it till it was all gone, and there was seldom if ever, even a bowl left for the freezer. (He would eventually stop making it because he was gaining weight too fast.) He kept tending it carefully and several times he made additional trips to the freezers to add more ice.

We all sat around the Lucky Buck Ranch sunken living room, each devouring the most awesomely refreshing Luckey homemade ice cream, each holding our own oversized dessert bowl, oohing and aahing with every swallow of the icy cold treat on that hot summer's afternoon. Gary told them "Thank you" (for all the compliments), and then added, "Well, I'm just glad we ended up with enough ice to make it come out right!" It took all the ice I could find in the freezers without having to drive to town to get more.

One of the girls said, "This is even better than I remembered, it's really good, did you do anything different?" Gary and I looked at each other, our eyes got as big as saucers, my eyes locked together with his. In a very weak sounding voice he replied, "Yes, it is good, isn't it, Betty, wouldn't you say this is even rather, *"sensational"? Then I remembered that was how he'd referred to the ice from the sky, sensational.*

That day I got on the computer and finally did what I had been putting off doing for many months, and checked the news the week we had discovered that ball of ice. Sure enough, another identical ball of ice was discovered **the very same day** in North Florida, up in the panhandle. It was also a ball of ice that almost could have hit a man on his head that day. It tested as a reported, "tether-ball-sized' ball of ice originating from a jet plane who had discarded their bathroom wastes from such a high altitude they never amagined it would hold together all the way to earth!

That homemade ice cream would go down in the Luckey family history as the most notorious batch that Gary ever made. "What flavor was it?" someone asked, "Vanilla Bean"? "Nope," Gary answered, "that'n thar was Vanilla Pee!" Of course now, if you happen to be unfamiliar with how homemade ice cream is made, the ice is only used to freeze it from the *outside* of the cannister, but still just the thought it was processed by frozen urine, is shockingly repulsive (unless you just really love it like we did!)

THE PLATFORM SHOES:

When the girls were in high school we never seemed to ever have enough money for clothes and shoes. Well, Libby, Sheri and I each had a pretty good pair of shoes or two, but I'd found a pair at Goodwill one day we each loved and somehow they fit all of us! They were sorta rustic, with natural fibers, neutral colors, high platform open heel, and a hippie-looking style that was very much in vogue those days. I paid five dollars for them, and they were worth every penny!

The best part about them was how good they made you look in them regardless of what you had on, but were they comfortable! You would not have thought so to look at them, but you could wear them all day without even thinking about taking them off, now that's unusual. Well, one of the girls would want to wear them to school, and someone else needed them for a date, and I wanted them with my uniform on the midnight shift. So, guess what? Those shoes got worn *somewhere*, 24/7!

I have no idea what country they were made in, but they would not wear out. One day I thought it was time we got rid of them after a couple of years, so we'd quit juggling them around so. They were starting to show fraying along the edges, and it's bad enough to be poor, you don't want to look poor, too!

I'm afraid I got so accustomed to hearing the old country sayings, I forget when they should or shouldn't be repeated. See, its kinda neat that when we get older we can excuse about anything we do as elderly "moments". If people talk about my book and say that I probably shared a lot of things too personal to be sharing, I'll just rationalize, they're right, I should have written it when I was younger, but then you wouldn't catch the part about how sometimes it takes a lifetime to finally learn by all those mistakes.

We had almost needed a schedule on the fridge to keep track of who got the shoes next. Oh, and here's another major componant in this, Niki Lynn was maybe three or four and she could be heard clomping around in them through the house when everyone was home and nobody was going to town in them. I mean to tell you, those shoes saw some action.

It was sad the day I put them along with some old clothes into the Goodwill box. We were all going to miss them, but I figured they were "tellin' on us" and we needed new shoes. From that day on I missed them and so did we all. A few weeks later I was in Goodwill and there to my astonishment, were the platform shoes for sale for a dollar, way up on the top clearance shelf!

As I paid the dollar, the frowning cashier said, "Oooo, I could never, ever, be able to wear a heel that high in a million years. They have got to be so miserably uncomfortable, wouldn't you think so? I'll just give them to you, Ms. Luckey, they look like thay could fall apart. No telling how long they'll last".

"Yep," I smiled and replied, "Thank you, and I'll bet if these shoes could talk we would not believe where all they've been!"

You wanna know the truth? Those shoes *did* talk to me in this respect, the Lord said to me that when we were created we were like those shoes. We became so used and abused and covered with sin and dirt and ravels that we needed rescuing. Many of us got thrown away in some form or another, sold into a slavery or bondage of sinful living all planned by the devil. Then Jesus came and *He bought us back! He turns us into new creatures all clean and pure.*

That day I took them home, trimmed off the uneven fraying on the edges with my sharpest pocketknife, put Lemon Pledge on the wooden part, and vigorously brushed them with a little piece of denim, and they looked brand new! You wouldn't believe how happy the girls' eyes lit up when they saw them. "Yay...it looks like a brand new pair, Mom!" and off Niki ran with them on, going clump, clump clump, across the room once again, good for at least another year!

"THE RED SPIKED HIGH HEEL PUMPS" When Sheri was probably thirteen, we were out on a shopping trip with my parents. They were buying us each something we might see and really need or want. There were no malls yet, so it was a trip to south West Palm Beach where several discount clothing and department stores existed before the north county finally developed.

Each of the children picked something out, including me, and we were waiting on Sheri to find something, *anything,* but the bright red high heeled pumps she kept clutching to her heart like a "treasure" to her chest. I could see my Dad asking my Mom, something like...well, why not let her have them if it's going to make a young lady so happy....and Mother, with her frown that said....no, that's rediculous. But every suggested item we would find and show Sheri, she would shake her head at. We were all getting hungry and trying to speed things up, when finally, my Mother put her arm around my little girl and said, "Sheri, you probably won't have a place to wear them, but you do look adorable in them, and if your mother says its ok, then, if they will make you happy, we want you to have them."

Oh, my goodness, she was so happy I thought she'd cry, and if Tifton and Niki didn't eat soon, they *might* cry, and when Libby, who had shown Sheri every cute piece of clothing in the whole store, looked so relieved, I gave in. We hurried outside where my Dad sat waiting for us in his van, reading his Bible, and smiled as Sheri excitedly held up high the big bag with the red shoes in it.

The shoes, needless to say, got so wore out looking that they never lasted long enough to make it two or three more years to the impromtu concert that occurred one night in our yard at the ranch, stage, floodlights, full band and all. Sheri was the rock star for the event and her outfit was cool...but no shoes to go with it. I heard her telling her sisters that her old red heels she'd thrown away would have been perfect, when I had an idea.

They dried just in time, too! A big crowd was gathering near the bonfire, the guitars were tuning up, and Gary was still finding additional extension cords everyone was needing for speakers or lighting, when in walked Sheri. Her wardrobe was great, makeup to perfection, and bright red spiked heels that set off the whole look like dynamite! Wow.

I had just painted my old white high heel Easter shoes with a can of eighty eight cent Kmart spray paint, *and since the sun had just set,* they looked good as new. I thanked God for always providing for every need!

"MRS. LUCKEY! THERE'S A SOUL TO SAVE!" (I will also entitle the last chapter with this because I'll have even more to say about it later.)

Roger Primm, our neighbor one mile a way, living at "Far Out Farm" has called me three times in his life, or awakened me in the night, and I have already told you how he miraculously was able to help provide one hundred concert Bibles once for Sheri to throw out to her audience. He was confined in the hospital watching television. I was home and had prayed that evening for money to purchase the Bibles with. Evidently, the Lord had Wheel of Fortune pull his late mother's submitted entry card out of thousands minutes later, and when he heard her name announced, he called me desparately needing me to break into his house to call the TV station within ten minutes! I did, and it gave us the money for all the Bibles needed early the following morning.

Those Bibles were probably responsible for an unknown number of souls who may have been saved when they received them. We heard reports of what a blessing they were and one girl said because of that Bible she caught that night, it had turned her life around. Even a newspaper article that week mentioned Sheri had thrown out Bibles to the thankful crowd.

Time before that, Roger had called me from a small central Florida hospital where he was taken by ambulance. On a hunting trip he had stopped in the fog on the highway to assist at the scene of a wreck that had just occurred, when another truck came along, it collided into Roger pinning him against his truck and the trooper had said it looked like it had almost nearly cut him in half!

At the small country hospital he was taken to by ambulance, he heard workers saying that he wasn't going to make it. He didn't want to die there where he didn't know anyone, all alone, and with probably inferior care for such serious injuries. He sounded urgent on the phone as he asked me to get him out and get him to Jupiter Hospital at least a couple of hours away. I heard myself tell him I would do so immediately.

Of course I had no idea who to call and it was already late at night. As soon as we hung up I opened the phone book and turned to physicians names in the yellow pages. I prayed, "Jesus, show me the one!" As God is my Judge, on three or four pages of medical names, only one of them sort of stood out supernaturally, so I called it. The doctor who answered said it was a miracle he picked up that ringing phone. I told him there was a Jupiter "good ol' boy" who was dying, who had no insurance that I knew of and no doctor, and needed urgent help. He wrote down Roger's information and said he'd let me know something in a few minutes.

The phone rang and it was the doctor. He said this, (it makes me cry even now remembering the moment). "Mrs. Luckey I have an ambulance leaving the little town he's in right now and they are bringing him to Jupiter Hospital tonight". That awesome doctor would continue to see Roger through many surgeries ahead, save his life, and stay with him throughout his rehab following a leg amputation and many challenges. Roger would recuperate, wear a tux, and marry! He is still alive today and gives God all the Glory for sparing his life. Roger was a "soul we saved"... God saved! But wait, there's more! lol

The first event happened years before when he was out all night partying with friends and I was home sound asleep. I smelled beer and I heard Roger's voice, and he was shaking my blanket covered shoulder as I lay there next to my sleeping husband. He was urgently saying, "Mrs. Luckey, (he had always called me *Miz'* Luckey), wake up, its Roger, wake up!" He had walked right into our unlocked front door when no one had heard the knocking and calling.

"Come on, Miz Luckey, in the living room, WE HAVE A SOUL TO SAVE!" I put on my robe and joined him in the other room where another young man waited, humbled, rescued from coming too close to committing suicide, and delivered into a room full of believers who prayed with him into God's Kingdom. He prayed the prayer to accept Jesus into his life and his heart, and we all sang Gospel songs till the sun came up.

Sheri and Gary joined in with us and we played a country album someone had just given us about salvation, and we all sang with our new brother in Christ, "Ain't Givin' Up Now!" I have never heard that song since, but it was the perfect song for that night we had someone who was givin' up for real and we had a "soul to save!"

To this day, if I pass out tracts, for instance, I will still hear Roger's voice, or whenever I need some immediate motivation to get up and go to church, or get to a revival service, or visit with some lost folks, or *write a book*, or rise and shine to start the day.....I will hear..."Get up Miz. Luckey, "We gotta soul to save!"

ANGELS ON ASSIGNMENT:

When the new book came out, "Angels on Assignment" by Charles and Frances Hunter, I could not put it down. It was about the angels at work in our lives and the true testimonies of people who could tell how they had performed miracles for the Glory of God in their normal every day lives. Their purpose was to promote activity that would lead people to the Lord. I was fascinated because I was experiencing so many similar supernatural happenings in my own life,

When Libby's fiance, Chris Primm, who was Roger's younger brother, was planning one day to marry her, he had told me this. "Mrs. Luckey I want to marry Libby after I turn twenty-one, because I feel like I'm not going to make it to my 21st birthday,"and he didn't. "I don't want to change her name, maybe leave her with a child, but I want you to know how much I love her."

I was home alone reading the book the day he unexpectedly pulled up in the yard with a truck full of fishing buddies. He just needed to stop by to pick up his hat and sunglasses he'd left in Libby's room. Surprisingly, his friends all came inside with him and plopped down on the sofas arranged in a square with a coffee table in the center. I had placed my book on that table and prayed, "Lord I won't tell them all about you today unless one of them asks me about the book". I will take that as a signal from You, that I am to share the Gospel message with them right now.

I chatted happily with the guys a minute when one of them asked what I was reading. Well that was what that book was about, witnessing to the lost at every opportunity, especially when the Lord sets up divine appointments to do so, which He does. I knew immediately this was one of those, and He had given me my sign.

I told the six young men absolutely *everything in a nutshell!* They all listened so intently and Chris conveniently remained down the hallway where he heard everything I told them. As they left they each thanked me and I knew I had been given the chance to share the Gospel and it had been so well received. As Chris donned his glasses and cap he looked at me and said "Thank you, Mrs. Luckey," as he walked out the door. I hadn't done anything except share Jesus with his buddies, and he was thanking me for it. I realized it would have taken him only a minute to get his stuff, but he had lingered so I'd have the time to do it!

I would see the six men two weeks later as they served as pallbearers carrying Chris's body at the funeral. The Lord had prepared them all that day for what was ahead, Chris as well. I could only thank Him. The book had been released in 1979 and he was killed driving my pickup truck with Libby in it, in 1980. There were even more miraculous stories connected to his passing and how it affected our whole family because we were all close to him. He was planning on taking Tifton fishing the following morning on Island Way in Tequesta, and Tifton was heartbroken at the age of 14. The doctor had said Libby had only a broken collar bone, but he was wrong, her heart was broken also.

The following year on Easter Sunday morning I was returning from the sunrise service on the beach when I heard the Lord tell me explicity to drive over to **Tammy Wynette's** home on the ocean and leave "Angels on Assignment" at her door. It was in my truck and I knew where her house was, so I did it immediately. Of course, I was a little hestitant not knowing what I would do when I got there with it, so I asked God to please help me. I mean, how strange for someone you don't know to come to your private residence very early on an Easter morning?!

As I pulled into the front driveway someone was walking out the door so I rolled down my window and handed the book out of it as I greeted them, saying, "The Lord wants me to leave this for Tammy, if you would please see she gets it." Within the next year Tammy returned it to me in the mail with a thank you note how thoughtful for me to leave it for her and that it had been a blessing to her. I was sad when I heard she had passed away but was glad I had been given the chance to share the Gospel with one of my favorite country singers.

I would later be the chaperone in Haiti with kids from our church and Georgette Jones was among them, she is the daughter of Tammy Wynette and George Jones. It was very special one night when she couldn't sleep so I stayed up with her and she sang song after song for me her parents had written that were love songs about her, their little girl. Who knew! I told her God also, wrote a love song to us and His name is Jesus.

TWENTY-FIVE NEW DRESSES:

Speaking of Haiti, while on the mission trip we had been instructed to wear cool, modest, inexpensive clothing and make plans to leave them there in Haiti when we left as part of our ministry to one of the most poverty stricken countries on earth, so we did. Actually, I had been wearing not much more than police uniforms for years and so just before the trip, Gary had me buy a new wardrobe at a discount store, but even that was a splurge for us, at the time.

When we left the mission field there, it was so exciting and rewarding to see the excitement on their faces as we left our laundry baskets overflowing with new-like clothing they would now launder and use, a souvenier of our time of ministry among them. On my flight home I hoped when Gary saw my empty suitcase he wouldn't be mad I'd given all of it away.

As I pulled up to the house I was thinking about my new job I was starting at the church that week as their new front office receptionist and security person and worried about what I'd ever wear! That was foolish, when the Bible says even the birds don't have to be anxious about what they'll wear or eat because their Heavenly Father takes care of them.... and how much more so, He will take care of us!

Gary said, "Oh, I forgot to tell you, Sue Clingan stopped by one day and dropped off something that's laying on the bed in there". It was twenty-five brand new "church" dresses with the tags still on them, perfect for a receptionist at the Maranatha Church of God in Palm Beach Gardens. They had been given to her by a wealthy lady she was working for who thought she might know someone they might fit. They were just my size. Yes, God clothed the birds, and He clothed me, too.

THE HEAVENLY TOWELS:

Once when we were moved out of the house we'd just sold, and about to move into the one we'd just built, we needed a place to live while our belongings were in storage, so we rented a motel room for a month. It was like resort living with the continental breakfasts, wonderful pool and recreational facilities, and playground for the children. We went through so many of their nice white towels in a month's time, I began to rationalize how we had spent such top dollar to be staying there, that surely they wouldn't mind if I accidently on purpose got some of them mixed in with the dirty laundry I'd be taking to the laundramat while we were there.

When we were making preparations to do just that on our final day there, I put all our laundry in big trash bags mixed with the nice, new looking white towels of all sizes that were going to look so good in the linen closet at the new house. After all, I needed new towels and couldn't afford to go buy them, especially after all the expenses we were dishing out to make the change of residence.

I started backing out of the motel parking lot when I heard a familiar voice. He said something like, "Betty, aren't you forgetting something?" I told the Lord yes, but that I thought He'd understand? Maybe? Or forgive me ahead of time? "Thou shall not steal", He said. Busted. I stopped the truck and gazed up at the sky saying I was sorry, so sorry. He asked me to keep looking up. Sometimes we just *need to look up,* I've learned. I gasped!

"What's wrong Mama?" I heard Libby asking. Up in the sky as far as the east was from the west, were tall stacks of Heavenly towels of every size and pastel color, (mostly shades of lavender, my favorite) as far as I could see! They were made to appear even more beautifully colored as they reflected the wonderful sunset colors from the pink, golden, and orchid clouds above. "It's a vision, a real vision the Lord is giving me of towels. Thousands of gorgeous top of the line, fluffy pretty towels, reminding me I forgot something important!" Libby sort of nonchalantly raised her eyebrows.

God spoked to me. "OK, Betty, you have a choice here, do you want your white ones, or would you rather have *these*?"

I pulled around to the maid's laundry room where two women employees were working with the door standing open. I told them we were about to leave but I had mistakenly, (it was about to be a mistake, alright!), mixed their towels in with my laundry so I'd be taking a few minutes to sort them out. The kids helped me in the back of the truck and the ladies helped carry 'their' white towels over to the big commercial size washing machine.

For the rest of my entire lifetime if there was *anything* I would ever be tempted to take that didn't belong to me....all I had to do was remember all those Heavenly towels and how God sure knows how to keep us clean, (and get us dry!) and keep us on the right mountain roads.

CELEBRITIES:

PERRY COMO had a home in the Jupiter Inlet Colony and a weekly televised program singing all his great hits so popular at that time. I was going to school with his niece, who was singing with me in the high school choir. I asked her if we could pull a real Christmas surprise for everyone and visit Perry Como's front yard when we went caroling in a few days. She set it up and I think we even surprised the choir teacher, Mr. Hupp.

When we slowly drove through the Colony and pulled into his driveway the group of twenty all whispered, "This is Perry Como's house!" and when he and his lovely wife, Roselle, actually stepped outside their front door, inviting us to come inside, I thought someone might pass out! Perry Como was a household name to everyone in those days.

They were so gracious and served us pastries and hot cocoa on the back patio. When our choir leader asked him to sing for us, he laughed and declining, told us that he was there to hear us sing and requested Silent Night. As we sang he put his arm around his wife and wiped tears from his eyes.

One Thanksgiving my mother had put the turkey in the oven and suggested we go over to the Jupiter beach to swim and sunbathe while the dinner cooked. We could see a tanned man in nothing but khaki shorts jogging from a distance toward us, his Catholic metal swinging from side to side from the chain around his neck. Mother said, "Oh, my goodness, we're here alone on this whole beach with none other than Perry Como! As he passed us, she said, "Happy Thanksgiving, Mr. Como!" He smiled and waved and said, "Happy Thanksgiving to each of you!"

We had a lot of friends who said they would frequently see him at the Jupiter Post Office, but this was our first encounter with the famous man. It was Perry who sang one of Gary's favorites, making it the number one song on the Hit Parade, "Catch a Falling Star, and Put it in your Pocket".

Libby would always ask Gary to sing it for her, and he loved to! I can still hear his voice and it would bring back so many happy family moments together. When Niki, Ernie, and Daphne flew in from Minnesota, he sang it for them before they left, one last time. *We will hear him singing it again, gang.*

People would also see **BURT REYNOLDS** at the Jupiter Post Office. Now Burt and his parents had a ranch close to our pasture and Mr. Reynolds, Burt's dad would pull Gary's truck out for him with his tractor when he got stuck. Gary's dad and Burt's dad were friends and the daddy had introduced us to Burt one day at his ranch, when Burt had come riding up on a horse.

But my favorite time was one day we were there with Mr. and Mrs. Reynolds when I needed to use the phone to have my dad come pick me up. Papa Reynolds was taking Gary back to our truck with his tractor. Burt's mother allowed me and my children to go inside and to use the phone in his fabulous batchelor quarters that was a cabin attached to the main house by a long veranda. Everything inside was so strickingly decorated in black and a deep rich bright red.

However, the best time was the day I was trying to ride down Jupiter

Farms Road and two horseback riders were blocking me from passing, so, careful that I wouldn't spook the horses, I drove behind them slowly, keeping a little distance. Then I realized just who they were. It was Burt on a horse, accompanied by a beautiful **DINAH SHORE**, the famous singer and actress!

She was dressed totally in all bright yellow western wear, including her riding pants, belt and buckle, ruffled long sleeved blouse, yellow boots and cowboy hat! It really showed off her dark tan, white teeth (they were both laughing), her nice figure, and the sunshine lit the outfit up like a radiant sunbeam! When they glanced at me they both waved and moved over so I could slowly pass. Not before getting to see how attractive they both looked and noticing how cute and flirty they were with each other. Now that would have been a real photo some media buff would have wanted to capture, and I was all alone with the two celebrities on a lonely country dirt road. Now, Burt was, of course, handsome, but Dinah was absolutely, dazzling, and didn't look a day over thirty years of age!

During my two years working as a security guard at Trinity Broadcast Network, and singing in the choir, my favorite guest singer was **DOTTIE RAMBO.** When she was there and would sing her original music she had written and recorded, together with her testimony of how she happened to put such outstanding lyrics and melody together, it was anointed like none other. When she was there, no one ever left that auditorium the same as when they'd come in.

Our choir had one of the finest backstage facilities in the business of ministry, and we would use the huge room to put on our choir robes over our clothing, with ample mirrors for makeup, hair styling, and primping. One night I had inadvertently, just carrying it nonchalantly in my hand, taken my can of hair spray with me to my seat up in the choir loft, oh no, it could be a real problem and no time to get rid of it, so I set it down on the floor by my chair. Why in the world I had done something like that was beyond me, and I was glad our robes camoflaged any items, such as a purse, from the television cameras. If anyone saw the can, I was sure I'd be in serious trouble. I could just see it rolling across the stage during a serious alter call, seen "coast to coast and around the world!" Why, I'd be fired. I would keep it hidden as best I could, and I prayed.

As the crowd was taking their seats in the grand auditorium, and the choir members were in our chairs behind the closed stage curtain, we would use that moment to pray as a group for the service along with our great choir director **Bill Morris.** It would be the final word to the choir just prior to the flood lights all bursting forth and the stage curtains opened before drum roll and the grand familiar announcer's voice would proclaim, "And now, from coast to coast and around the world, its time to Praise the Lord!" Now it was just a few minutes before this time when Bill would make any program announcements or changes, as the lights were starting to be lowered in the auditorium.

Suddenly, an stage hand ran from the side curtain and whispered something in an urgent manner to Bill, who promptly made a startling request: "We have a crisis here on the side stage, because someone needs hair spray this instant, and is urgently asking if anyone happens to have hair spray with them here on the stage!" There was no time for anyone to make a dash to the choir room.

With one swoop of my arm, I grabbed the can (I had been trying to conceal), holding it high above our heads and watched as Mr. Morris burst into laughter, and with immense relief, shaking his head, he said, "Only Betty Luckey would have a can of hair spray backstage, and would save the day, and solve Dottie Rambo's hair emergency, thank you Betty!"

Oh my goodness, I thought, my name and Dottie's name in the same sentence! Thank You, Jesus for this little "big" miracle in my life. I just helped my favorite singer, song writer of my whole lifetime! I don't think I have ever been what you'd call "star-struck" before, about any celebrity, except that night I discovered that I truly was, when my Walmart "Aqua Net" saved the show. And the very secret I was concerned with, would be the very thing I would proudly reveal to Bill and the whole choir.

I already told in a previous chapter how I came to move in with the famous HeeHaw comedian, **LULU ROMAN,** in Nashville one year, and what a blessing she'd been to me. I would drive her to the airport on occasion, serve as security or companion, attend a few of her rehearsals with her, and one night in particular she had wanted to slip into a row toward the back of the Grand Ole Opry, unnoticed, when the crowd did notice and gave her a standing ovation that didn't end until she announced, "Y'all can 'set' down now!" and everyone howled and clapped even longer. I had the upstairs in her lovely log home on a hill overloooking Nashville, where I would sleep in the daytime, patroling the TBN grounds during the night, singing in the TBN choir in the nightly evening service.

It would be Lulu who was with Dottie Rambo traveling in a tour bus on an all night ride to make it for a Mother's Day weekend concert in Texas, when the driver wrecked the bus, in Missouri, and Dottie went to be with the Lord on Mother's Day May 11, 2008.. My favorite of all her songwriter hit songs was, "We Shall Behold Him".

My mother used that beautiful recording at the Brighton Seminole Indian Reservation one time to act out with Indian sign language and dance movement, its powerful message about meeting Jesus one day "face to face", in all His Glory. It would break my heart to know we'd never see Dottie alive again, this side of Heaven, but rejoicing that she is with her Savior beholding Him face to face, and knows His Glory, for real! My Mama, too.

THE SURPRISE TRIP TO PTL:

Praise the Lord (PTL) Christian television network was the channel the TV was on most of the time. I had ordered a wonderful Bible, a one hundred dollar donation, for a Living Bible and King James Version dual Bible they would send to you with a promise to pay it later. I loved it and I began to save my money.

The program originated from studios in Charlotte, North Carolina, at their fantastic Christian resort, Heritage, USA. Every time the commercials came on, the kids and I would always look up from what we were doing and see people there staying in rented little log cabins with fireplaces, swimming with a water slide, picturesque hiking trails, sightseeing, eating at quaint little mountain restaurants, attending concerts and services at the huge auditorium, featuring the most popular musicians and Bible teachers of the time. We all wanted to go. It was all I could do at the time to save up a hundred dollars, there was no way we could afford to have room, meals, gas money, for a week in the North Carolina mountains. But I prayed for it anyway.

I had even asked Gary if we could all go on a mini vacation, and he said he had to work, but if I got the money somehow, I was free to take the kids and go. Wow, well, that was something, I prayed some more. I decided my first obligation was to pay for my Bible. I stopped by a bank that was convenient at the time, to buy a money order to mail in my Bible money.

The teller first asked me if I had an account there, otherwise it was against policy and she was not allowed to issue money orders for folks without accounts there. Sadly I said, no, I had no account there. Then as I turned to leave, she said let me run your name on my computer, and then asked me for my social security number. "Oh, you have an account, Ma'am" she said and read off to me all my information. I have no idea why I had money in an old account, probably when there had been a mortgage there when the kids were born, or something.

"How much is in my account?" I asked her. "Seven hundred" she said. "In that case here is the one hundred for my money order, and I'll withdraw my "savings" in small bills, please!" I think we skipped out of the bank, all of us, me and all four children, with huge smiles on our faces.

It was an awesome time on our trip, eating in the restaurants, sleeping in the cabin, hearing Phil Driscoll on his trumpet, and seeing the leaves changing on the trees, praying in the Upper Room, where we put Gary's picture on the wall, and looking in all the gift shops. I never did know if it was because there was money there from an old account, or if it was a banking error, but this I do know...it was an answer to my prayer, and we were Blessed! And...it would be the story I would tell if one of the kids said, "Hey, Mom, **tell us about the time** we went on our vacation!" Those were some *good ol' days, that was for sure!*

"Author's front door too remote on the mountain for the trick or treaters"

CHAPTER NINETEEN

NO MORE HALLOWEEN FOR ME!

"Wherefore come out from among them, and **be separate, saith the Lord,** *and touch not the unclean. And I will receive you. And I will be a Father to you, and ye shall be my sons and daughters, saith the Lord Almighty. Having therefore these promises, dearly beloved,* **let us cleanse ourselves from all filthiness of flesh and spirit,** *perfecting holiness in the fear of God.*
2Cor 6:17, 18, 7:1 KJV

There is a Bible verse in 1Corinthians 13:11 KJV, saying "When I was a child, I spake as a child, I understood as a child, I thought as a child; but when I became a man, I put away childish things". It's true we do foolish things that later in life we find it very hard to believe we could have ever been so naive, misinformed, or rebellious.

For me, one of those events was to decorate or dress up for Halloween. Back then, I didn't see it as evil or that I was celebrating a Satanic holiday or that it was conflicted with my strong Christian beliefs, it took some enlightenment. I "put it away", not so much as a foolish thing, as it is a dangerous and potentially deadly involvement, in which Satan will try to use it to steal your soul to Hell, a real place, created for him, not you!.

I'm sure some folks will read my book and think how could someone so spiritually following Jesus, do some things I remember Betty Luckey doing? There are several mistakes I made and there was a wonderful "reset", a repentance that took place as the Holy Spirit brought strong conviction and I did an "about face!", as the marchers say. Some corrections were thankfully immediate, while others took it, 'settling in' on layers, you might say.

One of those learning lessons got spread out over a few years from starting, to always go trick or treating and always dressing up, with church Halloween parties, then to Hallelujah parties, to no party...just revival! I used to decorate, then no decorating, just preparing some trick or treats, now I want no part of any part of it. The demonic realm became so real, so understood to be just as the Bible describes it to be, that I cannot in any way, shape, or form, give it recognition or celebration.

I laughed one day on television when Prophet Robin Dale Bullock told the story how he was waiting in an office and saw the candy bowl there for patrons to help themselves to, but when he picked it up to indulge, saw the Halloween image on the wrapper and set it back down. That's me, too! We both don't want anything that is, as the Bible puts it, "offered up, or consecrated to, or for memorial or dedication for, anything having to do with the enemy, Satan. Well it took awhile for it to set in, that everything Halloween was Satanic, but now I see it is.

There may still be people around who came to some of my early Halloween parties, one I can't forget because I had the whole thing sort of left to me to lead, after it was already publicized, at the last minute, and I had to think fast. Of course today my "fast" answer would be, "Sorry, not me!" with a nice smile! "I don't do Halloween!"

It was at our church in Palm Beach Gardens where my dad was pastor, and when I was given only a two hour notice, and I needed an hour of it just to drive to town. I grabbed a white sheet for a costume, a litter of several new kitttens our cat had recently, (I understood the person absent was to have provided prizes for the best costumes), and all the cookies in my kitchen, my orange Kool Aid packets, and my Bible. I made it just in time to see a fellowship room filling up with costumed children. I was thankful there were 'understanding' mothers there who helped me make the pitchers of drinks and had brought more cookies.

What the 'understanding' mothers may not have agreed with, naturally, was giving away real live meowing kittens as the awards for the best costumes, but they were so adorable they were the hit of the party, and are still responsible for the population of cats in Cabana Colony to this day!

Now maybe you will sympathize with me if you just imagine how you would spend the next hour entertaining fifty children with a Halloween theme. Well, I just relied on doing what I had done my whole life as a Sunday school teacher and I led them in every kid's chorus I knew, and they sang the songs enthusiasically at the top of their lungs to chase the evil spirits out.

I was wrapped in my sheet and I was carrying my Bible, remember, and I told a couple of spooky like stories, or illustrations with the happy ending of Jesus coming to the rescue and I used inspirational Scripture the witches, skeletons, pirates, and princesses in front of me, would understand. All in all it was a child evangelism meeting of great success and we all prayed together the typical Sinner's Prayer as we closed.

I got the shock of my life though, when a mother was leaving with her young son by the hand and I heard her asking him, "Did you have a good time?" "Yes Ma'am," he said, and then quite seriously, but with excitement in his voice, I heard him add, *"Mrs. Luckey was the Holy Ghost!"*

Oh, my Lord, God, again I ask, *please forgive me!* What examples have I set in my lifetime that would make me so ashamed of myself. Please help me correct them, Lord! It made me wonder just how many other children had been affected or had noticed or interpreted my "costume" as I had obviously somehow misrepresented myself that night. I certainly hoped no one else had thought or said I dressed up to be the Holy Ghost.

When Maranatha Church of God said they sure could use me at their youth Hallelujah party at the lovely home of one of the leaders, I went even though I needed to wear a costume if possible, they'd said. Since I had some white feathers and a fully-teased whiteish blonde wig, white Indian beads, and a simple long lacy white dress with a slip that went with it, I went as an "Indian Angel". I cringed when I heard it announced, "Now if you need anything this evening, see Mrs. Luckey by the door, just look for *Jan Crouch!*"

Let me step in right here and tell you something about Mrs. Jan Crouch, Co-founder with her husband, Paul, of Trinity Broadcast Network. She was one of my favorite people in the whole wide world.

There were few others who I ever knew in my lifetime, that I had more respect for and admiration. So that presumptuous remark was actually a compliment to me.

Jan was the greatest soul winner in the "whole wide world" because TBN not only reached our Continent for Jesus, but all the countries around the planet with the good news of the Gospel! When she'd give her testimony she would sometimes elude to the facts that brought her to rely on her beautiful hair styles, makeup, and clothing. Those things had helped provide her with additional boldness and self confidence to someone basically intimidated that she was now ministering before millions of people.

I was employed at the TBN compound near Nashville for almost two years, as the midnight shift security guard. What an assignment, thank You, Jesus! I walked through the gardens that were all lit up at night with millions of little twinkling lights in the trees and across the buildings. Multi colored floodlamps were showing off the lovely landscaping and bubbling waterfalls with softly playing beautiful Christian hymns and music coming from the many hidden speakers throughout the grounds, twenty-four hours a day.

Sometimes I drove my black pickup very slowly along all the driveways, or sat in the truck positioned in strategic places, but my favorite thing was to walk throughout all the grounds on the walkways checking doorknobs and buildings and from there, I could catch a very brief sight of the private courtyard attached to the Crouch's personal living quarters when they were not in California.

Our precious Jan could be seen walking, strolling, standing, on her patio or porch area and garden, that little Bible she always carried, in her hand, praying softly with tears pouring down her cheeks, speaking aloud, but I stayed at such a distance, of course, and couldn't have been able to make out or hear the words, and names, but *she really prayed!*

I know she had no idea I was able to see her, and it caused me to never leave the area when I knew she was praying outside like that. I made sure no one was in the vacinity and that she was secure and safe, but would never have allowed her awesome prayertime to be disturbed or interrupted. No wonder their ministry was so blessed and even now since their passing, those memories of that beautiful prayer warrior, pretty even without any wig or makeup, inspire me still. What will always stay with me, was her weeping. I had the Bible verse this morning about "Blessed is he who is weeping now because he will be rejoycing." Luke 6:21 KJV says, "Blessed are ye that hunger now; for ye shall be filled. Blessed are ye that weep now; for ye shall laugh".

Tifton may have been sixteen or seventeen when he stopped by the house to get ready for a Halloween party he'd just been invited to. He would only have a few minutes to dress up in something, and couldn't think of anything at the moment. Well right in front of us on the kitchen counter was an apron and rolling pin and Sheri finishing up some pumpkin pies. We had a fluffy black bathing cap that looked like a wig, and when you stretched and squeezed it on over your hair, it sort of made you look like you had an Afro hairstyle. We all looked at each other and one of us said, "Are you thinking what I'm thinking?"

I told Tifton if he wanted to be Aunt Jemima I could write her name on the apron, and we had some left over black paint that had been a part of a cammo kit for hunting, we offered to smear on his face, neck, arms and hands. I had a dress he could pull on over his jeans and western shirt, he could keep it tied at the waist to keep the dress from hanging down too long, and then he stuffed it with toss pillows. I used a wide magic marker to write the lettering big enough on the apron that people could read it well.

The Aunt Jemima commercials were very popular at that time, and it was also a period of time in our political and cultural history that the racial climate seemed peaceful, congenial, and would find Tifton, posing as the famous television pancake cook, even to his black classmates, a hilarious costume and certainly not offensive, or he would not have done it.

This is another one of those examples, folks, about...would you ever, *ever,* do such a thing *now? No way!* And y'all probably were smart enough to not have done it back then, because things went south, *fast!* It soon proved not to be a good idea by any means. If I only knew then what I know now. Even now, I don't like to see people dressing up as Indians, but back then it wasn't considered to be offensive. Please Lord forgive us for all our misgivings, the ones we're aware of and the ones we're not aware of. I no longer have any part, any longer, of anything connected to Halloween.

Sheri had helped him into his pillow-stuffed clothing, apron, black foundation, black curly wig, and then she handed him her big heavy, wooden rolling pin, the finishing prop. What was humerous was he was wearing his cowboy boots with this outfit, his daddy's red kerchief tied on the wig, and watching him get into his truck, I just shook my head as he drove toward town, and prayed for his protection.

Beeline Highway in Palm Beach County is a long lonely stretch of four-lane roadway that can be quite isolated. Tifton soon saw though, that he was not alone, but that a pickup truck with three unruly "tricksters" or harrassers, were riding close beside him instead of passing. They were young men wearing caps and sunglasses, grinning at him and yelling something. At first he tried ignoring them and kept his window up.

Tifton reached down under his seat and got out his loaded revolver, placing it on the seat next to him, beside his rolling pin. It was never clear to me if the culprits thought they were messing with a real woman or if they knew they had a party-goer in costume, but either way, it turned down right deadly serious when the fella by the window stuck a gun out and pointed it at Tifton, who was already driving well above the speed limit.

Tifton, then pointed his gun at the other man and when he did, they took off faster than ever and somewhere up ahead disappeared out of sight. Remember there were no cell phones yet and it would be another ten minutes before there was a gas station with a phone. He wasn't sure if they were going to show up again, or if they were going to call police, (which he learned later they had, and reported he had pulled a gun on them), so he stopped by the payphone in front of the gas station and dialed 911.

Not two minutes later a Sheriff's patrol car pulled up with his window down, screeched to a halt, looked at Tifton, and with his radio microphone in his hand, he said on it, *"What I got here, Sarg, is... Aunt Jemima... in a phone booth... with a loaded 44!"*

Thankfully, he would only be late for a party, and have a delay before getting his gun back, being a minor, but the trick or treat part of the incident could have been much worse. Actually, several hard lessons were learned from the incident, and I felt guilty later even just knowing I was supposed to be the "adult in the room", a much smarter mama than to be allowing such a thing. I would never ever want to make anyone think I held any disrespect for their tribe, race, religion, or culture. We live and learn. Thank You, God, that you help prevent us from the grief we sometimes deserve. That's truly what Grace is all about.

Well, twenty one years prior to that I dressed up too, actually thinking no one was going to know it was me, but everybody soon knew. I was very pregnant with Libby who was born on December 6, 1961. I had seen in the newspaper that there would be a big Halloween promotion on that Saturday at the Southdale Shopping Center down in West Palm Beach the last weekend in October. The timing couldn't be more perfect if I could win the "best costume first prize" which they said was fifty dollars. That was huge in my life at that time. Our insurance paid for all the obstetric care and the hospital, but the doctor had a co-pay amount he expected of fifty dollars before the baby came.

Now I had a brainstorm and believed I could think up the best costume ever in spite of being eight months pregnant. I think Gary was impressed that I was willing to try to win the money, and it would be a big financial relief to him especially. I noticed he just laughed about it and probably didn't really believe I was going to follow through, until that day. My preparations were detailed. I would use another shower cap or bathing cap for this costume, also.

The first thing I did was pull down a lot of Spanish moss from the oak trees in our yard. Pa Luckey told me that moss had little bugs and lice in it and if he was me he'd spray it good and rinse it well before putting it on my head. That's when I hung it on the clothes line with clothespins and used bug spray, then after it dried, I rinsed it all off with a hose and let it dry again.

When it was ready I sewed the moss onto my swim cap so that when I put the cap on my head, the gray moss would be a wig that would trail down to my knees from the top of my head. I even had some of it in front hiding parts of my face. I didn't know what I was becoming until I found I had a lot of green food coloring which I spread all over my face and neck, my legs and feet, and arms and hands, using cold cream first as moisturizer. I wore a Hawaiian mumu, the oversize dress with just an opening for your head and arms, that also went down to my knees, and I was barefoot.

Because I was eight months along I was pretty big in front. Gary told me he was afraid that at a community Halloween event there might be someone who would assume I had a pillow under the dress and attempt to punch it, or something, so he volunteered to stay close to me during the "parade" of contestants who would be walking in a large circle in the parking lot, in front of the judge's table.

I made a sign I hung from a piece of pink yarn that said, "**EXPECTANT GHOUL**", allowing it to hang on my backside. In front I kept my hands holding little pale blue baby booties I was knitting. I would plan to walk around the circle slowly, tilting my head back slightly with eyes opened as wide as I could keep them open, sort of zombie looking. I would go round and round in the judge's circle knitting the booties and humming "Rockabye Baby" with an eerie, shakey-voice sound to it.

I was actually very relieved to have Gary with me because there were energetic unsupervised kids running around, a dog or two, and I kept a weird feeling that maybe this wasn't such a great idea after all.

The event was covered with a full crew of news media, television cameras with big bright lights, reporters with smaller cameras and little lights, and a ton of news people with clipboards and tape recorders. Gary did a good job of dodging them and didn't want anyone to notice him in the crowd, especially didn't want any Pratt and Whitney Aircraft folks from work, who would undoubtedly be there, to know he was married to the ghoul, who'd fathered the baby ghoul! I didn't tell him at the time, but as he was attempting to disguise himself with sunglasses and a cowbot hat pulled down on his forehead, he actually looked more like he was a "cowboy" costume contestant, than a cattleman trying to (unsuccessfully) hide in the crowd.

The procession of contestants began and the announcer at the microphone, who was standing in front of spotlights, explained there would be four or five catagories, who would be chosen first, but that there would be the fifty dollar prize awarded lastly, to the best overall costume. I began slowly walking between a pirate in front of me, and a pretty Hawaiian dancer in a grass-skirt, covered bikini. There may have been a hundred costumes in all, or more. It's not easy to see that good with Spanish moss in your eyelashes.

Occasionally I would not see Gary who was supposed to be next to me as close as posible, and I began to realize that he had "positioned" himself to actually walk closer behind the dancer! Ooo ...I started getting more annoyed by the moment, as I felt an angry jealousy creep into my own creepiness. I thought he was watching her more than he was me! I felt so jealous I really got into the ghoul character and hummed the rockabye lullaby louder than ever with the meanest of eyes! You need to be reminded that pregnant women can feel a lot more emotional insecurity during those times, so I'm sure it had some bearing on my frustration.

I reminded myself of our Christian drama coach, who, when we were in rehearsals for the church dramas and musicals, would say, ok, now do that one more time, this time with *ENERGY!* Yep, glancing back he was watching the dancing and I was livid, and I gave my little dramatic dramatization lots of energy!

The winners had already been pulled out of the crowd, and the dancer became one of those. It was announced that the contestants would no longer be circling, and that the winner was to be announced, and come to the microphone. "Our winner tonight for the best over-all costume is....the EXPECTANT GHOUL"! The crowd cheered and clapped and I was so delighted I was receiving the money and my doctor bill would be paid in full, I gladly stepped up to the microphone and as he asked me to introduce myself, I could see Gary glancing again at the dancer, so instead of saying Betty Luckey.......I replied, *"MRS. GARY LUCKEY"!*

Oh...that felt so good! "Ok," said the announcer, "is Mr. Ghoul here tonight, will Mr. Gary Luckey please come to join us?" I saw my sheepishly looking husband come to the mic, face red with blushing, but grinning from ear to ear, as the cameras flashed and reporters everywhere wrote down his name. He hugged me in front of everyone, kissing me on my green cheek, and now *the dancer looked jealous! I* not only had the handsome cowboy, I got him *and* the check for fifty dollars!

There was another Halloween several young people will never forget. It was a quiet night in our rural neighborhood, so far out in the country from town, my closest neighbors a mile away had named their ranch, "Far Out Farm". There were no trick or treaters so my family sat around the campfire in our front yard eating my huge pile of Reese's peanut butter cups, along with about six neighborhood teenagers. I sat down on the porch swing we had hanging from a tree branch, and joined them.

The topic for discussion at that moment was just how much fun it had been when they were little, to be able to dress up and go door to door every year. I could see how bored they all looked, eating candy, throwing the little orange and brown paper wrappers in the fire to watch them burn, and staring at the flames. I decided (evidently without pre-thought or praying about it), to surprise them. I said, "Hey, y'all, I have enough white sheets for each of you, and a Publix bag to put your loot in, let's go to town and go trick or treatin'!" Oh what exuberance and laughter, well, if you could just picture what some of those guys were going to look like wrapped in a sheet you'd be laughing, too. Minutes later I was driving my truck with Niki up in the front with me, and the kids on hay bales in the back of my pickup.

Where I used to take my four youngun's to do this, was at the big fancy condominiums where retirees really welcomed kids and had prepared for them, seldom getting many. I would park in the parking lot where I could sit in the truck and watch them at each door. The folks loved to see the costumes and to have little children knocking on their doors and, ...well, on second thought, the senior population might not be too relaxed to see a group of teenagers draped in sheets at their private domain, so I had a brainstorm!

I would take them to a place they had never been, well, not at nightime, all lit up, anyway, PALM BEACH! I had been with my parents so many times when they'd had out-of-state guests and gave them a tour of the area. It was always so interesting to drive up into the driveways of the gorgeous estates on Palm Beach and see the exquisite homes and lush landscaping. We would show folks where the Kennedy's lived and others. Dad would start on the ocean and show his visitors Mar-a-lago and then work our way back toward the Palm Beach Inlet with all the boats and fishermen, and then have them window shop along Worth Avenue, before leaving the island.

Well, now that would be my plan that night and as our country western music was blaring from the radio, we were close to the bridge to Palm Beach and I spotted a nice looking hitch-hiker with his thumb out. I pulled over much to the delight of all the kids, the kind fella with the sweet smile climbed in the rear. I told him I didn't know where he wanted to go but that he could get off at any time, if that would help any, he nodded and smiled some more.

I swung into the iron gated entry of one large tropical looking mansion and the kids jumped out clutching their sheets, rang the doorbell, but no one answered so we continued on. The gates were closed at Mar-a-lago so we looked for the next driveway when all at once we were surrounded by flashing red and blue lights, white spotlights, and uniformed officers with their hands resting on their gunbelts. "Everybody out, line up against the truck, get your identification ready, leave your sheets in the back on the hay, Ma'am, your license, insurance and registration!" I wasn't sure how many patrol cars had us hemmed in across from the ocean seawall, but I figured it was their entire force on duty that night.

What happened next was so funny that none of us could gain our composure and one of the girls told the men it was cold out there in the ocean wind and could they please put their sheets back on, so they all redressed in their "costumes" once again, and looked more like a truckload of tattered angels. We all laughed some more. The hitchiker looked white as a ghost with fear and we never saw him smile again, he was just wide-eyed as his hand shook handing his ID card to the cop.

The officer advised me of the town's soliciting restrictions and that trick or treating was forbidden there. The policemen with him took their ID cards to their cars to help run them and to speed things up. Each one was asked to give their name, address and age, one at a time. Every name or address struck us so funny, we would double over hysterically at each one. The cops thought we were making it all up, and they would repeat after what we'd said, questioning our answers. They also assumed we were high. The cops never cracked a smile. They even told us the statute numbers for giving false information and we all howled some more. I would try to opologize, but then could not help but burst into laughter!

"Lucky Buck Ranch?"....."Far Out Farm?"...."Best Ranch?"..."Wind in the Vines?"...."Wind in the Pines?"..."Bet Luckey? Luckey,Bet?"...."Hungryland Slough?".... "Dan the Best?"..."Oh, Dan Best" "Miss Primm?"..."Oh, Chris Primm?"...."Tipton Luckey?"..."Oh, Tifton Luckey"...."Livvy Luckey?"..."OK, Libby Luckey" ..."Cherry Luckey?"..."Oh, Sheri Luckey?"...."She's cold?"..."Oh, you said, Nikole?"

With the ocean wind blowing so hard and together with the crashing sounds of the waves it was too hard for the officer to understand our answers, which kept striking us so funny. Besides, the wind was whipping a dozen sheets with flapping and snapping as if they were strung on a clothesline in a hurricane! You get the idea. We were released to leave.... without our tour of Worth Avenue, after all, and escorted across the bridge by a patrol car with his lights still flashing.

When we passed the spot where I had picked up the hitchiker, he tapped on the back rear window for me to go ahead and let him out. He thanked all of us for the best Halloween he had ever had, and we got to see his nice smile one more time. I'm sure he had never been so relieved than he was to get out of my truck. As I pulled slowly away I asked him once more if he was sure I couldn't drop him off somewhere esle? I heard him answer as he waved goodbye, "Thanks Mrs. Luckey, but, *No more Halloween for me!*"

As I said, it was the most fun Halloween we would ever have. It was all in good fun even without getting Palm Beach's great "trick or treat" candies and goodies, we'd dreamed they'd have awaiting for all of us, lol. None of us had ever laughed so hard, even if my country kids didn't get to tour and see the elaborate and famous estates there as I had planned.

Our little homes back at Lucky Buck Ranch, Far Out Farm, and The Best Ranch, actually couldn't be beat anywhere on earth. We had, actually, everything we'd ever need right there, cozy, happy, country homes with campfires, lots of love, good neighbors, and more Reese's Peanut Butter Cups waiting for us in an old calfing bucket with a rubber nipple on it!

Years before that one, there was also a Halloween when we lived at Square Lake in Palm Beach Gardens, when I'd taken our children to the condominium tour, leaving Gary at home with a ballgame to watch. When I'd left the house, I had told him that if he happened to get trick or treaters, I had a tray full of Halloween cupcakes all ready on the table in the kitchen. He forgot all about them.

When I got home I saw all the cupcakes still on the tray, so I asked, "No trick or treaters, huh?"

Gary replied, "Yes, surprisingly, quite a few, and its a good thing there were no more, I gave away all the change I could find!"

By the time I had spent years praying for people to be delivered from evil spirits, had given countless talks and sermons on the demonic realm around us, and had prayed exorcism of victims, homes, barns, and churches, I was well versed in doctrines that taught the powers of Satan to be actively at work to "steal, kill, and destroy" us and our families. There was no way Halloween was something fun or to be carelessly indulging in.

I heard too many first hand stories from former occult members who had repented, found Jesus, and renounced the devil, ashamed and forgiven of horrible activities their Satanic worship had entrapped them into, even involving murders and human sacrifice.

The Bible teaching could not be more clear, that all witchcraft, sorcery, related practices, divination (desiring to seek foretelling, predicting the future through other sources other than God's prophetic voice), use of curses, spells, and wizards and witches, those who practice magic arts, mediums and spiritists, holding seances, necromancer (one who consults the dead to foretell the future), human sacrifice and child sacrifice, baby murder such as those dedicated in Satanic worship. It may be difficult to discifer between some abortion as we know it, and what the Bible teaches with reference to Baal worship.

Satan had attempted to prevent the birth of Jesus, the promised Messiah by having babies killed by the Pharoh, and also to prevent when Moses was born but was spared when he was hidden in the water basket. In other words, killing babies has always been on the devil's agenda. Now Satanic sacrifice continues as millions of babies are slaughtered on earth every year. God doesn't allow it to continue, he sends judgement. He wants and demands mankind on the earth to respect and protect His Creation.

Praise God, that women who have aborted their children can come to Him as the Holy Spirit brings convictiction, and be so completely forgiven as if it had never happened. He washes us clean from our all of our sins whenever we humble ourselves before Him and receive His sacrificial forgiveness. His death on the cross paid for our disobediance to God's laws, but He gives us a new beginning. Hallelujah!

Of course I stopped having anything to do with Halloween because I want nothing to do with Satan or any of the evils that represent his ungodliness and his vicious attack against each one of us. Just like the poor old hitchhiker had said, as he was so glad to get out of my truck, "*No more Halloween for me!* I agree.

"Author's grandson, welder Justin Savacool, parents Libby and Jeff"

CHAPTER TWENTY

MIZ LUCKEY, WAKE UP! WE GOTTA SOUL TO SAVE!

*This is what the Lord says, 'Let not the wise boast of their wisdom, or the strong boast of their strength, or the rich boast of their riches, but let the one who boasts, boast about this: **that they have the understanding to know Me,** that **I am the Lord,** Who exercises kindness, justice, and righteousness on earth, **and in these I delight!** Jeremiah 9:23,24 NIV*

When Roger Primm, a dear old family friend had awakened me in the middle of the night with such urgency in his voice, it would result minutes later, in my living room at Lucky Buck Ranch, in the salvation of one of his buddies, when he had exclaimed, *"We've gotta soul to save!"* That same message would be one the Lord would resonate throughout the events of my lifetime from that moment on to motivate me not to waste another minute, and that time is of the essence!

In the verse above, one of my favorites, it would be that same *"kindness, justice and righteousness"* that God delights in, that I would always crave and delight in, as well. Those being the elements this lost world is also knowingly or unknowingly, craving as I am. The Good News is that He is anxious to provide it!

Someone recently reminded me that I had predicted we were about to be hit with something unlike anything we had known before. I knew God was telling me it was time for me to leave Florida and move high into the mountains to prepare, but I had no idea it would be called a coronavirus. I knew its effects were going to be just as devastating as they were, though, and that we needed to keep our eyes on Jesus, and completely hang on tight to our faith in Him only.

I was aware there were difficult days ahead, but I had no idea the extent of loss that was coming to our family personally. We would lose our grandson Justin in an automobile accident at the reservation and he'd be taken to Heaven instantly without warning. The Florida funeral took us back to the Ortona Cemetery where Justin had once said at a funeral with tears running down his cheeks, "Grandma, I feel like I know everybody here!" as he looked at all the gravestones around us.

It was good to have had a very happy moment with him when he graduated as an certified welder and became employed by a prestigious company in Orlando. It was there we took the picture above with his proud parents, Libby and Jeff.

It was at his funeral Gary and I both contracted the COVID-19. We would both be hospitalized, where I would survive after ten days there, but Gary would not. It wasn't long afterwards that his heartbroken daddy, Jeff Savacool passed away and now it would be Sean whose heart would break to lose the three men in his life all so close together, and Libby as well. Jeff had just completed the wooden cross he made for the curve on Reservation Road with Justin's initials. We never know how long we have and this is what motivated me to reach as many for Jesus while there's still time. Is there still time? We never know.

We have right now, today is the day of salvation. Pa Luckey, (James, Gary's dad), died in his sleep in 2005, healthy and happy after a brisk walk in the neighborhood, a relaxing ballgame to watch with a bowl of ice cream, he lay down in bed and then drifted off to sleep and right into Heaven.

I was asked about a month ago what I sensed next and I gave them an answer, besides the economy, war. I knew, and its true, that things already, would not ever be the same again, and I sense sorrows yet to come, especially as I keep the news fixed on my television set up in my loft, usually with the sound muted. Sometimes I'll have the news posted on the screen throughout the night so I can glance at in case I see something of significance as I get up at times throughout the night. I guess its just part of being a "watchman" at the gate or up in the watch tower. But I am filled with a peace knowing God is in control and will bring justice and open the eyes of the deceived.

The Ukrainian war, the world and national crisis, has brought me to my knees and to tears and to pray like I never have before. It has already changed me and even though the clothing you see on me is frequently a uniform of denim, flannel, and moccasins, I am certainly draped "spiritually" in sackcloth and ashes. I have sent money, prayers, and shed grief stricken tears of anguish for my heartbroken brothers and sisters (of this earth) over there, and here. I am trusting God to come with His mighty angels and His Power and Glory to show this world, in all it's pain and suffering, His judgment and justice....and I think it won't be long now.

Yes, and like the verse above, in Jeremiah 9:24, I *delight for it!* Do you know what it is to delight *for it? Same as how we delight in it!* At times I have the sense of such joy ahead when with the multitude of angelic hosts, we will sing praises of rejoicing and thanks to God for what He is going to do. You'll see. At the same time, I truly anticipate a jubilant time ahead with revivals, healing and prosperity.

He will make all of this right, folks, take heart. From the government, to the border and drug crisis, to the war atrocities, He will restore and heal. From the shaking of the earth, its quakes and to its storms of thunder, its winds and waters, He will shelter, save, and deliver. From the corruption and violence, to the evils and destruction, He will cleanse and bring justice.

I can thank Him ahead of time, and I can find joy deep down in my heart for the delight it will be. Remember the chorus we sang in Sunday school centuries ago? *"I have the joy, joy, joy, joy down in my heart, down in my heart, down in my heart I have the joy, joy, joy, joy, down in my heart, down in my heart to stay!"* (Written by George W Cooke, 1926).

But also never forget what the following verses say, as well, that Jesus gives us the 'the *Peace, that passes understanding'*.....and then also the one about, we know the '*devil doesn't like it, but He, Jesus, is down in our heart'*........and ' *I have the love of Jesus, love of Jesus, down in my heart, down in my heart to stay!'* Oh how He loves you and me and He's going to see us through all the difficult times ahead, hang on, keep trusting in Him!

When we moved to Cherokee County NC, I had the happiest heart to know I would be close enough to the Cherokee Indian Reservation to go there and minister where and when needed. I could make myself available to help with ministry, play piano, teach in Bible school, or any number of things the Lord might want to assign me to. I was bubbling over with evangelistic ideas and songs in my spirit to share with people who might need me. When it looked like I might not have opportunities open for me there, I asked God why was He not sending me to the Indian people He had called me to? I heard Him give me His direct and clear message:

"Betty, instead of you going where they are, I am going to bring them to you, where you are." I am giving you a book to write and it will begin a pilgrimage of some Native American tribal hunger for the messages within these pages that can meet the desperate needs of the people to find salvation in Christ, peace in a world that knows no peace, and healing from the bondage of Satan and his addictions, death, and hopelessness. These are the souls to save, and I have awakened you to send my urgent messages to each of them to find Me while there is yet time!" Then He added, I think with a big smile, "*Miz Luckey, wake up, there's a lot of souls I have to save!*"

I don't believe that message is for me, alone, but for everyone reading those words at this time. He is calling all of us to no longer put off becoming the men and women of God He created us to be in the first place, no longer so preoccupied with the "stuff" in our lives that prevents us from our higher calling, but we are to hear His voice calling one and all, to put your name where it says, 'Miz Luckey', because that's where your name goes, too. He is waking us up from our naps and slumbering and is bringing to our minds at least one soul we will soon have an opportunity to help lead to Jesus Christ.

The Verse in Matthew 28:18,19 and 20, is known as the Great Commission. It gives you and me the authority, the credentials, to obey it as believers, like when it says, *in the new First Nations Version of the Bible:* *"CREATOR-SETS-FREE" (Jesus), said, "ALL THE AUTHORITY OF THE SPIRIT-WORLD ABOVE AND THE EARTH BELOW HAS BEEN GIVEN TO ME" He told them. "SO NOW I AM SENDING YOU INTO ALL THE NATIONS TO TEACH THEM HOW TO WALK THE ROAD WITH ME. YOU WILL REPRESENT ME AS YOU PERFORM THE PURIFICATION CEREMONY (Baptism) WITH THEM INITIATING THEM INTO THE LIFE OF BEAUTY AND HARMONY REPRESENTED, IN THE NAME OF THE FATHER, SON, AND HOLY SPIRIT. YOU WILL TEACH THEM ALL THE WAYS THAT I HAVE INSTRUCTED YOU TO WALK IN." 'CREATOR SETS FREE', (JESUS), THEN LOOKED INTO THEIR FACES WITH LOVE AND GREAT AFFECTION. HE LIFTED HIS HANDS TOWARD THEM AND SPOKE THESE FINAL BLESSSING WORDS OVER THEM: "NEVER FORGET," He said as He began to rise up into the spirit-world above. "I WILL ALWAYS BE WITH YOU, YOUR INVISIBLE GUIDE, WALKING BESIDE YOU, UNTIL THE NEW AGE HAS FULLY COME!' AHO ! MAY IT BE SO!*

The unforgettable day my mother took us to Salamanca, NY, to the Allegheny (Seneca Indian) Reservation where we were to meet Rev. Ralph Elliot Bowen, Pastor of the Red House Baptist Church, we had no idea we would find such favor with him and his family. He and his wife Delores (Dee) would come stay in our home in Florida on a trip later on.

He was a highly decorated warrior in the US Army Air Corp during several of the foreign World War II engagements and at age 98, just before his passing, he received the special recognition from the New York State Senate Veteran's Hall of Fame for Heroic WWII Service on Oct. 2, 2020.

Bowen was a direct descendant of the famous and honorable Seneca War Chief "Cornplanter", and a member of the Snipe Clan. Chief Cornplanter was the half brother to "Handsome Lake", the Iroquois Prophet who had the vision of the three spirit visitors who gave him new standards on which to base his faith, a new religion for the Native people.

The importance of this was to be that the three were joined by a fourth visitor, who would change Handsome Lake's life forever. **He showed him the holes in His hands and His feet, as well as the hole where a sword had pierced his side.** Handsome Lake was commissioned by the Lord to share the Good News with his tribe and it transformed their beliefs from then on, and he was considered a Prophet by his people from that day forward.

Brother Bowen had shared with us the significance of a last days revival that would happen just before the Lord Jesus returns. It would be embraced by Indian people all over the country and preached widely by them and accepted.

Someone else had told me identically the same thing. Rev. Dr. Billy Yairda Barnett, the great Baptist preacher from Oklahoma, who I had the privilege to go pick up at the Palm Beach International Airport once for a revival. Pastor Wonder Johns was scheduled for an important doctor's appointment on the same day, so he asked me if I would do the honors of traveling to West Palm Beach and bringing him back to Brighton Reservation to preach the revival. What an honor for me!

Funny story happened at the airport. I had never met the prominent Brother Barnett personally, but he was one of the highest ranking executives for the annual Falls Creek Baptist Conference Center's Indian Assembly in Davis, OK., among countless other influential credentials. He was full-blooded Muskogee Creek, Bird Clan, founding pastor of Seminole Indian Nations in 1975. Wonder said he had told him all about me and the miracles the Lord had performed in my life, and to make a small sign with his last name on it to hold up in the crowd, when the passengers debarked from the plane, so I did.

To my surprise there was quite a large group of others, awaiting the plane, many of whom carried small signs like I did with names on them. We stood together as a group sort of off to the side, making room for the arrivals from Oklahoma to pass in front of us. My cardboard sign said in large letters, with my widest magic marker, "BARNETT".

One of the others in the group announced that he could hear the passengers headed our way and everyone began to hold up their signs high above all their heads. All of us stood quietly, without speaking, when one of the first passengers to disembark, a tall, good-looking, young fella, looked my way and said loudly, "Hey, can I be 'Barnett'?" Everyone turned to stare at me. I quickly shot back, "I don't know, can you *preach*?" Everybody howled! The laughing old man standing next to me holding a Holiday Inn sign, said, "That was a good one!"

All the way to Brighton Brother Barnett had me tell one true story after another of the great things God had done in my life and it was his final comment that day, that would be such an encouragement in my years to come. He had said, he believed I had a special blessing on my life for evangelism to Native peoples and that around the turn of the century, as predicted by medicine people and prophets early on and before that time, there would be special dispensation, or act of Divine providence, by which God would do miraculous things in future Indian bloodlines through their strong faith in Jesus Christ.

I explained to him that my agnostic (at that time) husband told me he thought I was clairvoyant, or gifted in the supernatural, or it was merely coincidental that these things would happen to me. "No", Brother Billy insisted, shaking his head, "It was handed down to you and there will be even more such amazing things as the last days approach. Indian people are going to begin to *wake up* and bring the Good News of the Gospel to this lost world that is dying without hope and without Jesus."

The Lord has blessed our present family with spiritual gifts like He had in our ancestors before us. I delight to see evidence that my children, grandchildren, and great grandchildren radiate the glory of God at work in their lives. My oldest granddaughter, Tiffani Luckey, who is Tifton's daughter, has been experiencing more recently the appearance of eagles and other birds just since her grandfather, Gary, passed away.

When there were difficult days of grieving, the Holy Spirit seemed to use the eagle that Gary loved so, (as well as all the various birds he was always pointing out to us), to help bring comfort and encouragement to Tiffani right at the exact moment when she most needed it. Following his funeral she walked into the room where I was speaking about our life on earth together with her grandpa, and a red Cardinal and a bright blue Jay landed on the window sill right beside us. It was as if their message was this, "Cheer up everyone! Life after death is real in Heaven! Gary is alive and well! All is happy and colorful, with joyfulness and song, flying high with our Creator, awaiting all of you to come on Home!"

We were proud of her achievements in high school and college. Not only was she the most beautiful young lady in her graduating classes, (her grandpa and I thought), but so skilled in several categories. Her athletic strengths were proven as a cheerleader when she participated in the most advanced and difficult, specialized team formations and maneuvers. She received her diploma at the University of Florida in Gainesville, a Bachelors of Science in Business and Communications, with a specialization in Leadership Development. She is an active real estate agent in south Florida and I see her, like an eagle who flies high in the sky above the valleys of this life, destined for the mountaintops with God.

I was with a close Seminole friend of mine one day in Okeechobee, Florida as we watched an eagle fly along the shoreline and perch on the highest tree in sight. Augustina ("Tina") Gopher Gore had met me down at the pier on Lake Okeechobee where we sat on a bench and got all caught up on the news. Tina was a half sister to our Pastor Wonder Johns and was actively involved in our First Indian Baptist Church. She loved Christian movies and drama. So much so, that one day, in spite of not feeling at all well, she would come to the evening church service so as not to miss the Gospel movie being shown. During it, she would stretch out on the pew she was sitting on, and unnoticed at the time by the congregation, who sat in the darkened sanctuary watching the film, she would drift off to sleep and right into the arms of Jesus, her Savior.

It had been a few months since we'd had taken time to just sit and visit. So we picked a beautiful and relaxing spot to do it. She told me about an old Seminole prophecy that some day before Jesus would return, there would be a miracle revival among the Native people. Even more, she had said, it will be led by Indians and be known all over the world.

She said it had been passed down by word of mouth, which was the Indian way to pass along more accurately the true history and prophecies. Many books written by non-native people, she said, did not always tell truthfully what had actually transpired, and that what your elders heard from their elders, would be spoken with no falsehoods out of respect and for its historical value. Sometimes it was just the language barriers that were to blame for the discrepancies. She shared that one such story that was not written but had been shared orally by generations. She said it concerned the very lake there in front of us, which contained a "golden bell"and a prophetic word.

She began by saying one of her favorite songs in the hymn book was "When They Ring those Golden Bells for You and Me". She said the song reminded her about the golden bell of great value that would someday be found in Lake Okeechobee. She said the prophecy stated that some day the water level of the lake would be lower than normal and that the bell made out of pure gold would be exposed, however, no one was to search for it. It was a mystery.

She said when it was found, it meant Jesus was close to returning. I would ask the Lord for a meaning and I felt that this was my answer. The bell has already been found and is represented by the wealth already dispensed monthly in tribal dividends. The success of the Seminole Tribe has not been the result of any governmental payments to the tribe, and not solely because of the gaming they sponsor here and abroad, but because of successful business investment and profitable and wise knowledge in a multitude of enterprises. The tribal business raising cattle, sugar cane, citrus, sod, fruit and vegetable farming, as well as, hotel resorts, sports management, tobacco, rodeos and tourism had paid off. The Tribe owns the Hard Rock Hotels all over the world as well as the gaming operations connected to them. t

No one in the decades and centuries of the past could ever have imagined how each member of the tribe would be allotted such personal wealth, probably nonexistent in any other country on earth. How did it come about? With prayer that was connected to all their wise business investments. Pastor Wonder Johns had told me that when the Seminole Tribe of Florida organized it was done with sincere prayer on the part of the leaders and the people. Meetings began and ended in prayer. Important matters and difficult issues were made a matter of prayer, and Christian congregations on all five reservations would include those things in their individual prayer gatherings.

When I had first joined the Brighton First Indian Baptist Church, I joined the ladies' sewing group that met on Tuesdays. I was not a seamstress or craftswoman like they were, by any means, but as we made things to sell at festivals, the money generated was donated to all the various annual missions offerings and WMU projects for the Southern Baptist Convention. I would join in on all the praying there and listened as the elder grandmothers prayed for their families while they operated their little black Singer sewing machines in one of the Sunday school classrooms.

They would pray that their sales of the beautiful Indian handmade clothing would meet the mission goals they'd set, and it always did! They would give the money so sacrificially and cheerfully! Why I remember the certificate that arrived at the church from the SBC once awarding recognition for their mission giving as being such an unusually abundant amount compared to the number of people in the congregation. This had been consistent all through their church history.

The ladies prayed for school shoes their grand kids and great grand kids needed desperately. They prayed for their old cars and trucks that needed repairing, for food to cook for church fundraising, for clothing, gas and expenses, and a variety of prayer needs, but mainly for revival among he people. No wonder the Lord would bless the tribe, they obeyed their Creator, loved Him, and served Him. They had not only prayed, they would work, *and they wept.*

If a hundred years and more ago, such wealth could be expressed or illustrated, there could be no such example of how it could possibly come about. It would be as if the Seminoles had "discovered a valuable solid gold item, a relic, as if it was a *bell*," it would be capable of being rung and heard long distances, in other words, known all over the world. And these days in which the profits became historically overly abundant, it occurred ironically at a time when the lake had never been so low along the shore, and at a time when the last days signs are so readily multiplying at alarming rates. The earthquakes, wars, plagues, famines, and violence are greater than ever before, also, corruption, evil, and trouble, prevailing world wide. I told Tina *I believed the "Golden Bell" prophetic sound was already ringing loud and clear.*

There is a line in the lyrics of the golden bell song that inspired me to write a marching song for little kids. It appears in the chorus when it says:

When They Ring the Golden Bells (by Daniel de Marbelle 1887)
Don't you hear the bells, now ringing?
Don't you hear the angels singing?
Tis' a Glory Hallelujah Jubilee! In that far off sweet forever
Just beyond the shining river,
When they ring the golden bells, for you and me!

If you happen to know the tune to "If You're Happy and You Know it Clap Your hands" you can put my lyrics to it and sing and march! I used the line, *"It's a Glory Hallelujah Jubilee!"* And so this is what I named it:

<u>The Glory Marching Song!</u> (by Betty Swan Luckey 2021)

It's a Glory Hallelujah Jubilee, It's a Glory Hallelujah Jubilee!
The Blood that Jesus bled for me, has paid my sins and set me free,
It's a Glory Hallelujah Jubilee!

It's a Glory Hallelujah Jubilee, It's a Glory Hallelujah Jubilee!
Jesus rose up from the dead, on the third day, like He said,
It's a Glory Hallelujah Jubilee!

It's a Glory Hallelujah Jubilee, It's a Glory Hallelujah Jubilee!
I know He's coming back here soon, to take me flying passed the moon!
It's a Glory Hallelujah Jubilee!

It's a Glory Hallelujah Jubilee, It's a Glory Hallelujah Jubilee!
We'll go to Heaven in the sky, All God's children, you and I!
It's a Glory Hallelujah Jubilee!

If you are using my song and need additional marching time, just go right into all those familiar verses of "If You're Happy and You Know it!" I can't emphasize more how urgent it is to begin teaching little children right now the Bible and to learn to trust Jesus. Our country is overrun with unbelief and doubt. It reminds me how "Prophet Handsome Lake" could only turn his life around and his skepticism, by seeing Jesus Himself, the holes in his hands, feet, and in His side. Just like Thomas in the Bible.

Acts 20:26 says that Jesus heard Thomas saying he could only believe if he could actually see the wounds on Jesus who had risen from the dead after He had been crucified. Jesus showed him the holes and made him place his fingers there. Thomas saw and believing, he cried out, "My Lord and my God!"

Then Jesus said, and He is referring to us, you and me, *"Blessed are they who have not seen, and yet have believed!" (From John 20:29b KJV)*

My final word to all the Indian nations, fellow chiefs, Jesus warriors, followers of Jesus everywhere, walking, marching, climbing, and traveling with Him on His Holy mountain. Obey Him and His words He speaks in Acts 26:16....are they, "Wake UP! We gotta soul to save?"....... almost! Here is what Jesus is saying to us at this very hour:

"ARISE, AND STAND UPON THY FEET: FOR I HAVE
APPEARED UNTO THEE FOR THIS PURPOSE. TO MAKE
THEE A MINISTER AND A WITNESS OF THESE THINGS
WHICH THOU HAST SEEN, AND OF THOSE THINGS
IN THE WHICH I WILL APPEAR UNTO THEE!"
Acts 26:16 KJV

And this is how it reads in the First Nations Version, an Indigenous Translation of the New Testament:

"Now rise up! Stand to your feet! I have chosen you to be my
servant, a witness who will tell others what you have seen
with your own eyes and what I will reveal to you!"
-Acts 26:16 FNV

What He will reveal to us.....what He revealed to me today was that He moved me not to just the mountains, but to the section of Cherokee, County, North Carolina, to a rural area named "Bellview". Now, my view from the loft window, in my tower, is of my Notla Baptist Church with the steeple, and the bell inside, that rings every Sunday morning to announce the start of the eleven o'clock service. Yesterday, Pastor Jerry Morrow called to ask me to resume playing every Sunday just before it rings, for about ten minutes as a music prelude to the worship. I had been doing that before the Covid19 pandemic had begun altering the church schedules.

It was an answer to my prayers, I was missing it because as a pianist, it was a major part of my worship and my Bloodhounds were beginning to wish I'd quit playing quite so much for them here at home. Sometimes they would jump up on the couch and cover their heads with their paws and let out a single moan. The male is "Hank" and the female is "Gracie" Nohna (Cherokee Indian word for "Grace". The sermon entitled, "Grace,

Grace" inspired her name, and is preached by Brother Jentezen Franklin, of Free Chapel in Gainesville, Georgia, available on line and on YouTube.) They are now the proud parents of a litter of seven perfect little black and tan puppies. God's blessings overflow!

His blessings were also overflowing one day back in the late 1940's when the Seminoles were honored with a special visitor. He was also one of my favorite evangelists, and it was Rev. Billy Graham, when he had visited the Brighton Seminole Reservation in Florida and preached before the tribal members who gathered there from all the reservations in the state. They gave him a magnificent welcome that day and it was followed with a huge outside dinner, the food displayed on long tables beneath the thatched roof chickee pavilions.

News media was there in full force, reporters interviewing him, photographers flashing pictures, but the highlight of the day would be when Brother Graham unexpectedly swooped up one little Seminole boy and hugged and held him up for the crowds to see. It caused all the people to cheer and clap. It would be something the little boy would never forget, because now he was an old man telling me all about the story. Before he passed away, the Indian man said it had been the most important day of his whole life, and *he would be one of those "souls who was saved."*

When we were asked in school once to name our "hero", someone we admired more than anyone else in the world, I wrote his name on my paper. I remember that other kids sitting around my desk were struggling to think of a hero, so they leaned over my paper and copied the name I had written. One or two of them on the other side of the room even, called out to me asking how I spelled Graham. The teacher who compiled the list later that day, announced that Billy Graham had received more votes than anyone else. My classmates looked sheepishly in my direction. I'm afraid some of them had no idea who he was. Well I surely did admire him and had listened to him preaching on the radio for many years.

I had also rededicated my life once when the famous preacher came to Connie Mack Field in West Palm Beach. I could hardly wait to get to have a closer look at him when I went forward during the invitation, but as I got down in front by the alter, I was so overcome by the anointing there, and my personal prayer, that I forgot to look up and see him so close.

It would be later when I would attend one of his gigantic meetings in a huge arena with my parents that would be the most memorable day in my life as I got a really close up look at him and I have to tell you what happened. I think it was at the Southern Baptist Convention in Miami, and I was attending with my Mother and Dad. I must have been in my senior year.

I could hardly wait to find our seats and was so hoping we would be close to the front, when reality set in pretty fast, as we frantically looked for any seat at all! An usher offered his assistance and we followed him past layers of rows of filled seating, and then sections of rows, as we climber higher and higher to the top of the highest seats way up in the balcony nearest the ceiling!

I was so frustrated and disappointed! Dad made a comment about I must love the seats because they were as high as you could go, and he knew how much I loved to be in the highest place of all. No, I explained, this just wasn't going to do! It was not only hot up there with little air circulation, but we were already thirsty, and unlike some others around us, had not thought to bring bottled water or a thermos. Not only that, but the bleachers in the highest balcony were hard and uncomfortable even for a teenager.

I complained to my parents that I had come to *see him*, not just *hear* him, and it would be very difficult to see him at all from that distance. I prayed for God to come to my rescue and I asked my parents if it was okay if I could walk down to the front and see if there was just one seat along the way, and they said I could try, and that they would keep an eye on me to see if I found one. I also had a brainstorm of an idea.

Before I got up I turned my name tag over and wrote **PRESS** on it as boldly as I could, pinning it to my blouse. Then I stuck my pencil in my ear, and carried a stack of papers I had picked up in the lobby at the registration table. My parents watched me wide-eyed as I made my way.... way down, to the front.

The press box was an elaborately designed area directly beneath the podium, a boxed in area with a gate and a security guard standing in front of it. Instead of speaking to the officer, I looked at him in a brief second as I nodded at him and he just merely swung open the gate for me to enter! Before me were two long oak tables with icy cold pitchers of ice water surrounded by drinking glasses. Around the tables were *empty* padded swivel chairs and only one of those was taken.

He was a Miami Herald reporter, a middle aged man with graying temples who looked identical to the movie star, Peter Falk who played Colombo. He had real credentials hanging from a thin strap around his neck, a clipboard and pen on the table in front of him and a chunky, expensive-looking camera beside it. He glanced at me and we nodded, professionally-like, and I took a seat at the opposite end of his table. The opening music, comments and announcements, became almost a blur as I became so excited at my luxurious whereabouts and the momentary arrival of my lifelong hero!

Why, aside from Colombo, I was about to be closer to Billy Graham than anyone there! I had the very finest seat in the whole place, padded, swivel, comfortable seats, cool air conditioning, and icy cold water to drink from in real glass tumblers, to boot! I almost said "Thank You, Jesus" right out loud! When he was finally introduced, the convention went ballistic with standing ovation and applause and I caught myself just before overreacting as well! When we sat down, I was amazed at Brother Graham's sparkling eyes, and clear voice, and he looked so close that had I wanted to, I could have probably reached and touched his shoe.

I kept Colombo in the corner of my eye and because I had never been briefed on "press protocol," I drank water whenever he did, wrote on paper when he did, and only moved my chair slowly whenever he did. Once when Brother Graham made such an awesome statement the whole assembly stood with thunderous applause, I caught myself doing the same and I saw the reporter glance in my direction with a raised eyebrow. Oops, I had to be more discreet. Well it was not that I was being too deceptive, after all, I was editor of the high school newspaper in Jupiter, and assistant editor of the year book, I rationalized.

I just knew that my parents had seen where I was seated and they were undoubtedly staring in unbelief from their high perch above the flood light clouds along the ceiling. When it was over I saw Colombo putting on the jacket he'd hung on the back of his chair and as we gathered our belongings, he kindly opened the press box gate for me to pass through, and said, "Well, did you get your story?" I answered, "Yes, did you get yours?"

With that, he shifted the shoulder strap on his camera, and glanced back at me as he started to hurry off, and said, "Yes, I did, but....*something tells me the real story tonight,* was in the *PRESS BOX!"*

That was very true, the real story was that I had gotten to see and hear the greatest evangelist in my day, who had truly answered the call of God when he was told, "Mister Billy!, *wake up, we have a soul to save!"*

I have enjoyed the first full year of the Murphy, North Carolina Worship Tent revival and the following 3,000 seat tent which replaced the first one to enable larger crowds. Evangelist D.R. Harrison conducted two weeks of services until a violent wind came through town on Friday, the last night, and just prior to the people arriving, the storm destroyed the tent. Losing the tent did not take down the strong local desire for having souls saved in Cherokee County, though, and the meetings continued on at the First Baptist Church nearby.

What a blessing to see how all the churches, regardless of denomination, prayed, worshiped, and worked so beautifully together in harmony and unity and how so many folks were saved in all the services. Every thought of any barriers, differences, theological and doctrinal issues, were put aside by all those who were attending, and every heart focused on the peace and love of Jesus and our mutual love for one another.

It brought back to me all the tent meetings I had been to since my birth, by my family and others, the sounds of the canvas flapping in a breeze, the smell of wood chips and saw dust, the light bulbs strung overhead and the hard old wooden or metal folding chairs we had to sit on. But oh, when the great revival music began, and the crowds would sing, clap, shout and laugh, the Holy Spirit filled the place with such excitement you just wouldn't want to be anywhere else in the whole world at that moment!

There were always two places that would come to my mind as a perfect atmosphere for evangelistic gathering, and it was, inside a big tent or around a fire. Many people would find themselves uncomfortable attending evangelistic events in a church, but there was something so inviting and fun in a tent or sitting around a campfire. I think I had always had visions and dreams of one day helping to provide just that, or even a huge meeting barn, where all my cowboy and Indian friends would feel like coming, just as they were, casually dressed, for Christian fellowship and to meet Jesus.

One of the memories I cherish is the Seminole Indians with the spurs still on their boots, cowboy hats on their heads, and a Bible in their hands, spurs jingling as they walked across the room to find a seat. I loved attending Cowboy Church in LaBelle, Florida, and in Nashville, Tennessee, where they used their western hats to pass around to collect the offerings. Well, don't let it surprise ya none, if my next book is, "The Jesus Barn" and I will be telling you about all the lost cowpokes, Native people, and others, whose lives were gloriously transformed. I think I'm *waking up*, this old *Miz' Luckey,* here, because there's still some *"souls to save!"* and very little time left to do it. Just listen with me carefully a moment 'cause I think I can hear a golden bell beginning to ring and a trumpet about to blow!

My daughter Sheri and her husband Simon Bjorn, are also answering God's call to save souls with music they're writing, playing and singing, with their band "Wedding Party". When I helped name the band many years ago, it was to remind us, that we, as followers of Jesus, are the Bride of Christ, and we await His return as our anticipated coming Bridegroom. Their band plays at Christian concerts and annual festivals such as Audio-feed near Champaign, Illinois, and they lovingly refer to me as the matriarch of the band. I am proud of them for the way they minister to the audience, not as performers who only entertain, but they testify that Jesus has come to save sinners to eternal life and deliver us from sin and death, and have an open alter for all those who will accept Him as their personal Savior.

My message I leave to each and every reader is that you will seek the Lord while He may be found, live your life to its fullest, *high upon Jesus' Mountain,* and every morning the moment you open up your eyes, you'll hear His urgent call, **Wake up!** *(your name)* **There's a SOUL TO SAVE!**

CHAPTER TWENTY-ONE

THE "HOUND OF HEAVEN" (SEARCH AND RESCUE)

*"Behold, I will send for many fishers, saith the Lord, and they shall fish them; and after **will I send for many hunters, and they shall hunt them from every mountain,** and from every hill, and out of the holes of the rocks, For mine eyes are upon all their ways; they are not hid from My face, neither is their iniquity hid from Mine eyes."*
-Jeremiah 16:16, 17 KJV

D id you ever try to hide from a Bloodhound? Just try to. Their ears are so long and their hearing so keen, they can almost hear where you're hiding. But they truly have noses unlike any other dog, that will direct them immediately to your smell. They are thorough as well, and will trace every move you made, nose to the ground, right to your side.

It's amusing for me to watch my two dogs from my windows in the loft bedroom overlooking our property. For instance, if a visitor left our house, stopped to look at Sheri and Simon's garden, dropped their sunglasses and stooped to pick them up, walked around their truck before getting in it, left our yard, stalled to punch in the gate code, and exited the property, it was then the dogs are let out after the gate shuts itself securely.

277

As I watch from my window I would see both dogs race faster than the speed of light, bolt out the door, check out the garden, stop to smell the ground where something had been dropped, run around in a circle the outline of the visitor's spot where they had been parked, race to the post with the gate keypad, both dogs smelling the keypad simultaneously, racing then to the closed gate, sniffing it sufficiently as they gaze down our long driveway as if to be sure the visitor was indeed gone and had left the area.

Speaking of that gate...a few weeks ago while Hank, the male, and Gracie, (his wife and mother of his seven puppies), were hanging out on the second level porch. I watched them from the glass door as they lay resting with their heads down. Suddenly both heads shot up frozen, listening one second, then bolting down two flights of stairs like lightning, into the black night, passed trees and bushes and down to the gate barking ferociously!

The barking was above and beyond their normal watchdog bark as when alerting to a neighbor or normal vehicle approaching, no, it was much different. Somehow they sensed trouble and they were right. I have never in my life heard such intense howling, snarling, growling and warning in my life! There was a car parked at the gate with its headlights on with a woman in it and several people with her, and it was past midnight. The story given from the open driver's side window, was questionable and they wanted to come inside our gate to look for someone. They were pretty much insisting on it, but Simon handled it well, while attempting to subdue the dogs, who incidentally, never stopped, making the conversations all but impossible. The people hesitated but left reluctantly, and I was never so proud of my son-in-law, and especially our dogs, who held their ground!

It reminded me how invaluable the ears, eyes, and noses *and instincts* are of a Bloodhound. They are made for and equipped with everything it takes for saving lives and have been my favorite breed my whole life. But there's something more as well. Much more. There is a sense to Hank and Gracie they have, that seems to me to be so connected to the Holy Spirit. All of their abilities appear to be so God given, God blessed, and for His purposes and for our protection. I know I include them in my prayers, covering them in prayer, thanking the Lord daily for giving them to us.

Those two dogs have actually been covered in prayer since before we got them. We have anointed them with oil and spoken to them frankly about God and oh, have they been sung to about Bloodhounds and Jesus! We had prayed for the right puppy and the Lord led us to a Tennessee farm in the mountains where we bought Gracie in 2020, shortly after my husband passed away. Then one day Sheri had a serious "talk" with her a year later because she was looking a little bit sad and lonely. She then prayed with Gracie about getting a new friend and God put her in touch with a man who was just beginning a new Christian ministry and needed to find a good home for him. What a match made in Heaven!

Gracie has been smiling ever since, and Hank also. They pretty much could have the run of the whole fenced in, almost eleven acres, but inside the house, Simon connected several large pens, a big one for the parents, each, and one cage for all the babies, at least for now. Gracie and Hank's crates are sometimes available with the doors kept open and they go inside voluntarily where their blankets and toys are, as they wish. They have always stayed inside the house with us when they're not out romping around the yard and investigating. I wanted my readers to have some background on them because there is nothing ordinary about them. I'll tell you why.

When I brought Gracie home the first day, I was still grieving for Gary and she would comfort me. She knew. There has never been a time I was feeling lonely and sad she didn't sense it and rush to my side and be loving or do funny things to make me laugh. Hank, in spite of being extremely macho, I mean as a lead detective, he would have the highest rank of authority anywhere, he is faithfully compassionate, gentle, and caring. Just don't threaten me, Sheri or Simon in any way. He is a warrior and so is his bride, Gracie. He is totally self confident and stoic like an Indian chief.

There have been things too difficult to try to explain that we have seen, heard, including dreams, visions, and manifestations, the dogs were also confirming with their responses, but we will save it for another book. But, what I have to leave you with, is that, according to the Bible prophecies and God's teachings, we have ahead of us a joyful time of revival and a return to the things of God; but, for a time of judgment and persecution that could also lie ahead, it would be wise to prepare.

I wanted to begin such preparation many years ago when I was new to law enforcement. Being a K9 officer was always my long range career goal, and if I couldn't work a canine unit, I would just as soon dispatch. Actually, that pretty much tells it in a nutshell. Gary strongly opposed the idea and had a variety of sensible reasons for how he felt. He never wavered. It involved the cattle, his own personal hunting, and the difficulty of keeping a Bloodhound on a ranch in the woods loaded with game. In other words, it would be complicated for us, and he was right. Even though I was disappointed I gave it to the Lord, and like always, He gave me a supernatural peace about it, and it made me stronger still in other important ways, in the Lord.

The longing to have a Bloodhound for my own, never left me, though, and what a happy surprise in LaBelle, one day, when he said we could finally have one. The family all chipped in for me to buy my first one, "Bo", (short for Bo Diddley) and then our second one later, "Belle" (short for LaBelle) and I was brokenhearted Bo was hit by a truck and when Belle died of a canine medical condition. It wasn't until Gary passed away, that Sheri could see how much another dog would help fill the void in my life, and there's nothing like a little puppy with long ears and a wrinkled face, with that pitiful look, to make you smile. I named her Gracie because of God's grace to us, that undeserved, unconditional, merit, favor and mercy! Her middle name is Nohna, which is grace in Cherokee. "Grace, Grace" is a favorite sermon of Jentezen Franklin that Gary and I had just been so blessed by when we found it on Youtube.

Bloodhounds gave me peace of mind that if our family ever might need to try to locate one of us in an emergency crisis, we'd be ready. If our county ever had a disaster, or if missing people needed to be located or bodies searched for, we were prepared. In the meantime, having a Bloodhound meant we had the best watch dog with the keenest senses and intuition.

My Aunt Betty had a sermon I heard her preach when I was very young. She would describe how God will seek us out to get our attention to hear Him, follow Him and obey His ways. She called it "The Hound of Heaven". I'm sure that those words were also the inspiration for many a famous preacher to title a sermon with, because He desires that no one perish. This was also the title of a very famous writing in those days.

"The Hound of Heaven" was first published in 1893 by an English poet by the name of Francis Thompson. Three hundred and fifty years prior to his poem, it was Martin Luther who referred to God as the Hound of Heaven. Luther described the surety of God's preserving those who are in Christ, and the inability for the true believe to be lost to death, that God's pursuit of man is relentless.

The Bible itself doesn't use those words together but it certainly portrays from Genesis to Revelation the Creator's love for us so great that He gave His only begotten Son, Jesus, so we would believe and have eternal life: *"For God so loved the world that He gave His only begotten Son, that whosoever believeth in Him should not perish, but have everlasting life".* John 3:16 KJV. The teachings and revelations of God's Holy Word tell us how unmistakably God **searches** our hearts and **rescues** us from sin, death, Hell, and the grave...and that He went to the cross to secure our salvation.

As committed followers of Christ, we too, are commissioned and anointed to seek the lost and snatch them from darkness, the pit, and the flames. We are to be like the Hound of Heaven also, and pursue the lost sheep as does our Heavenly Shepherd, who rescues the lost and says to us to feed His sheep.

Sometimes I have sat with Gracie and Hank and told them about why God made them with special abilities and why they're equipped to help save people. I have taught them their purpose and how important it is. They listen intently looking directly into my eyes. I think that when their seven healthy new puppies were born on April 29, 2022, they discovered their purpose would, also include bringing another generation of Bloodhounds into the world and into a valuable service. I have been so relieved to see each puppy go to special homes, mostly to search and rescue agencies with officers and EMS personnel dedicated to saving lives.

The importance of having these dogs trained and ready can't be stressed enough when it comes to even the urgency of present day crisis situations our generation is dealing with. I recently spent a day weeping in my living room with our friend John Swindell, as we watched the televised funeral service of his precious cousins in Texas, the Collins family, who were murdered at the hands of a Mexican Mafia cartel member who was an escaped fugitive.

The beloved grandfather and his four grandsons were discovered stabbed and shot at their ranch in Centerville, and the moving funeral service at their Baptist church was a tribute to their consecrated faith in Jesus Christ and knowledge of the eternal life He promises. Even the eleven year old boy had asked to be baptized in the family swimming pool that very same week he was murdered and what a testimony it was to all his classmates as well as people everywhere who heard the story.

When that fugitive was finally located and killed by law enforcement I had already been following the story for weeks since his escape, but I failed to catch any reports that showed any K9 Units. Hopefully they were used. I'm also disappointed as I also look for dogs being used on the border influx of migrants to help stop the flow of illegal drugs into the country.

Bloodhounds are experts to discover and capture illegal drug traffickers and if they had only been on the border scene from the beginning, maybe we wouldn't have a fentanyl invasion like we do. I frequently find myself asking as I watch news reports, "Where are the dogs????"

That, too, has touched my family, and is listed in the blood report for my precious grandson Justin who wrecked his car in 2020. It makes *my own blood* boil knowing fentanyl is flowing into American veins to kill us purposefully, and knowing Satan is behind it all, makes me preach the Gospel harder than ever! Justin was the best driver I ever knew, not because I taught him, I had watched him closely throughout his driving career. When he crashed in broad daylight into a farm tractor on Reservation Road in Glades County, it was because he had passed out very abruptly.

Close friends of his (and mine), would kindly share a picture with me of the monumental complexity of his life that day, but it would be the picture of Justin, his smile, his voice, and his activity in the "Heavenlies," that would turn my grief into pure joy! The Lord has allowed such an amazing revelation of the reality of who he is at this time in his life, that I dance in victory celebration because of who God has made him in Eternity! I believe it was the Hound of Heaven that heard who was searching, and Who found, and Who rescued him.

Just as God searches our hearts and knows us intimately, where there are no hiding places we can hide from Him, so it is with these amazing dogs who relentlessly pursue the most hidden places where people cannot even go. The Bloodhounds can detect many feet beneath the ground and even depths of water, the substances they are trained to know and alert to.

Dogs are happiest when they are obeying their trainers and working at the jobs that they're programmed to do. They love the finding and the rescuing. It's what they are designed to do. That's true with all of us.

When we follow Jesus, He leads us into all sorts of adventurous exploits and missions and it will keep us happy and fulfilled to be doing so.

Well, now the following huntin' story doesn't exactly fit that good right here, but it is about hound dogs and a rescue. I'll tell you a little of how it goes, but its best to pull it up on a computer or your phone sometime and get it straight from its story teller.

Gary began to love Bloodhounds like I do and his favorite country comedy performer was Jerry Clowers who recorded his hunting stories back in the 1970's . His favorite story Jerry would tell was one about his hounds he always took coon hunting. It is one of my fondest memories of my late husband, watching him laugh so hard he'd have to use his cowboy bandanna handkerchief to wipe the tears from his eyes from laughing so hard. He probably repeated that story right up until he passed away and he always laughed as hard as when he heard it for the first time almost fifty years ago:

Old Jerry Clowers said there "was two things" they did in the Mississippi backwoods when they weren't raisin' corn, they went to revivals...and they went coon huntin'. Oh, and on this one particular day, they'd also had a rat killin' that day, so it was three things to do in the swamps there. He tells about a man named John who comes along with Mr. Baron, the wealthy land owner, whose property John is living on. Now, John is a tree climber and he believed in giving them coons a fightin' chance, so John would climb up into the thick branches where the treed up coon was. All the hounds would be ferociously barking at the base of the tree, while John was supposed to take a pointed stick and jab the raccoon, causing him to fall below into the pack of hound dogs.

Such a loud ruckus ensued with the treed animal screaming, snarling and hissing, poor ole John's voice could hardly be heard yelling for Jerry to shoot. What happened when John attempted to jab the coon? *It wasn't a coon,* but a *lynx,* or what they referred to in those parts as a souped up wildcat! That wild thing had tusks and claws and he and John were wrapped up tangled in the top of that tall tree in a painful wrestling match with John hollering and Jerry yelling. "Shoot, Jerry, shoot!" he shouted. Jerry yelled back, "I can't! I can't see you for all the branches and I might *hit you* instead!" John said, "Shoot anyhow, *one of us* has got to have some relief!"

"The Author's Jeep Gladiator Mojave with her 2021 Christmas Tree"

CHAPTER TWENTY-TWO

THE BARN AT JESUS' MOUNTAIN

———————◆———————

*"Fear not; I am the first and the last: I am He that liveth, and was
dead; and, behold, I am alive for evermore, Amen; and have the
keys of hell and of death. 19) Write the things which thou hast seen,
and the things which are, and the things which shall be hereafter;"
-Revelation 1:18, 19 KJV*

On the evening of Wednesday night on May 11, 2022, the anniversary of the very birthday when my late grandson, Justin Howard Savacool, Libby's son, was born in 1984, (turning me proudly into a grandmother for the first time), I fell asleep in prayer. With tears on my pillow, I had asked the Lord if there was anything I had forgotten or anything at all He wanted me to add to my manuscript, as I came to the closure of my autobiography. Then, I fell promptly to sleep. I was awakened at 5:45 AM .

I heard the Lord's familiar voice answer, "Yes".

I sat up, immediately alert, without even a drop of my dark Folgers Black Silk coffee, but I said, "Yes....., what?"

He said, "There *is* something!"

Recalling then my prayer, I said, "What did I leave out?"

"The Barn." He replied.

"What Barn", said I.

"My Jesus Barn. The Barn on Jesus' Mountain"! I heard His voice say. "Oh, *that barn!*" I replied with eyes opened wide.

"The one I'd always daydreamed about since I was a teenager, maybe?"

I used to draw barns with a huge stage and floodlights in all the colors, mounted from the ceiling, with room for church meetings, Christian concerts, jam sessions and prayer gatherings. Pews, folding chairs, wooden benches, and rows of hay bales, were some of the seating options. Sometimes the decor was rustic pioneer, Native American, or western cowboy themes. Outside there would be room for portable toilets if not the real deal, old fashioned outhouse, and an ample fire-pit or space for bonfires to gather around. I had always desired having a place prepared that would draw folks there because it was casual and comfortable, with lower lighting, especially for people who had an aversion to crowded church buildings.

"No, this one!" I heard the Lord say.

For the following....maybe as much as an hour...maybe a fraction of that, I don't really know.... I sat motionless seated on the side of my bed, tears flowing in awe, and my heart leaping with such joy that I cannot see how in the world I'll be able to describe it to you. I have to take what I saw and heard and rewrite it into a compact, understandable, interpretation for my readers. For starters, I do not know what to call what happened. If I was asleep and it was a dream, how come I was aware of sitting on my bed without any coffee. I was awake.

Had it been a vision...well, I just never had one before with such an amazing and unusual opening introduction....and I had merely asked Him a simple question. Yes, it was a vision, but more likely would be better labeled, a *revelation,* because it seemed more like a prophetic preview of a heart's desire of mine, except it was obviously taking place in Heaven, not here. Of course, the perfect name for the final thoughts to leave you with can be appropriately named **Revelation**...after all, that's what **He called His final chapter**, right? I'm smiling.

The details were people and what they said or did that I would never imagine in my own mind, so that makes me as excited to relive what I saw as you are now curious to know what it was I saw. Maybe I'm not supposed to try to categorize *how* it came to me, but just tell you where I was this morning, when suddenly I was somewhere else.

The Jesus Barn

I drove my 2021 Jeep Gladiator Mojave (4x4 truck) up the mountain road that was like driving above the famous Ten Commandments at Fields of the Wood in Cherokee County, North Carolina, quite close to where I live. (I love driving to its highest point to enjoy the view and picnic tables). But at the top of *this* mountain was a tremendous barn. It was made of beautiful, rustic old brown wood in a quaint and idyllic historic or vintage design. My Jeep was the only one in the Snazzberry Pearl (maroon-like raspberry color) and there were more Jeep Gladiator trucks there of every hue, style, combination and condition.

Notation: I understand you need a word of explanation concerning the Jeep trucks. For the past twenty-five years, probably, Gary and I drove new F150 4x4 trucks we were proud of, that we traded in for new ones. I thanked God for those. Prior to that I knew what it was like to arrive at destinations in whatever it took to get me there, and I thanked the Lord for those, too. You know, the kind Native Americans fondly refer to as "Indian cars". It was the old, rusty cattle trailers I had to pull that were usually the most dilapidated-looking "Beverly Hillbilly" trailers you ever saw! I have to admit how embarrassed it made me feel parking it at the Okeechobee Livestock Market with a load of Brangus (Brahma and Angus) type, mixed Florida beef cattle. There were fine looking trailers there and mine was always the one that looked like it might not make it back home that day, or even out of the livestock parking lot.

So after Gary was gone to Heaven and it was time to trade in my F150, it was the new Jeep truck that struck me, easy to park, guaranteed to get you through every challenging road and off road condition, and so versatile, you could take the top off and get some sun and fresh air, or remove tailgate, doors and windshield and have a top of the line dune buggy. It was also great for climbing mountains or an unexpected steep hill. But for a new widow, it meant transportation security and I liked the rugged style. It was "me".

There was something though, that I hadn't counted on, and that was everyone, everywhere stopping to say how badly they wanted one just like it. One man, noticing the Jesus Scriptures I had posted on it stopped me today, just to admire it and share a joke. He asked, "Ya know how come we know Jesus drove a Chevy?" I shook my head. He continued, "He walked everywhere He went!" (Well, I suppose you could use whatever vehicle brand you preferred for the joke, I had always been pretty partial to the Fords we'd had).

It didn't make me feel good, though, when seeing my truck made them envious because I knew how it felt to be ashamed of my ride when it was all I could afford. *That's why....(I think),* my vision of my Heaven trip had everyone in my favorite vehicle. No one has it better than anyone else, but has exactly what they want. You are not being allowed to be a show-off, if everyone else has the same identical truck. You see, God was teaching me to rid my very being of every last bit of pride for the materialistic things in life and it was also God's way of teasing me about it, by rubbing it in. He keeps me humble.

End of Notation

The parking was on the grass in all directions down the sides of the hill and maybe there were a thousand Jeep Gladiator Mojaves. The drivers or owners of the trucks were inside the barn. There was a parking space by the front door and Brother Camillo "Cam" Castellana, pastor from Murphy, NC's Worship Tent, stood there waving to me and pointing to the parking spot. There were horses of all breeds and colors meandering about peacefully, grazing on the greenest grass, but wore no tack, awaiting their riders who were inside to celebrate and worship. Somehow I knew that the Jeeps required no gas, and the horses required no riding gear.

When smiling Pastor Jimmy Tanner from the Murphy First Baptist Church swung open the big heavy antique barn door, Lt. Richard "Stash" Atchison (my retired Florida Sheriff's Lieutenant from the 1990's in Martin County), got the other one and at once I could see how humongous the barn was inside. It was far bigger inside than it appeared outside. No, it was actually MUCH bigger on the inside than the outside. No "appearing" to it, it was literally, supernaturally, a phenomenon. From outside, it looked like the biggest hay barn you ever saw. From inside, it looked like the rows of pews continued with no ends to them.

Huge chandeliers that were kerosene lamps on wagon wheels sparkled and glowed from high above, crossing the old wooden ceiling and also hung low from metal chains closer to the audience below. There did not appear to be windows but huge openings along the side walls making the mountain views a part of the room. The only glass window was the tremendous stained glass image of my brother's (Lawrence Swan), that appears on the front cover of my book. It was located above the stage and speaker's stand. Dazzling, brilliant colors reflected from his geometrically designed original he entitled, "Mountain Top". The stained glass colors encircled the barn with an amazing kaleidoscopic effect from hundreds (or thousands or millions) of flickering lamp lights. It was a thrilling and fascinating "light show" of new, supernaturally implemented phenomena. So would the music, the fellowship, and the total atmosphere be, with *everything* within that barn.

There is a certain smell I have always loved. The barn had the smell. Did you ever walk into a really old house made of original pines, cypress, or cedar, and it smelled so good you just had to stop still and take it all in? That was the smell, aside from the sweet Honeysuckle vines along the board fences outside by the front doors. There was also an occasional whiff of good-smelling hay in the air, coming from the uniquely designed seating up on the stage. Those are things I just "knew" but it was *who* was sitting inside awaiting the event to begin, was all I could actually try to focus on. Every row of thickly padded hand crafted pews went on seemingly endlessly, and everyone I *ever* knew was there, smiling, nodding, chattering, chuckling, and visiting with all of those around them...*everyone!*

Cam's wife, Rachelle Castellana, wearing jeans and cowboy boots, was down by the stage probably doing what she always does...making sure the lights, sound, people and pastors are provided for and ready to start, praying all the while! I joined her in front of the stage waving to everybody as I did, then found my seat along the front row where Gary and the kids had my seat saved on the end of the row on the center aisle. All my blood kinfolk I have ever known, and even the ones I had yet to meet, were there in the seats surrounding me and I nodded and smiled to their waving and applause. We would all be visiting and hugging each other later, *and forever.*

Let me tell you who filled all the sections of pews....my school classmates, my teachers, from public school as well as Sunday school teachers and Vacation Bible school classes, police training and college. My fellow employees from a lifetime of working in law enforcement and Christian service. My churches, and their Pastors, from several states and missionaries I had helped in other countries were there including the converts we had ministered to. Everyone was there from the Wounded Knee Christmas party we had at the Pine Ridge Lakota Sioux Indian Reservation in South Dakota! From all across the country were all the community attendants from stores, restaurants, medical facilities, gas stations, banks....I'm tellin' ya, *everybody* I *ever* witnessed to!

But oh, the Blessing beyond all Blessings was going to be, hugging all my closest love ones who had already been in Heaven awhile now, and the elderly parents, grandparents, great grands I never met, the aunts, uncles and cousins, all together once again in the happiest and most joy-filled place I had ever seen and could not have ever imagined! I joined hands with Gary and all our children and our parents in the first rows.

There were the most unique seats resembling thrones lined up across the stage. They appeared to be constructed from bales of high quality hay made into custom plush spongy-soft padding, placed on frames of solid red cedar log chairs with comfortable backs and armrests, covered with Seminole Indian-quilted covers that smelled like a cedar chest. They were a combination of "elegant, rustic, and whimsy". What in the world is an elegant, but rustic, and whimsical furnishing? I have no idea, but I sure like it, a lot!

People were still arriving and the musicians began their sound checks and tuning-up all at once and all the tuning-up already sounded with perfection, the harmony and sounds we were about to discover and explore, truly something "out of this world".

Prophet Robin Dale Bullock played his electric guitar (that required no electricity, incidentally), and resembled his "Eleventh Hour" prophetic chords and sounds the Holy Spirit flows through him on YouTube. Pastor Jentezen Franklin was tuning up with his sax and Phil Driscoll, his trumpet. Johnny Swindell was ready with his shofar and my daddy stood beside him holding his ram's horn, smiling at me and the congregation. Emmy Lou Harris was sitting on a hay bale in front of the stage with her fiddle and that alone was blessing my boots off. I actually did not know or realize I was a guest of honor at a Heavenly event until the lights were lowered and the audience's voices were reduced to excited whispers. Someone said there would first be a procession of Indian chiefs down the center aisle and then the celebration would start after "He" arrived. But first I would say a few words, introduce a few people, and a special song, before His appearance.

Someone else whispered, "He?" Another answered, "Yes, **Jesus** is coming and He's on the way as we speak! We think He might even arrive in his real metallic Jeep stripped down to the dune buggy style with the top off, and come riding it down the center aisle right up onto the stage!" I heard voices go "ooh and aah" including lots of laughter at that suggestion, and yet they said it like they had seen Him, do stuff like that before! I loved seeing Jesus in movies where He was portrayed having a joyful time, like dancing in a wedding scene, and I knew Jesus, personally, first hand, to have a better sense of humor than anyone else had ever had.

All of a sudden the orchestra band began in unison as various musicians seated throughout the audience all over as far as you could see, picked up their instruments they'd brought and played in perfect harmony, a never before heard melody, as a long line of Indian chiefs walked in single file down the main aisle to the center stage ramp, up to their "thrones". First in line were the chiefs in my grandfather, Papa Weakland's photograph from earth, at the 1930's Chautauqua County church revival.

They were followed in royal procession by so many Indian chiefs I couldn't quite recognize all of them, but the following tribal pastors and leaders who had especially befriended me, the ones I'd spent time with, had ministered with, and who had Spiritually influenced my life, were all wearing impressive Eagle-feathered and beaded leather headdresses and warbonnets.

As a casual, friendly, warmly gesture, they touched my shoulder or the top of my head as they passed my seat in front. There was Pastor Salaw Hummingbird, Rev. Billy Barnett, Brother Dan Bowers, Rev. Ralph Bowen, Rev. Chief Billy Osceola, Pastor JD Fish, Pastor Walter Taylor, Brother Chad Huff, Sammy Gopher, Joe Henry Tiger, Joe John, Joe Lester John, Roger Smith, Jack Smith Jr and Sr, Howard and Jack Micco, Pastor Paul Buster, Pastor Tim Walters, Wallace Tommie, Eugene Tommie, Earl Taylor, Norman Bowers, Rev. Norman Benz, Anthony Fish, Pastor Stanley Hollow-horn, and Brother Coleman Josh. Taking their seats of prominence were also Gator Sapp, Tito Nieves, Gerald Meisenheimer, and Rev. Joe Bishop.

Not to be forgotten, were these lovely ladies in their tribal skirts and bead work who followed to their seats along the front and *who had always gone out of their way to minister to me personally, whether or not they were aware of it.* There are many more, but too many to name, but they know who they are, and they are loved as well. Noticeably present were Martha Jones, Julie John, Agnes Jumper, Agnes Bert, Dee Huff, Happy Jones, Elsie Smith, Brenda Hummingbird, Lois Micco, Shula Jones, Belinda Taylor, Lillian Bowers, Mary Louise Johns, Rosie Billie Buck, Leona Smith, Wanda and Lois Smith, Leoma Taylor, Elsie Bowers, Edna, Bobbi

Lu, and Rachel Bowers, Onnie Osceola, Emma and Carolyn Fish, Sandy Buck, Samantha Jimmie, Cecelia Thomas, Alice Snow, Alice Sweat, Tina Gore, and Delores Bowen.

So many more as well, like my Seminole Police officers, Angela Comito, Vanessia Baker, and Theresa Bass were precious co-workers, friends and sisters in the Lord. Lay ministers who always kept me in prayer like Bob and Loretta Young, and Louise Sargent, Doris Nave, Mabel Bain, Walter and Lillian Doering, and, too many to attempt to list. Thank You Lord for all the friends, neighbors, like Patsy Anderson, Rhonda Taylor, Bianca White, Bonnie, Billy, and Brian Keasler, Glenda Allen, Eddie Coleman and his family, fellow church members, and the precious personal family He has so Blessed me with!

So now you kind of get the picture...the unity and love of everyone in one place under one roof all praising the Lord, happy, smiling, and joyful, not in a tent, a church, arena or an auditorium, but an awesome barn! That was my kind of atmosphere where I felt comfortable and like "home". I suppose the celebration event was similar to what everyone in Heaven might experience after having made a recent arrival there, I don't know, sort of a grand reunion with the folks who had played a significant role of sorts in each of our lives.

The barn resembled the gorgeous barn beautiful Ginger and my son Tifton Luckey had chosen for their lovely, country mountain wedding, last July 17 just out side Murphy, North Carolina. The "McGuire's Millrace Farm" barn they were married in exhibited that same elegance and ambiance with the chandeliers from the rafters, candlelight, extraordinary floral appointments and music.

Now the program begins.....My eyes scan the crowd and I'm delighted to see all my favorite musicians in the audience, the singers and song writers, famous evangelists, the prophets, and the last Indian has come down the aisle wearing a tribal headdress, and it is none other than my dear Seminole Pastor Wonder Johns, who escorts me to the stage to say a few words.

After making a few introductions I had my great Papa Weakland come receive an Indian Warbonnet as a gift from the head Seneca senior Chief in the group, the chiefs my grandfather had personally led to the Lord. He then placed it on Papa's head and he took his place in a throne beside his dear old Indian friends from long, long ago, looking just as I had remembered them in that old photograph he'd shown me as a little girl.

I then had my mountain church pastor in North Carolina, Rev. Jerry Morrow sing "He was There All the Time", as his lovely wife, Trudy, played the piano. He wept at times, as he always does, at places throughout the songs he sings, *as did Johnny Cash*, seated halfway back in the crowd, and I saw Johnny take a black bandanna from his back jeans pocket, and wipe his eyes. Preacher Morrow had touched the heart of God with his commitment to the Lord, and my heart, as well,...and even the heart of one of greatest famous country singers on planet Earth. The song was anointed and moving.

Now it was time for Jesus to arrive and people were straining their necks looking toward the doors, but also wondering if he would come flying in on a solid gold Jeep Gladiator Mojave truck, or just pop in like at the Upper Room or out on the sea surprising the disciples, *when all of a sudden* He stood up from his hay-bale throne, **right there in front of us on the stage** where had been sitting all along, with all the other chiefs, wearing an Indian headdress with the very finest assortment of Eagle feathers, he grinned ear to ear and waved to the standing ovation and the thunderous applause of the startled, enthusiastic crowd before Him, and taking the microphone He said the title words of the song just sung, and said, *"I was there all the time!"*

Of course it brought down the house, as they say, and His words, the music, and the worship that followed is reserved for an eternal moment I have yet to see. His presence, so sacred and Holy it was then met with no one left standing, I am sure, but in reverence, we most likely lay prostrate on the barn wood floor or kneeling. There would then be worship, praises, and singing, I knew, but, for now, I was suddenly aware the celebration was over and Jesus had departed, but the fellowship would continue outside the barn, forever.

As the crowd was filing out the door, hugging and visiting, I whispered to my handsome grandson, Justin, something *I had always whispered to him* on earth, his whole life, since he was just a little tyke, "I'm *really* gettin' hungry, how 'bout you?!"

To that, his countenance lit up like a Christmas tree, and he answered back, "Oh yeah, Grandma, that's *right,* you haven't even gotten to *see* the

DINNER BARN yet, have ya, come on, *they're waitin' on us!"* At just that moment, who should come racing our way but a canine stampede which included Tucky, Bo, Belle, Gracie and Hank, tails wagging, ears flapping, Bloodhound howls filling the air with puppy praises for eternity, and we heard Gary's voice say once again, "You better hurry, we're a'waitin' on ya'll, ...like one dog waits on another at suppertime!"

"Now unto Him that is able to keep you from falling, and to present you faultless before the presence of His Glory with exceeding joy, to the only wise God our Saviour, be glory, and majesty, dominion and power, both now and ever. Amen"
Jude 1:24,25 KJV

"Betty Swan Luckey"

ABOUT THE AUTHOR

Betty Swan Luckey

Betty Luckey was born Elizabeth (Betty) Winsom Swan on March 16, in 1943 in Jamestown, NY, to Sherman Winsom Swan and Dorothy Weakland Swan. Her dad was called by God to preach while he was in the Army Air Force when she was a baby. Immediately following his military assignment, they would moved to Louisville, KY, to live at the Southern Baptist Theological Seminary until her dad's graduation. Her dad pastored the First Baptist Churches in Midway and in Paris, Ky.

When she was thirteen the First Baptist Church of West Palm Beach called her dad to pastor the First Baptist Church of Lake Park, Florida, that was their mission at that time. It was there she met her husband, Gary Luckey. They would have four children, ten grandchildren and two great grandsons. They had homes and ranches in Palm Beach County, Okeechobee, and Highlands County, living at their ranch near LaBelle before settling in North Carolina.

Betty spent almost thirty years in law enforcement, as a 911 operator, a police officer, a Sheriff's Auxilliary deputy, and as a security guard in Nashville at Trinity Broadcast Network. Gary retired from Pratt and Whitney Aircraft in 2000, and Betty in 2004 from the Seminole Indian Police Department at Brighton Reservation, near Okeechobee, Florida.

She was a pastor's secretary, church pianist, and adult Sunday school teacher at the First Indian Baptist Church at *Brighton.* She and Gary also owned and operated two restaurants there. In 2019 they moved from

Florida and settled into their log home in the Smoky Mountains near Murphy, NC. It was there they became active members at Notla Baptist Church together, singing in the choir.

Gary passed away from the Caronavirus in 2020 and Betty wrote her second book. The first one was published in 2005 about miracles in her life, and was entitled *"Operation: Devil's Garden"* by Elizabeth Swan Luckey.

The Lord Bless thee and keep thee, the Lord make His face to shine upon thee, and be gracious unto thee; The Lord lift up His Countenance upon thee and give thee Peace.
Numbers 6:24-25 KJV

Printed in the United States
by Baker & Taylor Publisher Services